The Fall of Troy

Smyrnaeus Quintus

Contents

INTRODUCTION	7
BOOK I:	11
BOOK II	47
BOOK III	74
BOOK IV	104
BOOK V	126
BOOK VI	151
BOOK VII	175
BOOK VIII	201
BOOK IX	219
BOOK X	239
BOOK XI	257
BOOK XII	275
BOOK XIII	296
BOOK XIV	316

THE FALL OF TROY

BY

Smyrnaeus Quintus

INTRODUCTION

Homer's "Iliad" begins towards the close of the last of the ten years of the Trojan War: its incidents extend over some fifty days only, and it ends with the burial of Hector. The things which came before and after were told by other bards, who between them narrated the whole "cycle" of the events of the war, and so were called the Cyclic Poets. Of their works none have survived; but the story of what befell between Hector's funeral and the taking of Troy is told in detail, and well told, in a poem about half as long as the "Iliad". Some four hundred years after Christ there lived at Smyrna a poet of whom we know scarce anything, save that his first name was Quintus. He had saturated himself with the spirit of Homer, he had caught the ring of his music, and he perhaps had before him the works of those Cyclic Poets whose stars had paled before the sun.

We have practically no external evidence as to the date or place of birth of Quintus of Smyrna, or for the sources whence he drew his materials. His date is approximately settled by two passages in the poem, viz. vi. 531 sqq., in which occurs an illustration drawn from the man-and-beast fights of the amphitheatre, which were suppressed by Theodosius I. (379-395 A.D.); and xiii. 335 sqq., which contains a prophecy, the special particularity of which, it is maintained by Koechly, limits its applicability to the middle of the fourth century A.D.

His place of birth, and the precise locality, is given by himself in xii. 308-313, and confirmatory evidence is afforded by his familiarity, of which he gives numerous instances, with many natural features of the western part of Asia Minor.

With respect to his authorities, and the use he made of their writings, there has been more difference of opinion. Since his narrative covers the same ground as the "Aethiopis" ("Coming of Memnon") and the "Iliupersis" ("Destruction of Troy") of Arctinus (circ. 776 B.C.), and the "Little Iliad" of Lesches (circ. 700 B.C.), it has been assumed that the work of Quintus "is little more than an amplification or remodelling of the works of these two Cyclic Poets." This, however, must needs be pure conjecture, as the only remains of these poets consist of fragments amounting to no more than a very few lines from each, and of the "summaries of contents" made by the grammarian Proclus (circ. 140 A.D.), which, again, we but get at second-hand through the "Bibliotheca" of Photius (ninth century). Now, not merely do the only descriptions of incident that are found in the fragments differ essentially from the corresponding incidents as described by Quintus, but even in the summaries, meagre as they are, we find, as German critics have shown by exhaustive investigation, serious discrepancies enough to justify us in the conclusion that, even if Quintus had the works of the Cyclic poets before him, which is far from certain, his poem was no mere remodelling of theirs, but an independent and practically original work. Not that this conclusion disposes by any means of all difficulties. If Quintus did not follow the Cyclic poets, from what source did he draw his materials? The German critic unhesitatingly answers, "from Homer." As regards language, versification, and general spirit, the matter is beyond controversy; but when we come to consider the incidents of the story, we find deviations from Homer even more serious than any of those from the Cyclic poets. And the strange thing is, that each of these deviations is a manifest detriment to the perfection of his poem; in each of them the writer has missed, or has rejected, a magnificent opportunity. With regard to the slaying of Achilles by the hand of Apollo only, and not by those of Apollo and Paris, he might have pleaded that Homer himself here speaks with an uncertain voice (cf. "Iliad" xv. 416-17, xxii. 355-60, and xxi. 277-78). But, in describing the fight for the body of Achilles ("Odyssey" xxiv. 36 sqq.), Homer makes Agamemnon say:

> "So we grappled the livelong day, and we had not refrained
>   us then,
> But Zeus sent a hurricane, stilling the storm of the battle
>   of men."

Now, it is just in describing such natural phenomena, and in blending them with the turmoil of battle, that Quintus is in his element; yet for such a scene he substitutes what is, by comparison, a lame and impotent conclusion. Of that awful cry that rang over the sea heralding the coming of Thetis and the Nymphs to the death-rites of her son, and the panic with which it filled the host, Quintus is silent. Again, Homer ("Odyssey" iv. 274-89) describes how Helen came in the night with Deiphobus, and stood by the Wooden Horse, and called to each of the hidden warriors with the voice of his own wife. This thrilling scene Quintus omits, and substitutes nothing of his own. Later on, he makes Menelaus slay Deiphobus unresisting, "heavy with wine," whereas Homer ("Odyssey" viii. 517-20) makes him offer such a magnificent resistance, that Odysseus and Menelaus together could not kill him without the help of Athena. In fact, we may say that, though there are echoes of the "Iliad" all through the poem, yet, wherever Homer has, in the "Odyssey", given the outline-sketch of an effective scene, Quintus has uniformly neglected to develop it, has sometimes substituted something much weaker--as though he had not the "Odyssey" before him!

For this we have no satisfactory explanation to offer. He may have set his own judgment above Homer--a most unlikely hypothesis: he may have been consistently following, in the framework of his story, some original now lost to us: there may be more, and longer, lacunae in the text than any editors have ventured to indicate: but, whatever theory we adopt, it must be based on mere conjecture.

The Greek text here given is that of Koechly (1850) with many of Zimmermann's emendations, which are acknowledged in the notes. Passages enclosed in square brackets are suggestions of Koechly for supplying the general sense of lacunae. Where he has made no such suggestion, or none that seemed to the editors to be adequate, the lacuna has been indicated by asterisks, though here too a few words have been added in the translation, sufficient to connect the sense.

--A. S. Way

BOOK I:

How died for Troy the Queen of the Amazons, Penthesileia.

When godlike Hector by Peleides slain
Passed, and the pyre had ravined up his flesh,
And earth had veiled his bones, the Trojans then
Tarried in Priam's city, sore afraid
Before the might of stout-heart Aeacus' son:
As kine they were, that midst the copses shrink
From faring forth to meet a lion grim,
But in dense thickets terror-huddled cower;
So in their fortress shivered these to see
That mighty man. Of those already dead
They thought of all whose lives he reft away
As by Scamander's outfall on he rushed,
And all that in mid-flight to that high wall
He slew, how he quelled Hector, how he haled
His corse round Troy;--yea, and of all beside
Laid low by him since that first day whereon
O'er restless seas he brought the Trojans doom.
Ay, all these they remembered, while they stayed
Thus in their town, and o'er them anguished grief
Hovered dark-winged, as though that very day
All Troy with shrieks were crumbling down in fire.

Then from Thermodon, from broad-sweeping streams,
Came, clothed upon with beauty of Goddesses,
Penthesileia--came athirst indeed
For groan-resounding battle, but yet more
Fleeing abhorred reproach and evil fame,
Lest they of her own folk should rail on her
Because of her own sister's death, for whom
Ever her sorrows waxed, Hippolyte,
Whom she had struck dead with her mighty spear,
Not of her will--'twas at a stag she hurled.
So came she to the far-famed land of Troy.
Yea, and her warrior spirit pricked her on,
Of murder's dread pollution thus to cleanse
Her soul, and with such sacrifice to appease
The Awful Ones, the Erinnyes, who in wrath
For her slain sister straightway haunted her
Unseen: for ever round the sinner's steps
They hover; none may 'scape those Goddesses.
And with her followed twelve beside, each one
A princess, hot for war and battle grim,
Far-famed each, yet handmaids unto her:
Penthesileia far outshone them all.
As when in the broad sky amidst the stars
The moon rides over all pre-eminent,
When through the thunderclouds the cleaving heavens
Open, when sleep the fury-breathing winds;
So peerless was she mid that charging host.
Clonie was there, Polemusa, Derinoe,
Evandre, and Antandre, and Bremusa,
Hippothoe, dark-eyed Harmothoe,
Alcibie, Derimacheia, Antibrote,
And Thermodosa glorying with the spear.

The Fall of Troy

All these to battle fared with warrior-souled
Penthesileia: even as when descends
Dawn from Olympus' crest of adamant,
Dawn, heart-exultant in her radiant steeds
Amidst the bright-haired Hours; and o'er them all,
How flawless-fair soever these may be,
Her splendour of beauty glows pre-eminent;
So peerless amid all the Amazons Unto
Troy-town Penthesileia came.
To right, to left, from all sides hurrying thronged
The Trojans, greatly marvelling, when they saw
The tireless War-god's child, the mailed maid,
Like to the Blessed Gods; for in her face
Glowed beauty glorious and terrible.
Her smile was ravishing: beneath her brows
Her love-enkindling eyes shone like to stars,
And with the crimson rose of shamefastness
Bright were her cheeks, and mantled over them
Unearthly grace with battle-prowess clad.

Then joyed Troy's folk, despite past agonies,
As when, far-gazing from a height, the hinds
Behold a rainbow spanning the wide sea,
When they be yearning for the heaven-sent shower,
When the parched fields be craving for the rain;
Then the great sky at last is overgloomed,
And men see that fair sign of coming wind
And imminent rain, and seeing, they are glad,
Who for their corn-fields' plight sore sighed before;
Even so the sons of Troy when they beheld
There in their land Penthesileia dread
Afire for battle, were exceeding glad;
For when the heart is thrilled with hope of good,

All smart of evils past is wiped away:
So, after all his sighing and his pain,
Gladdened a little while was Priam's soul.
As when a man who hath suffered many a pang
From blinded eyes, sore longing to behold
The light, and, if he may not, fain would die,
Then at the last, by a cunning leech's skill,
Or by a God's grace, sees the dawn-rose flush,
Sees the mist rolled back from before his eyes,--
Yea, though clear vision come not as of old,
Yet, after all his anguish, joys to have
Some small relief, albeit the stings of pain
Prick sharply yet beneath his eyelids;--so
Joyed the old king to see that terrible queen--
The shadowy joy of one in anguish whelmed
For slain sons. Into his halls he led the Maid,
And with glad welcome honoured her, as one
Who greets a daughter to her home returned
From a far country in the twentieth year;
And set a feast before her, sumptuous
As battle-glorious kings, who have brought low
Nations of foes, array in splendour of pomp,
With hearts in pride of victory triumphing.
And gifts he gave her costly and fair to see,
And pledged him to give many more, so she
Would save the Trojans from the imminent doom.
And she such deeds she promised as no man
Had hoped for, even to lay Achilles low,
To smite the wide host of the Argive men,
And cast the brands red-flaming on the ships.
Ah fool!--but little knew she him, the lord
Of ashen spears, how far Achilles' might
In warrior-wasting strife o'erpassed her own!

The Fall of Troy

But when Andromache, the stately child
Of king Eetion, heard the wild queen's vaunt,
Low to her own soul bitterly murmured she:
"Ah hapless! why with arrogant heart dost thou
Speak such great swelling words? No strength is thine
To grapple in fight with Peleus' aweless son.
Nay, doom and swift death shall he deal to thee.
Alas for thee! What madness thrills thy soul?
Fate and the end of death stand hard by thee!
Hector was mightier far to wield the spear
Than thou, yet was for all his prowess slain,
Slain for the bitter grief of Troy, whose folk
The city through looked on him as a God.
My glory and his noble parents' glory
Was he while yet he lived--O that the earth
Over my dead face had been mounded high,
Or ever through his throat the breath of life
Followed the cleaving spear! But now have I
Looked--woe is me!--on grief unutterable,
When round the city those fleet-footed steeds
Haled him, steeds of Achilles, who had made
Me widowed of mine hero-husband, made
My portion bitterness through all my days."

So spake Eetion's lovely-ankled child
Low to her own soul, thinking on her lord.
So evermore the faithful-hearted wife
Nurseth for her lost love undying grief.

Then in swift revolution sweeping round
Into the Ocean's deep stream sank the sun,
And daylight died. So when the banqueters
Ceased from the wine-cup and the goodly feast,

Then did the handmaids spread in Priam's halls
For Penthesileia dauntless-souled the couch
Heart-cheering, and she laid her down to rest;
And slumber mist-like overveiled her eyes [depths
Like sweet dew dropping round. From heavens' blue
Slid down the might of a deceitful dream
At Pallas' hest, that so the warrior-maid
Might see it, and become a curse to Troy
And to herself, when strained her soul to meet;
The whirlwind of the battle. In this wise
The Trito-born, the subtle-souled, contrived:
Stood o'er the maiden's head that baleful dream
In likeness of her father, kindling her
Fearlessly front to front to meet in fight
Fleetfoot Achilles. And she heard the voice,
And all her heart exulted, for she weened
That she should on that dawning day achieve
A mighty deed in battle's deadly toil
Ah, fool, who trusted for her sorrow a dream
Out of the sunless land, such as beguiles
Full oft the travail-burdened tribes of men,
Whispering mocking lies in sleeping ears,
And to the battle's travail lured her then!

But when the Dawn, the rosy-ankled, leapt
Up from her bed, then, clad in mighty strength
Of spirit, suddenly from her couch uprose
Penthesileia. Then did she array
Her shoulders in those wondrous-fashioned arms
Given her of the War-god. First she laid
Beneath her silver-gleaming knees the greaves
Fashioned of gold, close-clipping the strong limbs.
Her rainbow-radiant corslet clasped she then

About her, and around her shoulders slung,
With glory in her heart, the massy brand
Whose shining length was in a scabbard sheathed
Of ivory and silver. Next, her shield
Unearthly splendid, caught she up, whose rim
Swelled like the young moon's arching chariot-rail
When high o'er Ocean's fathomless-flowing stream
She rises, with the space half filled with light
Betwixt her bowing horns. So did it shine
Unutterably fair. Then on her head
She settled the bright helmet overstreamed
With a wild mane of golden-glistering hairs.
So stood she, lapped about with flaming mail,
In semblance like the lightning, which the might,
The never-wearied might of Zeus, to earth
Hurleth, what time he showeth forth to men
Fury of thunderous-roaring rain, or swoop
Resistless of his shouting host of winds.
Then in hot haste forth of her bower to pass
Caught she two javelins in the hand that grasped
Her shield-band; but her strong right hand laid hold
On a huge halberd, sharp of either blade,
Which terrible Eris gave to Ares' child
To be her Titan weapon in the strife
That raveneth souls of men. Laughing for glee
Thereover, swiftly flashed she forth the ring
Of towers. Her coming kindled all the sons
Of Troy to rush into the battle forth
Which crowneth men with glory. Swiftly all
Hearkened her gathering-cry, and thronging came,
Champions, yea, even such as theretofore
Shrank back from standing in the ranks of war
Against Achilles the all-ravager.

But she in pride of triumph on she rode
Throned on a goodly steed and fleet, the gift
Of Oreithyia, the wild North-wind's bride,
Given to her guest the warrior-maid, what time
She came to Thrace, a steed whose flying feet
Could match the Harpies' wings. Riding thereon
Penthesileia in her goodlihead
Left the tall palaces of Troy behind.
And ever were the ghastly-visaged Fates
Thrusting her on into the battle, doomed
To be her first against the Greeks--and last!
To right, to left, with unreturning feet
The Trojan thousands followed to the fray,
The pitiless fray, that death-doomed warrior-maid,
Followed in throngs, as follow sheep the ram
That by the shepherd's art strides before all.
So followed they, with battle-fury filled,
Strong Trojans and wild-hearted Amazons.
And like Tritonis seemed she, as she went
To meet the Giants, or as flasheth far
Through war-hosts Eris, waker of onset-shouts.
So mighty in the Trojans' midst she seemed,
Penthesileia of the flying feet.

Then unto Cronos' Son Laomedon's child
Upraised his hands, his sorrow-burdened hands,
Turning him toward the sky-encountering fane
Of Zeus of Ida, who with sleepless eyes
Looks ever down on Ilium; and he prayed:
"Father, give ear! Vouchsafe that on this day
Achaea's host may fall before the hands
Of this our warrior-queen, the War-god's child;
And do thou bring her back unscathed again

Unto mine halls: we pray thee by the love
Thou bear'st to Ares of the fiery heart
Thy son, yea, to her also! is she not
Most wondrous like the heavenly Goddesses?
And is she not the child of thine own seed?
Pity my stricken heart withal! Thou know'st
All agonies I have suffered in the deaths
Of dear sons whom the Fates have torn from me
By Argive hands in the devouring fight.
Compassionate us, while a remnant yet
Remains of noble Dardanus' blood, while yet
This city stands unwasted! Let us know
From ghastly slaughter and strife one breathing-space!"

In passionate prayer he spake:--lo, with shrill scream
Swiftly to left an eagle darted by
And in his talons bare a gasping dove.
Then round the heart of Priam all the blood
Was chilled with fear. Low to his soul he said:
"Ne'er shall I see return alive from war
Penthesileia!" On that selfsame day
The Fates prepared his boding to fulfil;
And his heart brake with anguish of despair.

Marvelled the Argives, far across the plain
Seeing the hosts of Troy charge down on them,
And midst them Penthesileia, Ares' child.
These seemed like ravening beasts that mid the hills
Bring grimly slaughter to the fleecy flocks;
And she, as a rushing blast of flame she seemed
That maddeneth through the copses summer-scorched,
When the wind drives it on; and in this wise
Spake one to other in their mustering host:

"Who shall this be who thus can rouse to war
The Trojans, now that Hector hath been slain--
These who, we said, would never more find heart
To stand against us? Lo now, suddenly
Forth are they rushing, madly afire for fight!
Sure, in their midst some great one kindleth them
To battle's toil! Thou verily wouldst say
This were a God, of such great deeds he dreams!
Go to, with aweless courage let us arm
Our own breasts: let us summon up our might
In battle-fury. We shall lack not help
Of Gods this day to close in fight with Troy."

So cried they; and their flashing battle-gear
Cast they about them: forth the ships they poured
Clad in the rage of fight as with a cloak.
Then front to front their battles closed, like beasts
Of ravin, locked in tangle of gory strife.
Clanged their bright mail together, clashed the spears,
The corslets, and the stubborn-welded shields
And adamant helms. Each stabbed at other's flesh
With the fierce brass: was neither ruth nor rest,
And all the Trojan soil was crimson-red.

Then first Penthesileia smote and slew
Molion; now Persinous falls, and now
Eilissus; reeled Antitheus 'neath her spear
The pride of Lernus quelled she: down she bore
Hippalmus 'neath her horse-hoofs; Haemon's son
Died; withered stalwart Elasippus' strength.
And Derinoe laid low Laogonus,
And Clonie Menippus, him who sailed
Long since from Phylace, led by his lord

Protesilaus to the war with Troy.
Then was Podarces, son of Iphiclus,
Heart-wrung with ruth and wrath to see him lie
Dead, of all battle-comrades best-beloved.
Swiftly at Clonie he hurled, the maid
Fair as a Goddess: plunged the unswerving lance
'Twixt hip and hip, and rushed the dark blood forth
After the spear, and all her bowels gushed out.
Then wroth was Penthesileia; through the brawn
Of his right arm she drave the long spear's point,
She shore atwain the great blood-brimming veins,
And through the wide gash of the wound the gore
Spirted, a crimson fountain. With a groan
Backward he sprang, his courage wholly quelled
By bitter pain; and sorrow and dismay
Thrilled, as he fled, his men of Phylace.
A short way from the fight he reeled aside,
And in his friends' arms died in little space.
Then with his lance Idomeneus thrust out,
And by the right breast stabbed Bremusa. Stilled
For ever was the beating of her heart.
She fell, as falls a graceful-shafted pine
Hewn mid the hills by woodmen: heavily,
Sighing through all its boughs, it crashes down.
So with a wailing shriek she fell, and death
Unstrung her every limb: her breathing soul
Mingled with multitudinous-sighing winds.
Then, as Evandre through the murderous fray
With Thermodosa rushed, stood Meriones,
A lion in the path, and slew: his spear
Right to the heart of one he drave, and one
Stabbed with a lightning sword-thrust 'twixt the hips:
Leapt through the wounds the life, and fled away.

Oileus' fiery son smote Derinoe
'Twixt throat and shoulder with his ruthless spear;
And on Alcibie Tydeus' terrible son
Swooped, and on Derimacheia: head with neck
Clean from the shoulders of these twain he shore
With ruin-wreaking brand. Together down
Fell they, as young calves by the massy axe
Of brawny flesher felled, that, shearing through
The sinews of the neck, lops life away.
So, by the hands of Tydeus' son laid low
Upon the Trojan plain, far, far away
From their own highland-home, they fell. Nor these
Alone died; for the might of Sthenelus
Down on them hurled Cabeirus' corse, who came
From Sestos, keen to fight the Argive foe,
But never saw his fatherland again.
Then was the heart of Paris filled with wrath
For a friend slain. Full upon Sthenelus
Aimed he a shaft death-winged, yet touched him not,
Despite his thirst for vengeance: otherwhere
The arrow glanced aside, and carried death
Whither the stern Fates guided its fierce wing,
And slew Evenor brazen-tasleted,
Who from Dulichium came to war with Troy.
For his death fury-kindled was the son
Of haughty Phyleus: as a lion leaps
Upon the flock, so swiftly rushed he: all
Shrank huddling back before that terrible man.
Itymoneus he slew, and Hippasus' son
Agelaus: from Miletus brought they war
Against the Danaan men by Nastes led,
The god-like, and Amphimachus mighty-souled.
On Mycale they dwelt; beside their home

The Fall of Troy

Rose Latmus' snowy crests, stretched the long glens
Of Branchus, and Panormus' water-meads.
Maeander's flood deep-rolling swept thereby,
Which from the Phrygian uplands, pastured o'er
By myriad flocks, around a thousand forelands
Curls, swirls, and drives his hurrying ripples on
Down to the vine-clad land of Carian men
These mid the storm of battle Meges slew,
Nor these alone, but whomsoe'er his lance
Black-shafted touched, were dead men; for his breast
The glorious Trito-born with courage thrilled
To bring to all his foes the day of doom.
And Polypoetes, dear to Ares, slew
Dresaeus, whom the Nymph Neaera bare
To passing-wise Theiodamas for these
Spread was the bed of love beside the foot
Of Sipylus the Mountain, where the Gods
Made Niobe a stony rock, wherefrom
Tears ever stream: high up, the rugged crag
Bows as one weeping, weeping, waterfalls
Cry from far-echoing Hermus, wailing moan
Of sympathy: the sky-encountering crests
Of Sipylus, where alway floats a mist
Hated of shepherds, echo back the cry.
Weird marvel seems that Rock of Niobe
To men that pass with feet fear-goaded: there
They see the likeness of a woman bowed,
In depths of anguish sobbing, and her tears
Drop, as she mourns grief-stricken, endlessly.
Yea, thou wouldst say that verily so it was,
Viewing it from afar; but when hard by
Thou standest, all the illusion vanishes;
And lo, a steep-browed rock, a fragment rent

From Sipylus--yet Niobe is there,
Dreeing her weird, the debt of wrath divine,
A broken heart in guise of shattered stone.

All through the tangle of that desperate fray
Stalked slaughter and doom. The incarnate Onset-shout
Raved through the rolling battle; at her side
Paced Death the ruthless, and the Fearful Faces,
The Fates, beside them strode, and in red hands
Bare murder and the groans of dying men.
That day the beating of full many a heart,
Trojan and Argive, was for ever stilled,
While roared the battle round them, while the fury
Of Penthesileia fainted not nor failed;
But as amid long ridges of lone hills
A lioness, stealing down a deep ravine,
Springs on the kine with lightning leap, athirst
For blood wherein her fierce heart revelleth;
So on the Danaans leapt that warrior-maid.
And they, their souls were cowed: backward they shrank,
And fast she followed, as a towering surge
Chases across the thunder-booming sea
A flying bark, whose white sails strain beneath
The wind's wild buffering, and all the air
Maddens with roaring, as the rollers crash
On a black foreland looming on the lee
Where long reefs fringe the surf-tormented shores.
So chased she, and so dashed the ranks asunder
Triumphant-souled, and hurled fierce threats before:
"Ye dogs, this day for evil outrage done
To Priam shall ye pay! No man of you
Shall from mine hands deliver his own life,
And win back home, to gladden parents eyes,

Or comfort wife or children. Ye shall lie
Dead, ravined on by vultures and by wolves,
And none shall heap the earth-mound o'er your clay.
Where skulketh now the strength of Tydeus' son,
And where the might of Aeacus' scion?
Where is Aias' bulk? Ye vaunt them mightiest men
Of all your rabble. Ha! they will not dare
With me to close in battle, lest I drag
Forth from their fainting frames their craven souls!"

Then heart-uplifted leapt she on the foe,
Resistless as a tigress, crashing through
Ranks upon ranks of Argives, smiting now
With that huge halberd massy-headed, now
Hurling the keen dart, while her battle-horse
Flashed through the fight, and on his shoulder bare
Quiver and bow death-speeding, close to her hand,
If mid that revel of blood she willed to speed
The bitter-biting shaft. Behind her swept
The charging lines of men fleet-footed, friends
And brethren of the man who never flinched
From close death-grapple, Hector, panting all
The hot breath of the War-god from their breasts,
All slaying Danaans with the ashen spear,
Who fell as frost-touched leaves in autumn fall
One after other, or as drops of rain.
And aye went up a moaning from earth's breast
All blood-bedrenched, and heaped with corse on corse.
Horses pierced through with arrows, or impaled
On spears, were snorting forth their last of strength
With screaming neighings. Men, with gnashing teeth
Biting the dust, lay gasping, while the steeds
Of Trojan charioteers stormed in pursuit,

Trampling the dying mingled with the dead
As oxen trample corn in threshing-floors.

Then one exulting boasted mid the host
Of Troy, beholding Penthesileia rush
On through the foes' array, like the black storm
That maddens o'er the sea, what time the sun
Allies his might with winter's Goat-horned Star;
And thus, puffed up with vain hope, shouted he:
"O friends, in manifest presence down from heaven
One of the deathless Gods this day hath come
To fight the Argives, all of love for us,
Yea, and with sanction of almighty Zeus,
He whose compassion now remembereth
Haply strong-hearted Priam, who may boast
For his a lineage of immortal blood.
For this, I trow, no mortal woman seems,
Who is so aweless-daring, who is clad
In splendour-flashing arms: nay, surely she
Shall be Athene, or the mighty-souled
Enyo--haply Eris, or the Child
Of Leto world-renowned. O yea, I look
To see her hurl amid yon Argive men
Mad-shrieking slaughter, see her set aflame
Yon ships wherein they came long years agone
Bringing us many sorrows, yea, they came
Bringing us woes of war intolerable.
Ha! to the home-land Hellas ne'er shall these
With joy return, since Gods on our side fight."

In overweening exultation so
Vaunted a Trojan. Fool!--he had no vision
Of ruin onward rushing upon himself

And Troy, and Penthesileia's self withal.
For not as yet had any tidings come
Of that wild fray to Aias stormy-souled,
Nor to Achilles, waster of tower and town.
But on the grave-mound of Menoetius' son
They twain were lying, with sad memories
Of a dear comrade crushed, and echoing
Each one the other's groaning. One it was
Of the Blest Gods who still was holding back
These from the battle-tumult far away,
Till many Greeks should fill the measure up
Of woeful havoc, slain by Trojan foes
And glorious Penthesileia, who pursued
With murderous intent their rifled ranks,
While ever waxed her valour more and more,
And waxed her might within her: never in vain
She aimed the unswerving spear-thrust: aye she pierced
The backs of them that fled, the breasts of such
As charged to meet her. All the long shaft dripped
With steaming blood. Swift were her feet as wind
As down she swooped. Her aweless spirit failed
For weariness nor fainted, but her might
Was adamantine. The impending Doom,
Which roused unto the terrible strife not yet
Achilles, clothed her still with glory; still
Aloof the dread Power stood, and still would shed
Splendour of triumph o'er the death-ordained
But for a little space, ere it should quell
That Maiden 'neath the hands of Aeaeus' son.
In darkness ambushed, with invisible hand
Ever it thrust her on, and drew her feet
Destruction-ward, and lit her path to death
With glory, while she slew foe after foe.

As when within a dewy garden-close,
Longing for its green springtide freshness, leaps
A heifer, and there rangeth to and fro,
When none is by to stay her, treading down
All its green herbs, and all its wealth of bloom,
Devouring greedily this, and marring that
With trampling feet; so ranged she, Ares' child,
Through reeling squadrons of Achaea's sons,
Slew these, and hunted those in panic rout.

From Troy afar the women marvelling gazed
At the Maid's battle-prowess. Suddenly
A fiery passion for the fray hath seized
Antimachus' daughter, Meneptolemus' wife,
Tisiphone. Her heart waxed strong, and filled
With lust of fight she cried to her fellows all,
With desperate-daring words, to spur them on
To woeful war, by recklessness made strong.
"Friends, let a heart of valour in our breasts
Awake! Let us be like our lords, who fight
With foes for fatherland, for babes, for us,
And never pause for breath in that stern strife!
Let us too throne war's spirit in our hearts!
Let us too face the fight which favoureth none!
For we, we women, be not creatures cast
In diverse mould from men: to us is given
Such energy of life as stirs in them.
Eyes have we like to theirs, and limbs: throughout
Fashioned we are alike: one common light
We look on, and one common air we breathe:
With like food are we nourished--nay, wherein
Have we been dowered of God more niggardly
Than men? Then let us shrink not from the fray

See ye not yonder a woman far excelling
Men in the grapple of fight? Yet is her blood
Nowise akin to ours, nor fighteth she
For her own city. For an alien king
She warreth of her own heart's prompting, fears
The face of no man; for her soul is thrilled
With valour and with spirit invincible.
But we--to right, to left, lie woes on woes
About our feet: this mourns beloved sons,
And that a husband who for hearth and home
Hath died; some wail for fathers now no more;
Some grieve for brethren and for kinsmen lost.
Not one but hath some share in sorrow's cup.
Behind all this a fearful shadow looms,
The day of bondage! Therefore flinch not ye
From war, O sorrow-laden! Better far
To die in battle now, than afterwards
Hence to be haled into captivity
To alien folk, we and our little ones,
In the stern grip of fate leaving behind
A burning city, and our husbands' graves."

So cried she, and with passion for stern war
Thrilled all those women; and with eager speed
They hasted to go forth without the wall
Mail-clad, afire to battle for their town
And people: all their spirit was aflame.
As when within a hive, when winter-tide
Is over and gone, loud hum the swarming bees
What time they make them ready forth to fare
To bright flower-pastures, and no more endure
To linger therewithin, but each to other
Crieth the challenge-cry to sally forth;

Even so bestirred themselves the women of Troy,
And kindled each her sister to the fray.
The weaving-wool, the distaff far they flung,
And to grim weapons stretched their eager hands.

And now without the city these had died
In that wild battle, as their husbands died
And the strong Amazons died, had not one voice
Of wisdom cried to stay their maddened feet,
When with dissuading words Theano spake:
"Wherefore, ah wherefore for the toil and strain
Of battle's fearful tumult do ye yearn,
Infatuate ones? Never your limbs have toiled
In conflict yet. In utter ignorance
Panting for labour unendurable,
Ye rush on all-unthinking; for your strength
Can never be as that of Danaan men,
Men trained in daily battle. Amazons
Have joyed in ruthless fight, in charging steeds,
From the beginning: all the toil of men
Do they endure; and therefore evermore
The spirit of the War-god thrills them through.
'They fall not short of men in anything:
Their labour-hardened frames make great their hearts
For all achievement: never faint their knees
Nor tremble. Rumour speaks their queen to be
A daughter of the mighty Lord of War.
Therefore no woman may compare with her
In prowess--if she be a woman, not
A God come down in answer to our prayers.
Yea, of one blood be all the race of men,
Yet unto diverse labours still they turn;
And that for each is evermore the best

Whereto he bringeth skill of use and wont.
Therefore do ye from tumult of the fray
Hold you aloof, and in your women's bowers
Before the loom still pace ye to and fro;
And war shall be the business of our lords.
Lo, of fair issue is there hope: we see
The Achaeans falling fast: we see the might
Of our men waxing ever: fear is none
Of evil issue now: the pitiless foe
Beleaguer not the town: no desperate need
There is that women should go forth to war."

So cried she, and they hearkened to the words
Of her who had garnered wisdom from the years;
So from afar they watched the fight. But still
Penthesileia brake the ranks, and still
Before her quailed the Achaeans: still they found
Nor screen nor hiding-place from imminent death.
As bleating goats are by the blood-stained jaws
Of a grim panther torn, so slain were they.
In each man's heart all lust of battle died,
And fear alone lived. This way, that way fled
The panic-stricken: some to earth had flung
The armour from their shoulders; some in dust
Grovelled in terror 'neath their shields: the steeds
Fled through the rout unreined of charioteers.
In rapture of triumph charged the Amazons,
With groan and scream of agony died the Greeks.
Withered their manhood was in that sore strait;
Brief was the span of all whom that fierce maid
Mid the grim jaws of battle overtook.
As when with mighty roaring bursteth down
A storm upon the forest-trees, and some

Uprendeth by the roots, and on the earth
Dashes them down, the tail stems blossom-crowned,
And snappeth some athwart the trunk, and high
Whirls them through air, till all confused they lie
A ruin of splintered stems and shattered sprays;
So the great Danaan host lay, dashed to dust
By doom of Fate, by Penthesileia's spear.

But when the very ships were now at point
To be by hands of Trojans set aflame,
Then battle-bider Aias heard afar
The panic-cries, and spake to Aeacus' son:
"Achilles, all the air about mine ears
Is full of multitudinous eries, is full
Of thunder of battle rolling nearer aye.
Let us go forth then, ere the Trojans win
Unto the ships, and make great slaughter there
Of Argive men, and set the ships aflame.
Foulest reproach such thing on thee and me
Should bring; for it beseems not that the seed
Of mighty Zeus should shame the sacred blood
Of hero-fathers, who themselves of old
With Hercules the battle-eager sailed
To Troy, and smote her even at her height
Of glory, when Laomedon was king.
Ay, and I ween that our hands even now
Shall do the like: we too are mighty men."

He spake: the aweless strength of Aeacus' son
Hearkened thereto, for also to his ears
By this the roar of bitter battle came.
Then hasted both, and donned their warrior-gear
All splendour-gleaming: now, in these arrayed

The Fall of Troy

Facing that stormy-tossing rout they stand.
Loud clashed their glorious armour: in their souls
A battle-fury like the War-god's wrath
Maddened; such might was breathed into these twain
By Atrytone, Shaker of the Shield,
As on they pressed. With joy the Argives saw
The coming of that mighty twain: they seemed
In semblance like Aloeus' giant sons
Who in the old time made that haughty vaunt
Of piling on Olympus' brow the height
Of Ossa steeply-towering, and the crest
Of sky-encountering Pelion, so to rear
A mountain-stair for their rebellious rage
To scale the highest heaven. Huge as these
The sons of Aeacus seemed, as forth they strode
To stem the tide of war. A gladsome sight
To friends who have fainted for their coming, now
Onward they press to crush triumphant foes.
Many they slew with their resistless spears;
As when two herd-destroying lions come
On sheep amid the copses feeding, far
From help of shepherds, and in heaps on heaps
Slay them, till they have drunken to the full
Of blood, and filled their maws insatiate
With flesh, so those destroyers twain slew on,
Spreading wide havoc through the hosts of Troy.

There Deiochus and gallant Hyllus fell
By Alas slain, and fell Eurynomus
Lover of war, and goodly Enyeus died.
But Peleus' son burst on the Amazons
Smiting Antandre, Polemusa then,
Antibrote, fierce-souled Hippothoe,

Hurling Harmothoe down on sisters slain.
Then hard on all their-reeling ranks he pressed
With Telamon's mighty-hearted son; and now
Before their hands battalions dense and strong
Crumbled as weakly and as suddenly
As when in mountain-folds the forest-brakes
Shrivel before a tempest-driven fire.

When battle-eager Penthesileia saw
These twain, as through the scourging storm of war
Like ravening beasts they rushed, to meet them there
She sped, as when a leopard grim, whose mood
Is deadly, leaps from forest-coverts forth,
Lashing her tail, on hunters closing round,
While these, in armour clad, and putting trust
In their long spears, await her lightning leap;
So did those warriors twain with spears upswung
Wait Penthesileia. Clanged the brazen plates
About their shoulders as they moved. And first
Leapt the long-shafted lance sped from the hand
Of goodly Penthesileia. Straight it flew
To the shield of Aeacus' son, but glancing thence
This way and that the shivered fragments sprang
As from a rock-face: of such temper were
The cunning-hearted Fire-god's gifts divine.
Then in her hand the warrior-maid swung up
A second javelin fury-winged, against
Aias, and with fierce words defied the twain:
"Ha, from mine hand in vain one lance hath leapt!
But with this second look I suddenly
To quell the strength and courage of two foes,--
Ay, though ye vaunt you mighty men of war
Amid your Danaans! Die ye shall, and so

Lighter shall be the load of war's affliction
That lies upon the Trojan chariot-lords.
Draw nigh, come through the press to grips with me,
So shall ye learn what might wells up in breasts
Of Amazons. With my blood is mingled war!
No mortal man begat me, but the Lord
Of War, insatiate of the battle-cry.
Therefore my might is more than any man's."

With scornful laughter spake she: then she hurled
Her second lance; but they in utter scorn
Laughed now, as swiftly flew the shaft, and smote
The silver greave of Aias, and was foiled
Thereby, and all its fury could not scar
The flesh within; for fate had ordered not
That any blade of foes should taste the blood
Of Aias in the bitter war. But he
Recked of the Amazon naught, but turned him thence
To rush upon the Trojan host, and left
Penthesileia unto Peleus' son
Alone, for well he knew his heart within
That she, for all her prowess, none the less
Would cost Achilles battle-toil as light,
As effortless, as doth the dove the hawk.

Then groaned she an angry groan that she had sped
Her shafts in vain; and now with scoffing speech
To her in turn the son of Peleus spake:
"Woman, with what vain vauntings triumphing
Hast thou come forth against us, all athirst
To battle with us, who be mightier far
Than earthborn heroes? We from Cronos' Son,
The Thunder-roller, boast our high descent.

Ay, even Hector quailed, the battle-swift,
Before us, e'en though far away he saw
Our onrush to grim battle. Yea, my spear
Slew him, for all his might. But thou--thine heart
Is utterly mad, that thou hast greatly dared
To threaten us with death this day! On thee
Thy latest hour shall swiftly come--is come!
Thee not thy sire the War-god now shall pluck
Out of mine hand, but thou the debt shalt pay
Of a dark doom, as when mid mountain-folds
A pricket meets a lion, waster of herds.
What, woman, hast thou heard not of the heaps
Of slain, that into Xanthus' rushing stream
Were thrust by these mine hands?--or hast thou heard
In vain, because the Blessed Ones have stol'n
Wit and discretion from thee, to the end
That Doom's relentless gulf might gape for thee?"

He spake; he swung up in his mighty hand
And sped the long spear warrior-slaying, wrought
By Chiron, and above the right breast pierced
The battle-eager maid. The red blood leapt
Forth, as a fountain wells, and all at once
Fainted the strength of Penthesileia's limbs;
Dropped the great battle-axe from her nerveless hand;
A mist of darkness overveiled her eyes,
And anguish thrilled her soul. Yet even so
Still drew she difficult breath, still dimly saw
The hero, even now in act to drag
Her from the swift steed's back. Confusedly
She thought: "Or shall I draw my mighty sword,
And bide Achilles' fiery onrush, or
Hastily cast me from my fleet horse down

To earth, and kneel unto this godlike man,
And with wild breath promise for ransoming
Great heaps of brass and gold, which pacify
The hearts of victors never so athirst
For blood, if haply so the murderous might
Of Aeacus' son may hearken and may spare,
Or peradventure may compassionate
My youth, and so vouchsafe me to behold
Mine home again?--for O, I long to live!"

So surged the wild thoughts in her; but the Gods
Ordained it otherwise. Even now rushed on
In terrible anger Peleus' son: he thrust
With sudden spear, and on its shaft impaled
The body of her tempest-footed steed,
Even as a man in haste to sup might pierce
Flesh with the spit, above the glowing hearth
To roast it, or as in a mountain-glade
A hunter sends the shaft of death clear through
The body of a stag with such winged speed
That the fierce dart leaps forth beyond, to plunge
Into the tall stem of an oak or pine.
So that death-ravening spear of Peleus' son
Clear through the goodly steed rushed on, and pierced
Penthesileia. Straightway fell she down
Into the dust of earth, the arms of death,
In grace and comeliness fell, for naught of shame
Dishonoured her fair form. Face down she lay
On the long spear outgasping her last breath,
Stretched upon that fleet horse as on a couch;
Like some tall pine snapped by the icy mace
Of Boreas, earth's forest-fosterling
Reared by a spring to stately height, amidst

Long mountain-glens, a glory of mother earth;
So from the once fleet steed low fallen lay
Penthesileia, all her shattered strength
Brought down to this, and all her loveliness.

Now when the Trojans saw the Warrior-queen
Struck down in battle, ran through all their lines
A shiver of panic. Straightway to their walls
Turned they in flight, heart-agonized with grief.
As when on the wide sea, 'neath buffetings
Of storm-blasts, castaways whose ship is wrecked
Escape, a remnant of a crew, forspent
With desperate conflict with the cruel sea:
Late and at last appears the land hard by,
Appears a city: faint and weary-limbed
With that grim struggle, through the surf they strain
To land, sore grieving for the good ship lost,
And shipmates whom the terrible surge dragged down
To nether gloom; so, Troyward as they fled
From battle, all those Trojans wept for her,
The Child of the resistless War-god, wept
For friends who died in groan-resounding fight.

Then over her with scornful laugh the son
Of Peleus vaunted: "In the dust lie there
A prey to teeth of dogs, to ravens' beaks,
Thou wretched thing! Who cozened thee to come
Forth against me? And thoughtest thou to fare
Home from the war alive, to bear with thee
Right royal gifts from Priam the old king,
Thy guerdon for slain Argives? Ha, 'twas not
The Immortals who inspired thee with this thought,
Who know that I of heroes mightiest am,

The Danaans' light of safety, but a woe
To Trojans and to thee, O evil-starred!
Nay, but it was the darkness-shrouded Fates
And thine own folly of soul that pricked thee on
To leave the works of women, and to fare
To war, from which strong men shrink shuddering back."

So spake he, and his ashen spear the son
Of Peleus drew from that swift horse, and from
Penthesileia in death's agony.
Then steed and rider gasped their lives away
Slain by one spear. Now from her head he plucked
The helmet splendour-flashing like the beams
Of the great sun, or Zeus' own glory-light.
Then, there as fallen in dust and blood she lay,
Rose, like the breaking of the dawn, to view
'Neath dainty-pencilled brows a lovely face,
Lovely in death. The Argives thronged around,
And all they saw and marvelled, for she seemed
Like an Immortal. In her armour there
Upon the earth she lay, and seemed the Child
Of Zeus, the tireless Huntress Artemis
Sleeping, what time her feet forwearied are
With following lions with her flying shafts
Over the hills far-stretching. She was made
A wonder of beauty even in her death
By Aphrodite glorious-crowned, the Bride
Of the strong War-god, to the end that he,
The son of noble Peleus, might be pierced
With the sharp arrow of repentant love.
The warriors gazed, and in their hearts they prayed
That fair and sweet like her their wives might seem,
Laid on the bed of love, when home they won.

Yea, and Achilles' very heart was wrung
With love's remorse to have slain a thing so sweet,
Who might have borne her home, his queenly bride,
To chariot-glorious Phthia; for she was
Flawless, a very daughter of the Gods,
Divinely tall, and most divinely fair.

Then Ares' heart was thrilled with grief and rage
For his child slain. Straight from Olympus down
He darted, swift and bright as thunderbolt
Terribly flashing from the mighty hand Of
Zeus, far leaping o'er the trackless sea,
Or flaming o'er the land, while shuddereth
All wide Olympus as it passeth by.
So through the quivering air with heart aflame
Swooped Ares armour-clad, soon as he heard
The dread doom of his daughter. For the Gales,
The North-wind's fleet-winged daughters, bare to him,
As through the wide halls of the sky he strode,
The tidings of the maiden's woeful end.
Soon as he heard it, like a tempest-blast
Down to the ridges of Ida leapt he: quaked
Under his feet the long glens and ravines
Deep-scored, all Ida's torrent-beds, and all
Far-stretching foot-hills. Now had Ares brought
A day of mourning on the Myrmidons,
But Zeus himself from far Olympus sent
Mid shattering thunders terror of levin-bolts
Which thick and fast leapt through the welkin down
Before his feet, blazing with fearful flames.
And Ares saw, and knew the stormy threat
Of the mighty-thundering Father, and he stayed
His eager feet, now on the very brink

The Fall of Troy

Of battle's turmoil. As when some huge crag
Thrust from a beetling cliff-brow by the winds
And torrent rains, or lightning-lance of Zeus,
Leaps like a wild beast, and the mountain-glens
Fling back their crashing echoes as it rolls
In mad speed on, as with resistless swoop
Of bound on bound it rushes down, until
It cometh to the levels of the plain,
And there perforce its stormy flight is stayed;

So Ares, battle-eager Son of Zeus,
Was stayed, how loth soe'er; for all the Gods
To the Ruler of the Blessed needs must yield,
Seeing he sits high-throned above them all,
Clothed in his might unspeakable. Yet still
Many a wild thought surged through Ares' soul,
Urging him now to dread the terrible threat
Of Cronos' wrathful Son, and to return
Heavenward, and now to reck not of his Sire,
But with Achilles' blood to stain those hands,
The battle-tireless. At the last his heart
Remembered how that many and many a son
Of Zeus himself in many a war had died,
Nor in their fall had Zeus availed them aught.
Therefore he turned him from the Argives--else,
Down smitten by the blasting thunderbolt,
With Titans in the nether gloom he had lain,
Who dared defy the eternal will of Zeus.

Then did the warrior sons of Argos strip
With eager haste from corpses strown all round
The blood-stained spoils. But ever Peleus' son
Gazed, wild with all regret, still gazed on her,

The strong, the beautiful, laid in the dust;
And all his heart was wrung, was broken down
With sorrowing love, deep, strong as he had known
When that beloved friend Patroclus died.

Loud jeered Thersites, mocking to his face:
"Thou sorry-souled Achilles! art not shamed
To let some evil Power beguile thine heart
To pity of a pitiful Amazon
Whose furious spirit purposed naught but ill
To us and ours? Ha, woman-mad art thou,
And thy soul lusts for this thing, as she were
Some lady wise in household ways, with gifts
And pure intent for honoured wedlock wooed!
Good had it been had her spear reached thine heart,
The heart that sighs for woman-creatures still!
Thou carest not, unmanly-souled, not thou,
For valour's glorious path, when once thine eye
Lights on a woman! Sorry wretch, where now
Is all thy goodly prowess? where thy wit?
And where the might that should beseem a king
All-stainless? Dost not know what misery
This self-same woman-madness wrought for Troy?
Nothing there is to men more ruinous
Than lust for woman's beauty; it maketh fools
Of wise men. But the toil of war attains
Renown. To him that is a hero indeed
Glory of victory and the War-god's works
Are sweet. 'Tis but the battle-blencher craves
The beauty and the bed of such as she!"

So railed he long and loud: the mighty heart
Of Peleus' son leapt into flame of wrath.

The Fall of Troy

A sudden buffet of his resistless hand
Smote 'neath the railer's ear, and all his teeth
Were dashed to the earth: he fell upon his face:
Forth of his lips the blood in torrent gushed:
Swift from his body fled the dastard soul
Of that vile niddering. Achaea's sons
Rejoiced thereat, for aye he wont to rail
On each and all with venomous gibes, himself
A scandal and the shame of all the host.
Then mid the warrior Argives cried a voice:
"Not good it is for baser men to rail
On kings, or secretly or openly;
For wrathful retribution swiftly comes.
The Lady of Justice sits on high; and she
Who heapeth woe on woe on humankind,
Even Ate, punisheth the shameless tongue."

So mid the Danaans cried a voice: nor yet
Within the mighty soul of Peleus' son
Lulled was the storm of wrath, but fiercely he spake:
"Lie there in dust, thy follies all forgot!
'Tis not for knaves to beard their betters: once
Thou didst provoke Odysseus' steadfast soul,
Babbling with venomous tongue a thousand gibes,
And didst escape with life; but thou hast found
The son of Peleus not so patient-souled,
Who with one only buffet from his hand
Unkennels thy dog's soul! A bitter doom
Hath swallowed thee: by thine own rascalry
Thy life is sped. Hence from Achaean men,
And mouth out thy revilings midst the dead!"

So spake the valiant-hearted aweless son

Of Aeacus. But Tydeus' son alone
Of all the Argives was with anger stirred
Against Achilles for Thersites slain,
Seeing these twain were of the self-same blood,
The one, proud Tydeus' battle-eager son,
The other, seed of godlike Agrius:
Brother of noble Oeneus Agrius was;
And Oeneus in the Danaan land begat
Tydeus the battle-eager, son to whom
Was stalwart Diomedes. Therefore wroth
Was he for slain Thersites, yea, had raised
Against the son of Peleus vengeful hands,
Except the noblest of Aehaea's sons
Had thronged around him, and besought him sore,
And held him back therefrom. With Peleus' son
Also they pleaded; else those mighty twain,
The mightiest of all Argives, were at point
To close with clash of swords, so stung were they
With bitter wrath; yet hearkened they at last
To prayers of comrades, and were reconciled.

Then of their pity did the Atreid kings--
For these too at the imperial loveliness
Of Penthesileia marvelled--render up
Her body to the men of Troy, to bear
Unto the burg of Ilus far-renowned
With all her armour. For a herald came
Asking this boon for Priam; for the king
Longed with deep yearning of the heart to lay
That battle-eager maiden, with her arms,
And with her war-horse, in the great earth-mound
Of old Laomedon. And so he heaped
A high broad pyre without the city wall:

Upon the height thereof that warrior-queen
They laid, and costly treasures did they heap
Around her, all that well beseems to burn
Around a mighty queen in battle slain.
And so the Fire-god's swift-upleaping might,
The ravening flame, consumed her. All around
The people stood on every hand, and quenched
The pyre with odorous wine. Then gathered they
The bones, and poured sweet ointment over them,
And laid them in a casket: over all
Shed they the rich fat of a heifer, chief
Among the herds that grazed on Ida's slope.
And, as for a beloved daughter, rang
All round the Trojan men's heart-stricken wail,
As by the stately wall they buried her
On an outstanding tower, beside the bones
Of old Laomedon, a queen beside
A king. This honour for the War-god's sake
They rendered, and for Penthesileia's own.
And in the plain beside her buried they
The Amazons, even all that followed her
To battle, and by Argive spears were slain.
For Atreus' sons begrudged not these the boon
Of tear-besprinkled graves, but let their friends,
The warrior Trojans, draw their corpses forth,
Yea, and their own slain also, from amidst
The swath of darts o'er that grim harvest-field.
Wrath strikes not at the dead: pitied are foes
When life has fled, and left them foes no more.

Far off across the plain the while uprose
Smoke from the pyres whereon the Argives laid
The many heroes overthrown and slain

By Trojan hands what time the sword devoured;
And multitudinous lamentation wailed
Over the perished. But above the rest
Mourned they o'er brave Podarces, who in fight
Was no less mighty than his hero-brother
Protesilaus, he who long ago
Fell, slain of Hector: so Podarces now,
Struck down by Penthesileia's spear, hath cast
Over all Argive hearts the pall of grief.
Wherefore apart from him they laid in clay
The common throng of slain; but over him
Toiling they heaped an earth-mound far-descried
In memory of a warrior aweless-souled.
And in a several pit withal they thrust
The niddering Thersites' wretched corse.
Then to the ships, acclaiming Aeacus' son,
Returned they all. But when the radiant day
Had plunged beneath the Ocean-stream, and night,
The holy, overspread the face of earth,
Then in the rich king Agamemnon's tent
Feasted the might of Peleus' son, and there
Sat at the feast those other mighty ones
All through the dark, till rose the dawn divine.

BOOK II

How Memnon, Son of the Dawn, for Troy's sake fell in the Battle.

    When o'er the crests of the far-echoing hills
The splendour of the tireless-racing sun
Poured o'er the land, still in their tents rejoiced
Achaea's stalwart sons, and still acclaimed
Achilles the resistless. But in Troy
Still mourned her people, still from all her towers
Seaward they strained their gaze; for one great fear
Gripped all their hearts--to see that terrible man
At one bound overleap their high-built wall,
Then smite with the sword all people therewithin,
And burn with fire fanes, palaces, and homes.
And old Thymoetes spake to the anguished ones:
"Friends, I have lost hope: mine heart seeth not
Or help, or bulwark from the storm of war,
Now that the aweless Hector, who was once
Troy's mighty champion, is in dust laid low.
Not all his might availed to escape the Fates,
But overborne he was by Achilles' hands,
The hands that would, I verily deem, bear down
A God, if he defied him to the fight,
Even as he overthrew this warrior-queen

Penthesileia battle-revelling,
From whom all other Argives shrank in fear.
Ah, she was marvellous! When at the first
I looked on her, meseemed a Blessed One
From heaven had come down hitherward to bring
Light to our darkness--ah, vain hope, vain dream!
Go to, let us take counsel, what to do
Were best for us. Or shall we still maintain
A hopeless fight against these ruthless foes,
Or shall we straightway flee a city doomed?
Ay, doomed!--for never more may we withstand
Argives in fighting field, when in the front
Of battle pitiless Achilles storms."

Then spake Laomedon's son, the ancient king:
"Nay, friend, and all ye other sons of Troy,
And ye our strong war-helpers, flinch we not
Faint-hearted from defence of fatherland!
Yet let us go not forth the city-gates
To battle with yon foe. Nay, from our towers
And from our ramparts let us make defence,
Till our new champion come, the stormy heart
Of Memnon. Lo, he cometh, leading on
Hosts numberless, Aethiopia's swarthy sons.
By this, I trow, he is nigh unto our gates;
For long ago, in sore distress of soul,
I sent him urgent summons. Yea, and he
Promised me, gladly promised me, to come
To Troy, and make all end of all our woes.
And now, I trust, he is nigh. Let us endure
A little longer then; for better far
It is like brave men in the fight to die
Than flee, and live in shame mid alien folk."

So spake the old king; but Polydamas,
The prudent-hearted, thought not good to war
Thus endlessly, and spake his patriot rede:
"If Memnon have beyond all shadow of doubt
Pledged him to thrust dire ruin far from us,
Then do I gainsay not that we await
The coming of that godlike man within
Our walls--yet, ah, mine heart misgives me, lest,
Though he with all his warriors come, he come
But to his death, and unto thousands more,
Our people, nought but misery come thereof;
For terribly against us leaps the storm
Of the Achaeans' might. But now, go to,
Let us not flee afar from this our Troy
To wander to some alien land, and there,
In the exile's pitiful helplessness, endure
All flouts and outrage; nor in our own land
Abide we till the storm of Argive war
O'erwhelm us. Nay, even now, late though it be,
Better it were for us to render back
Unto the Danaans Helen and her wealth,
Even all that glory of women brought with her
From Sparta, and add other treasure--yea,
Repay it twofold, so to save our Troy
And our own souls, while yet the spoiler's hand
Is laid not on our substance, and while yet
Troy hath not sunk in gulfs of ravening flame.
I pray you, take to heart my counsel! None
Shall, well I wot, be given to Trojan men
Better than this. Ah, would that long ago
Hector had hearkened to my pleading, when
I fain had kept him in the ancient home!"

So spake Polydamas the noble and strong,
And all the listening Trojans in their hearts
Approved; yet none dared utter openly
The word, for all with trembling held in awe
Their prince and Helen, though for her sole sake
Daily they died. But on that noble man
Turned Paris, and reviled him to his face:
"Thou dastard battle-blencher Polydamas!
Not in thy craven bosom beats a heart
That bides the fight, but only fear and panic.
Yet dost thou vaunt thee--quotha!--still our best
In counsel!--no man's soul is base as thine!
Go to, thyself shrink shivering from the strife!
Cower, coward, in thine halls! But all the rest,
We men, will still go armour-girt, until
We wrest from this our truceless war a peace
That shall not shame us! 'Tis with travail and toil
Of strenuous war that brave men win renown;
But flight?--weak women choose it, and young babes!
Thy spirit is like to theirs. No whit I trust
Thee in the day of battle--thee, the man
Who maketh faint the hearts of all the host!"

So fiercely he reviled: Polydamas
Wrathfully answered; for he shrank not, he,
From answering to his face. A caitiff hound,
A reptile fool, is he who fawns on men
Before their faces, while his heart is black
With malice, and, when they be gone, his tongue
Backbites them. Openly Polydamas
Flung back upon the prince his taunt and scoff:
"O thou of living men most mischievous!
Thy valour--quotha!--brings us misery!

Thine heart endures, and will endure, that strife
Should have no limit, save in utter ruin
Of fatherland and people for thy sake!
Ne'er may such wantwit valour craze my soul!
Be mine to cherish wise discretion aye,
A warder that shall keep mine house in peace."

Indignantly he spake, and Paris found
No word to answer him, for conscience woke
Remembrance of all woes he had brought on Troy,
And should bring; for his passion-fevered heart
Would rather hail quick death than severance
From Helen the divinely fair, although
For her sake was it that the sons of Troy
Even then were gazing from their towers to see
The Argives and Achilles drawing nigh.

But no long time thereafter came to them
Memnon the warrior-king, and brought with him
A countless host of swarthy Aethiops.
From all the streets of Troy the Trojans flocked
Glad-eyed to gaze on him, as seafarers,
With ruining tempest utterly forspent,
See through wide-parting clouds the radiance
Of the eternal-wheeling Northern Wain;
So joyed the Troyfolk as they thronged around,
And more than all Laomedon's son, for now
Leapt in his heart a hope, that yet the ships
Might by those Aethiop men be burned with fire;
So giantlike their king was, and themselves
So huge a host, and so athirst for fight.
Therefore with all observance welcomed he
The strong son of the Lady of the Dawn

With goodly gifts and with abundant cheer.
So at the banquet King and Hero sat
And talked, this telling of the Danaan chiefs,
And all the woes himself had suffered, that
Telling of that strange immortality
By the Dawn-goddess given to his sire,
Telling of the unending flow and ebb
Of the Sea-mother, of the sacred flood
Of Ocean fathomless-rolling, of the bounds
Of Earth that wearieth never of her travail,
Of where the Sun-steeds leap from orient waves,
Telling withal of all his wayfaring
From Ocean's verge to Priam's wall, and spurs
Of Ida. Yea, he told how his strong hands
Smote the great army of the Solymi
Who barred his way, whose deed presumptuous brought
Upon their own heads crushing ruin and woe.
So told he all that marvellous tale, and told
Of countless tribes and nations seen of him.
And Priam heard, and ever glowed his heart
Within him; and the old lips answering spake:
"Memnon, the Gods are good, who have vouchsafed
To me to look upon thine host, and thee
Here in mine halls. O that their grace would so
Crown this their boon, that I might see my foes
All thrust to one destruction by thy spears.
That well may be, for marvellous-like art thou
To some invincible Deathless One, yea, more
Than any earthly hero. Wherefore thou,
I trust, shalt hurl wild havoc through their host.
But now, I pray thee, for this day do thou
Cheer at my feast thine heart, and with the morn
Shalt thou go forth to battle worthy of thee."

Then in his hands a chalice deep and wide
He raised, and Memnon in all love he pledged
In that huge golden cup, a gift of Gods;
For this the cunning God-smith brought to Zeus,
His masterpiece, what time the Mighty in Power
To Hephaestus gave for bride the Cyprian Queen;
And Zeus on Dardanus his godlike son
Bestowed it, he on Erichthonius;
Erichthonius to Tros the great of heart
Gave it, and he with all his treasure-store
Bequeathed it unto Ilus, and he gave
That wonder to Laomedon, and he
To Priam, who had thought to leave the same
To his own son. Fate ordered otherwise.
And Memnon clasped his hands about that cup
So peerless-beautiful, and all his heart
Marvelled; and thus he spake unto the King:
"Beseems not with great swelling words to vaunt
Amidst the feast, and lavish promises,
But rather quietly to eat in hall,
And to devise deeds worthy. Whether I
Be brave and strong, or whether I be not,
Battle, wherein a man's true might is seen,
Shall prove to thee. Now would I rest, nor drink
The long night through. The battle-eager spirit
By measureless wine and lack of sleep is dulled."

Marvelled at him the old King, and he said:
"As seems thee good touching the banquet, do
After thy pleasure. I, when thou art loth,
Will not constrain thee. Yea, unmeet it is
To hold back him who fain would leave the board,
Or hurry from one's halls who fain would stay.

So is the good old law with all true men."

Then rose that champion from the board, and passed
Thence to his sleep--his last! And with him went
All others from the banquet to their rest:
And gentle sleep slid down upon them soon.

But in the halls of Zeus, the Lightning-lord,
Feasted the gods the while, and Cronos' son,
All-father, of his deep foreknowledge spake
Amidst them of the issue of the strife:
"Be it known unto you all, to-morn shall bring
By yonder war affliction swift and sore;
For many mighty horses shall ye see
In either host beside their chariots slain,
And many heroes perishing. Therefore ye
Remember these my words, howe'er ye grieve
For dear ones. Let none clasp my knees in prayer,
Since even to us relentless are the fates."

So warned he them, which knew before, that all
Should from the battle stand aside, howe'er
Heart-wrung; that none, petitioning for a son
Or dear one, should to Olympus vainly come.
So, at that warning of the Thunderer,
The Son of Cronos, all they steeled their hearts
To bear, and spake no word against their king;
For in exceeding awe they stood of him.
Yet to their several mansions and their rest
With sore hearts went they. O'er their deathless eyes
The blessing-bringer Sleep his light veils spread.

When o'er precipitous crests of mountain-walls

Leapt up broad heaven the bright morning-star
Who rouseth to their toils from slumber sweet
The binders of the sheaf, then his last sleep
Unclasped the warrior-son of her who brings
Light to the world, the Child of Mists of Night.
Now swelled his mighty heart with eagerness
To battle with the foe forthright. And Dawn
With most reluctant feet began to climb
Heaven's broad highway. Then did the Trojans gird
Their battle-harness on; then armed themselves
The Aethiop men, and all the mingled tribes
Of those war-helpers that from many lands
To Priam's aid were gathered. Forth the gates
Swiftly they rushed, like darkly lowering clouds
Which Cronos' Son, when storm is rolling up,
Herdeth together through the welkin wide.
Swiftly the whole plain filled. Onward they streamed
Like harvest-ravaging locusts drifting on
In fashion of heavy-brooding rain-clouds o'er
Wide plains of earth, an irresistible host
Bringing wan famine on the sons of men;
So in their might and multitude they went.
The city streets were all too strait for them
Marching: upsoared the dust from underfoot.

From far the Argives gazed, and marvelling saw
Their onrush, but with speed arrayed their limbs
In brass, and in the might of Peleus' son
Put their glad trust. Amidst them rode he on
Like to a giant Titan, glorying
In steeds and chariot, while his armour flashed
Splendour around in sudden lightning-gleams.
It was as when the sun from utmost bounds

Of earth-encompassing ocean comes, and brings
Light to the world, and flings his splendour wide
Through heaven, and earth and air laugh all around.
So glorious, mid the Argives Peleus' son
Rode onward. Mid the Trojans rode the while
Memnon the hero, even such to see
As Ares furious-hearted. Onward swept
The eager host arrayed about their lord.

Then in the grapple of war on either side
Closed the long lines, Trojan and Danaan;
But chief in prowess still the Aethiops were.
Crashed they together as when surges meet
On the wild sea, when, in a day of storm,
From every quarter winds to battle rush.
Foe hurled at foe the ashen spear, and slew:
Screams and death-groans went up like roaring fire.
As when down-thundering torrents shout and rave
On-pouring seaward, when the madding rains
Stream from God's cisterns, when the huddling clouds
Are hurled against each other ceaselessly,
And leaps their fiery breath in flashes forth;
So 'neath the fighters' trampling feet the earth
Thundered, and leapt the terrible battle-yell
Through frenzied air, for mad the war-cries were.

For firstfruits of death's harvest Peleus' son
Slew Thalius and Mentes nobly born,
Men of renown, and many a head beside
Dashed he to dust. As in its furious swoop
A whirlwind shakes dark chasms underground,
And earth's foundations crumble and melt away
Around the deep roots of the shuddering world,

So the ranks crumbled in swift doom to the dust
Before the spear and fury of Peleus's son.

But on the other side the hero child
Of the Dawn-goddess slew the Argive men,
Like to a baleful Doom which bringeth down
On men a grim and ghastly pestilence.
First slew he Pheron; for the bitter spear
Plunged through his breast, and down on him he hurled
Goodly Ereuthus, battle-revellers both,
Dwellers in Thryus by Alpheus' streams,
Which followed Nestor to the god-built burg
Of Ilium. But when he had laid these low,
Against the son of Neleus pressed he on
Eager to slay. Godlike Antilochus
Strode forth to meet him, sped the long spear's flight,
Yet missed him, for a little he swerved, but slew
His Aethiop comrade, son of Pyrrhasus.
Wroth for his fall, against Antilochus
He leapt, as leaps a lion mad of mood
Upon a boar, the beast that flincheth not
From fight with man or brute, whose charge is a flash
Of lightning; so was his swift leap. His foe
Antilochus caught a huge stone from the ground,
Hurled, smote him; but unshaken abode his strength,
For the strong helm-crest fenced his head from death;
But rang the morion round his brows. His heart
Kindled with terrible fury at the blow
More than before against Antilochus.
Like seething cauldron boiled his maddened might.
He stabbed, for all his cunning of fence, the son
Of Nestor above the breast; the crashing spear
Plunged to the heart, the spot of speediest death.

Then upon all the Danaans at his fall
Came grief; but anguish-stricken was the heart
Of Nestor most of all, to see his child
Slain in his sight; for no more bitter pang
Smiteth the heart of man than when a son
Perishes, and his father sees him die.
Therefore, albeit unused to melting mood,
His soul was torn with agony for the son
By black death slain. A wild cry hastily
To Thrasymedes did he send afar:
"Hither to me, Thrasymedes war-renowned!
Help me to thrust back from thy brother's corse,
Yea, from mine hapless son, his murderer,
That so ourselves may render to our dead
All dues of mourning. If thou flinch for fear,
No son of mine art thou, nor of the line
Of Periclymenus, who dared withstand
Hercules' self. Come, to the battle-toil!
For grim necessity oftentimes inspires
The very coward with courage of despair."

Then at his cry that brother's heart was stung
With bitter grief. Swift for his help drew nigh
Phereus, on whom for his great prince's fall
Came anguish. Charged these warriors twain to face
Strong Memnon in the gory strife. As when
Two hunters 'mid a forest's mountain-folds,
Eager to take the prey, rush on to meet
A wild boar or a bear, with hearts afire
To slay him, but in furious mood he leaps
On them, and holds at bay the might of men;
So swelled the heart of Memnon. Nigh drew they,

Yet vainly essayed to slay him, as they hurled
The long spears, but the lances glanced aside
Far from his flesh: the Dawn-queen turned them thence.
Yet fell their spears not vainly to the ground:
The lance of fiery-hearted Phereus, winged
With eager speed, dealt death to Meges' son,
Polymnius: Laomedon was slain
By the wrath of Nestor's son for a brother dead,
The dear one Memnon slew in battle-rout,
And whom the slayer's war-unwearied hands
Now stripped of his all-brazen battle-gear,
Nought recking, he, of Thrasymedes' might,
Nor of stout Phereus, who were unto him
But weaklings. A great lion seemed he there
Standing above a hart, as jackals they,
That, howso hungry, dare not come too nigh.

But hard thereby the father gazed thereon
In agony, and cried the rescue-cry
To other his war-comrades for their aid
Against the foe. Himself too burned to fight
From his war-car; for yearning for the dead
Goaded him to the fray beyond his strength.
Ay, and himself had been on his dear son
Laid, numbered with the dead, had not the voice
Of Memnon stayed him even in act to rush
Upon him, for he reverenced in his heart
The white hairs of an age-mate of his sire:
"Ancient," he cried, "it were my shame to fight.
With one so much mine elder: I am not
Blind unto honour. Verily I weened
That this was some young warrior, when I saw
Thee facing thus the foe. My bold heart hoped

For contest worthy of mine hand and spear.
Nay, draw thou back afar from battle-toil
And bitter death. Go, lest, how loth soe'er,
I smite thee of sore need. Nay, fall not thou
Beside thy son, against a mightier man
Fighting, lest men with folly thee should charge,
For folly it is that braves o'ermastering might."

He spake, and answered him that warrior old:
"Nay, Memnon, vain was that last word of thine.
None would name fool the father who essayed,
Battling with foes for his son's sake, to thrust
The ruthless slayer back from that dear corpse,
But ah that yet my strength were whole in me,
That thou might'st know my spear! Now canst thou vaunt
Proudly enow: a young man's heart is bold
And light his wit. Uplifted is thy soul
And vain thy speech. If in my strength of youth
Thou hadst met me--ha, thy friends had not rejoiced,
For all thy might! But me the grievous weight
Of age bows down, like an old lion whom
A cur may boldly drive back from the fold,
For that he cannot, in his wrath's despite,
Maintain his own cause, being toothless now,
And strengthless, and his strong heart tamed by time.
So well the springs of olden strength no more
Now in my breast. Yet am I stronger still
Than many men; my grey hairs yield to few
That have within them all the strength of youth."

So drew he back a little space, and left
Lying in dust his son, since now no more
Lived in the once lithe limbs the olden strength,

The Fall of Troy

For the years' weight lay heavy on his head.
Back leapt Thrasymedes likewise, spearman good,
And battle-eager Phereus, and the rest
Their comrades; for that slaughter-dealing man
Pressed hard on them. As when from mountains high
A shouting river with wide-echoing din
Sweeps down its fathomless whirlpools through the gloom,
When God with tumult of a mighty storm
Hath palled the sky in cloud from verge to verge,
When thunders crash all round, when thick and fast
Gleam lightnings from the huddling clouds, when fields
Are flooded as the hissing rain descends,
And all the air is filled with awful roar
Of torrents pouring down the hill-ravines;
So Memnon toward the shores of Hellespont
Before him hurled the Argives, following hard
Behind them, slaughtering ever. Many a man
Fell in the dust, and left his life in blood
'Neath Aethiop hands. Stained was the earth with gore
As Danaans died. Exulted Memnon's soul
As on the ranks of foemen ever he rushed,
And heaped with dead was all the plain of Troy.
And still from fight refrained he not; he hoped
To be a light of safety unto Troy
And bane to Danaans. But all the while
Stood baleful Doom beside him, and spurred on
To strife, with flattering smile. To right, to left
His stalwart helpers wrought in battle-toil,
Alcyoneus and Nychius, and the son
Of Asius furious-souled; Meneclus' spear,
Clydon and Alexippus, yea, a host
Eager to chase the foe, men who in fight
Quit them like men, exulting in their king.

Then, as Meneclus on the Danaans charged,
The son of Neleus slew him. Wroth for his friend,
Whole throngs of foes fierce-hearted Memnon slew.
As when a hunter midst the mountains drives
Swift deer within the dark lines of his toils--
The eager ring of beaters closing in
Presses the huddled throng into the snares
Of death: the dogs are wild with joy of the chase
Ceaselessly giving tongue, the while his darts
Leap winged with death on brocket and on hind;
So Memnon slew and ever slew: his men
Rejoiced, the while in panic stricken rout
Before that glorious man the Argives fled.
As when from a steep mountain's precipice-brow
Leaps a huge crag, which all-resistless Zeus
By stroke of thunderbolt hath hurled from the crest;
Crash oakwood copses, echo long ravines,
Shudders the forest to its rattle and roar,
And flocks therein and herds and wild things flee
Scattering, as bounding, whirling, it descends
With deadly pitiless onrush; so his foes
Fled from the lightning-flash of Memnon's spear.

Then to the side of Aeacus' mighty son
Came Nestor. Anguished for his son he cried:
"Achilles, thou great bulwark of the Greeks,
Slain is my child! The armour of my dead
Hath Memnon, and I fear me lest his corse
Be cast a prey to dogs. Haste to his help!
True friend is he who still remembereth
A friend though slain, and grieves for one no more."

Achilles heard; his heart was thrilled with grief:

The Fall of Troy

He glanced across the rolling battle, saw
Memnon, saw where in throngs the Argives fell
Beneath his spear. Forthright he turned away
From where the rifted ranks of Troy fell fast
Before his hands, and, thirsting for the fight,
Wroth for Antilochus and the others slain,
Came face to face with Memnon. In his hands
That godlike hero caught up from the ground
A stone, a boundary-mark 'twixt fields of wheat,
And hurled. Down on the shield of Peleus' son
It crashed. But he, the invincible, shrank not
Before the huge rock-shard, but, thrusting out
His long lance, rushed to close with him, afoot,
For his steeds stayed behind the battle-rout.
On the right shoulder above the shield he smote
And staggered him; but he, despite the wound,
Fought on with heart unquailing. Swiftly he thrust
And pricked with his strong spear Achilles' arm.
Forth gushed the blood: rejoicing with vain joy
To Aeacus' son with arrogant words he cried:
"Now shalt thou in thy death fill up, I trow,
Thy dark doom, overmastered by mine hands.
Thou shalt not from this fray escape alive!
Fool, wherefore hast thou ruthlessly destroyed
Trojans, and vaunted thee the mightiest man
Of men, a deathless Nereid's son? Ha, now
Thy doom hath found thee! Of birth divine am I,
The Dawn-queen's mighty son, nurtured afar
By lily-slender Hesperid Maids, beside
The Ocean-river. Therefore not from thee
Nor from grim battle shrink I, knowing well
How far my goddess-mother doth transcend
A Nereid, whose child thou vauntest thee.

To Gods and men my mother bringeth light;
On her depends the issue of all things,
Works great and glorious in Olympus wrought
Whereof comes blessing unto men. But thine--
She sits in barren crypts of brine: she dwells
Glorying mid dumb sea-monsters and mid fish,
Deedless, unseen! Nothing I reck of her,
Nor rank her with the immortal Heavenly Ones."

In stern rebuke spake Aeacus' aweless son:
"Memnon, how wast thou so distraught of wit
That thou shouldst face me, and to fight defy
Me, who in might, in blood, in stature far
Surpass thee? From supremest Zeus I trace
My glorious birth; and from the strong Sea-god
Nereus, begetter of the Maids of the Sea,
The Nereids, honoured of the Olympian Gods.
And chiefest of them all is Thetis, wise
With wisdom world-renowned; for in her bowers
She sheltered Dionysus, chased by might
Of murderous Lycurgus from the earth.
Yea, and the cunning God-smith welcomed she
Within her mansion, when from heaven he fell.
Ay, and the Lightning-lord she once released
From bonds. The all-seeing Dwellers in the Sky
Remember all these things, and reverence
My mother Thetis in divine Olympus.
Ay, that she is a Goddess shalt thou know
When to thine heart the brazen spear shall pierce
Sped by my might. Patroclus' death I avenged
On Hector, and Antilochus on thee
Will I avenge. No weakling's friend thou hast slain!
But why like witless children stand we here

Babbling our parents' fame and our own deeds?
Now is the hour when prowess shall decide."

Then from the sheath he flashed his long keen sword,
And Memnon his; and swiftly in fiery fight
Closed they, and rained the never-ceasing blows
Upon the bucklers which with craft divine
Hephaestus' self had fashioned. Once and again
Clashed they together, and their cloudy crests
Touched, mingling all their tossing storm of hair.
And Zeus, for that he loved them both, inspired
With prowess each, and mightier than their wont
He made them, made them tireless, nothing like
To men, but Gods: and gloated o'er the twain
The Queen of Strife. In eager fury these
Thrust swiftly out the spear, with fell intent
To reach the throat 'twixt buckler-rim and helm,
Thrust many a time and oft, and now would aim
The point beneath the shield, above the greave,
Now close beneath the corslet curious-wrought
That lapped the stalwart frame: hard, fast they lunged,
And on their shoulders clashed the arms divine.
Roared to the very heavens the battle-shout
Of warring men, of Trojans, Aethiops,
And Argives mighty-hearted, while the dust
Rolled up from 'neath their feet, tossed to the sky
In stress of battle-travail great and strong.

As when a mist enshrouds the hills, what time
Roll up the rain-clouds, and the torrent-beds
Roar as they fill with rushing floods, and howls
Each gorge with fearful voices; shepherds quake
To see the waters' downrush and the mist,

Screen dear to wolves and all the wild fierce things
Nursed in the wide arms of the forest; so
Around the fighters' feet the choking dust
Hung, hiding the fair splendour of the sun
And darkening all the heaven. Sore distressed
With dust and deadly conflict were the folk.
Then with a sudden hand some Blessed One
Swept the dust-pall aside; and the Gods saw
The deadly Fates hurling the charging lines
Together, in the unending wrestle locked
Of that grim conflict, saw where never ceased
Ares from hideous slaughter, saw the earth
Crimsoned all round with rushing streams of blood,
Saw where dark Havoc gloated o'er the scene,
Saw the wide plain with corpses heaped, even all
Bounded 'twixt Simois and Xanthus, where
They sweep from Ida down to Hellespont.

But when long lengthened out the conflict was
Of those two champions, and the might of both
In that strong tug and strain was equal-matched,
Then, gazing from Olympus' far-off heights,
The Gods joyed, some in the invincible son
Of Peleus, others in the goodly child
Of old Tithonus and the Queen of Dawn.
Thundered the heavens on high from east to west,
And roared the sea from verge to verge, and rocked
The dark earth 'neath the heroes' feet, and quaked
Proud Nereus' daughters all round Thetis thronged
In grievous fear for mighty Achilles' sake;
And trembled for her son the Child of the Mist
As in her chariot through the sky she rode.
Marvelled the Daughters of the Sun, who stood

The Fall of Troy

Near her, around that wondrous splendour-ring
Traced for the race-course of the tireless sun
By Zeus, the limit of all Nature's life
And death, the dally round that maketh up
The eternal circuit of the rolling years.
And now amongst the Blessed bitter feud
Had broken out; but by behest of Zeus
The twin Fates suddenly stood beside these twain,
One dark--her shadow fell on Memnon's heart;
One bright--her radiance haloed Peleus' son.
And with a great cry the Immortals saw,
And filled with sorrow they of the one part were,
They of the other with triumphant joy.

Still in the midst of blood-stained battle-rout
Those heroes fought, unknowing of the Fates
Now drawn so nigh, but each at other hurled
His whole heart's courage, all his bodily might.
Thou hadst said that in the strife of that dread day
Huge tireless Giants or strong Titans warred,
So fiercely blazed the wildfire of their strife,
Now, when they clashed with swords, now when they leapt
Hurling huge stones. Nor either would give back
Before the hail of blows, nor quailed. They stood
Like storm-tormented headlands steadfast, clothed
With might past words, unearthly; for the twain
Alike could boast their lineage of high Zeus.
Therefore 'twixt these Enyo lengthened out
The even-balanced strife, while ever they
In that grim wrestle strained their uttermost,
They and their dauntless comrades, round their kings
With ceaseless fury toiling, till their spears
Stood shivered all in shields of warriors slain,

And of the fighters woundless none remained;
But from all limbs streamed down into the dust
The blood and sweat of that unresting strain
Of fight, and earth was hidden with the dead,
As heaven is hidden with clouds when meets the sun
The Goat-star, and the shipman dreads the deep.
As charged the lines, the snorting chariot-steeds
Trampled the dead, as on the myriad leaves
Ye trample in the woods at entering-in
Of winter, when the autumn-tide is past.

Still mid the corpses and the blood fought on
Those glorious sons of Gods, nor ever ceased
From wrath of fight. But Eris now inclined
The fatal scales of battle, which no more
Were equal-poised. Beneath the breast-bone then
Of godlike Memnon plunged Achilles' sword;
Clear through his body all the dark-blue blade
Leapt: suddenly snapped the silver cord of life.
Down in a pool of blood he fell, and clashed
His massy armour, and earth rang again.
Then turned to flight his comrades panic-struck,
And of his arms the Myrmidons stripped the dead,
While fled the Trojans, and Achilles chased,
As whirlwind swift and mighty to destroy.

Then groaned the Dawn, and palled herself in clouds,
And earth was darkened. At their mother's hest
All the light Breathings of the Dawn took hands,
And slid down one long stream of sighing wind
To Priam's plain, and floated round the dead,
And softly, swiftly caught they up, and bare
Through silver mists the Dawn-queen's son, with hearts

The Fall of Troy

Sore aching for their brother's fall, while moaned
Around them all the air. As on they passed,
Fell many blood-gouts from those pierced limbs
Down to the earth, and these were made a sign
To generations yet to be. The Gods
Gathered them up from many lands, and made
Thereof a far-resounding river, named
Of all that dwell beneath long Ida's flanks
Paphlagoneion. As its waters flow
'Twixt fertile acres, once a year they turn
To blood, when comes the woeful day whereon
Died Memnon. Thence a sick and choking reek
Steams: thou wouldst say that from a wound unhealed
Corrupting humours breathed an evil stench.
Ay, so the Gods ordained: but now flew on
Bearing Dawn's mighty son the rushing winds
Skimming earth's face and palled about with night.

Nor were his Aethiopian comrades left
To wander of their King forlorn: a God
Suddenly winged those eager souls with speed
Such as should soon be theirs for ever, changed
To flying fowl, the children of the air.
Wailing their King in the winds' track they sped.
As when a hunter mid the forest-brakes
Is by a boar or grim-jawed lion slain,
And now his sorrowing friends take up the corse,
And bear it heavy-hearted; and the hounds
Follow low-whimpering, pining for their lord
In that disastrous hunting lost; so they
Left far behind that stricken field of blood,
And fast they followed after those swift winds

With multitudinous moaning, veiled in mist
Unearthly. Trojans over all the plain
And Danaans marvelled, seeing that great host
Vanishing with their King. All hearts stood still
In dumb amazement. But the tireless winds
Sighing set hero Memnon's giant corpse
Down by the deep flow of Aesopus' stream,
Where is a fair grove of the bright-haired Nymphs,
The which round his long barrow afterward
Aesopus' daughters planted, screening it
With many and manifold trees: and long and loud
Wailed those Immortals, chanting his renown,
The son of the Dawn-goddess splendour-throned.

Now sank the sun: the Lady of the Morn
Wailing her dear child from the heavens came down.
Twelve maidens shining-tressed attended her,
The warders of the high paths of the sun
For ever circling, warders of the night
And dawn, and each world-ordinance framed of Zeus,
Around whose mansion's everlasting doors
From east to west they dance, from west to east,
Whirling the wheels of harvest-laden years,
While rolls the endless round of winter's cold,
And flowery spring, and lovely summer-tide,
And heavy-clustered autumn. These came down
From heaven, for Memnon wailing wild and high;
And mourned with these the Pleiads. Echoed round
Far-stretching mountains, and Aesopus' stream.
Ceaseless uprose the keen, and in their midst,
Fallen on her son and clasping, wailed the Dawn;
"Dead art thou, dear, dear child, and thou hast clad
Thy mother with a pall of grief. Oh, I,

The Fall of Troy

Now thou art slain, will not endure to light
The Immortal Heavenly Ones! No, I will plunge
Down to the dread depths of the underworld,
Where thy lone spirit flitteth to and fro,
And will to blind night leave earth, sky, and sea,
Till Chaos and formless darkness brood o'er all,
That Cronos' Son may also learn what means
Anguish of heart. For not less worship-worthy
Than Nereus' Child, by Zeus's ordinance,
Am I, who look on all things, I, who bring
All to their consummation. Recklessly
My light Zeus now despiseth! Therefore I
Will pass into the darkness. Let him bring
Up to Olympus Thetis from the sea
To hold for him light forth to Gods and men!
My sad soul loveth darkness more than day,
Lest I pour light upon thy slayer's head:

Thus as she cried, the tears ran down her face
Immortal, like a river brimming aye:
Drenched was the dark earth round the corse. The Night
Grieved in her daughter's anguish, and the heaven
Drew over all his stars a veil of mist
And cloud, of love unto the Lady of Light.

Meanwhile within their walls the Trojan folk
For Memnon sorrowed sore, with vain regret
Yearning for that lost king and all his host.
Nor greatly joyed the Argives, where they lay
Camped in the open plain amidst the dead.
There, mingled with Achilles' praise, uprose
Wails for Antilochus: joy clasped hands with grief.

All night in groans and sighs most pitiful
The Dawn-queen lay: a sea of darkness moaned
Around her. Of the dayspring nought she recked:
She loathed Olympus' spaces. At her side
Fretted and whinnied still her fleetfoot steeds,
Trampling the strange earth, gazing at their Queen
Grief-stricken, yearning for the fiery course.
Suddenly crashed the thunder of the wrath
Of Zeus; rocked round her all the shuddering earth,
And on immortal Eos trembling came.

Swiftly the dark-skinned Aethiops from her sight
Buried their lord lamenting. As they wailed
Unceasingly, the Dawn-queen lovely-eyed
Changed them to birds sweeping through air around
The barrow of the mighty dead. And these
Still do the tribes of men "The Memnons" call;
And still with wailing cries they dart and wheel
Above their king's tomb, and they scatter dust
Down on his grave, still shrill the battle-cry,
In memory of Memnon, each to each.
But he in Hades' mansions, or perchance
Amid the Blessed on the Elysian Plain,
Laugheth. Divine Dawn comforteth her heart
Beholding them: but theirs is toil of strife
Unending, till the weary victors strike
The vanquished dead, or one and all fill up
The measure of their doom around his grave.

So by command of Eos, Lady of Light,
The swift birds dree their weird. But Dawn divine
Now heavenward soared with the all-fostering Hours,
Who drew her to Zeus' threshold, sorely loth,

Yet conquered by their gentle pleadings, such
As salve the bitterest grief of broken hearts.
Nor the Dawn-queen forgat her daily course,
But quailed before the unbending threat of Zeus,
Of whom are all things, even all comprised
Within the encircling sweep of Ocean's stream,
Earth and the palace-dome of burning stars.
Before her went her Pleiad-harbingers,
Then she herself flung wide the ethereal gates,
And, scattering spray of splendour, flashed there-through.

BOOK III

How by the shaft of a God laid low was Hero Achilles.

When shone the light of Dawn the splendour-throned,
Then to the ships the Pylian spearmen bore
Antilochus' corpse, sore sighing for their prince,
And by the Hellespont they buried him
With aching hearts. Around him groaning stood
The battle-eager sons of Argives, all,
Of love for Nestor, shrouded o'er with grief.
But that grey hero's heart was nowise crushed
By sorrow; for the wise man's soul endures
Bravely, and cowers not under affliction's stroke.
But Peleus' son, wroth for Antilochus
His dear friend, armed for vengeance terrible
Upon the Trojans. Yea, and these withal,
Despite their dread of mighty Achilles' spear,
Poured battle-eager forth their gates, for now
The Fates with courage filled their breasts, of whom
Many were doomed to Hades to descend,
Whence there is no return, thrust down by hands
Of Aeacus' son, who also was foredoomed
To perish that same day by Priam's wall.
Swift met the fronts of conflict: all the tribes

The Fall of Troy

Of Troy's host, and the battle-biding Greeks,
Afire with that new-kindled fury of war.

Then through the foe the son of Peleus made
Wide havoc: all around the earth was drenched
With gore, and choked with corpses were the streams
Of Simois and Xanthus. Still he chased,
Still slaughtered, even to the city's walls;
For panic fell on all the host. And now
All had he slain, had dashed the gates to earth,
Rending them from their hinges, or the bolts,
Hurling himself against them, had he snapped,
And for the Danaans into Priam's burg
Had made a way, had utterly destroyed
That goodly town--but now was Phoebus wroth
Against him with grim fury, when he saw
Those countless troops of heroes slain of him.
Down from Olympus with a lion-leap
He came: his quiver on his shoulders lay,
And shafts that deal the wounds incurable.
Facing Achilles stood he; round him clashed
Quiver and arrows; blazed with quenchless flame
His eyes, and shook the earth beneath his feet.
Then with a terrible shout the great God cried,
So to turn back from war Achilles awed
By the voice divine, and save from death the Trojans:
"Back from the Trojans, Peleus' son! Beseems not
That longer thou deal death unto thy foes,
Lest an Olympian God abase thy pride."

But nothing quailed the hero at the voice
Immortal, for that round him even now
Hovered the unrelenting Fates. He recked

Naught of the God, and shouted his defiance.
"Phoebus, why dost thou in mine own despite
Stir me to fight with Gods, and wouldst protect
The arrogant Trojans? Heretofore hast thou
By thy beguiling turned me from the fray,
When from destruction thou at the first didst save
Hector, whereat the Trojans all through Troy
Exulted. Nay, thou get thee back: return
Unto the mansion of the Blessed, lest
I smite thee--ay, immortal though thou be!"

Then on the God he turned his back, and sped
After the Trojans fleeing cityward,
And harried still their flight; but wroth at heart
Thus Phoebus spake to his indignant soul:
"Out on this man! he is sense-bereft! But now
Not Zeus himself nor any other Power
Shall save this madman who defies the Gods!"

From mortal sight he vanished into cloud,
And cloaked with mist a baleful shaft he shot
Which leapt to Achilles' ankle: sudden pangs
With mortal sickness made his whole heart faint.
He reeled, and like a tower he fell, that falls
Smit by a whirlwind when an earthquake cleaves
A chasm for rushing blasts from underground;
So fell the goodly form of Aeacus' son.
He glared, a murderous glance, to right, to left,
[Upon the Trojans, and a terrible threat]
Shouted, a threat that could not be fulfilled:
"Who shot at me a stealthy-smiting shaft?
Let him but dare to meet me face to face!
So shall his blood and all his bowels gush out

About my spear, and he be hellward sped!
I know that none can meet me man to man
And quell in fight--of earth-born heroes none,
Though such an one should bear within his breast
A heart unquailing, and have thews of brass.
But dastards still in stealthy ambush lurk
For lives of heroes. Let him face me then!--
Ay! though he be a God whose anger burns
Against the Danaans! Yea, mine heart forebodes
That this my smiter was Apollo, cloaked
In deadly darkness. So in days gone by
My mother told me how that by his shafts
I was to die before the Scaean Gates
A piteous death. Her words were not vain words."

Then with unflinching hands from out the wound
Incurable he drew the deadly shaft
In agonized pain. Forth gushed the blood; his heart
Waxed faint beneath the shadow of coming doom.
Then in indignant wrath he hurled from him
The arrow: a sudden gust of wind swept by,
And caught it up, and, even as he trod
Zeus' threshold, to Apollo gave it back;
For it beseemed not that a shaft divine,
Sped forth by an Immortal, should be lost.
He unto high Olympus swiftly came,
To the great gathering of immortal Gods,
Where all assembled watched the war of men,
These longing for the Trojans' triumph, those
For Danaan victory; so with diverse wills
Watched they the strife, the slayers and the slain.

Him did the Bride of Zeus behold, and straight

Upbraided with exceeding bitter words:
"What deed of outrage, Phoebus, hast thou done
This day, forgetful of that day whereon
To godlike Peleus' spousals gathered all
The Immortals? Yea, amidst the feasters thou
Sangest how Thetis silver-footed left
The sea's abysses to be Peleus' bride;
And as thou harpedst all earth's children came
To hearken, beasts and birds, high craggy hills,
Rivers, and all deep-shadowed forests came.
All this hast thou forgotten, and hast wrought
A ruthless deed, hast slain a godlike man,
Albeit thou with other Gods didst pour
The nectar, praying that he might be the son
By Thetis given to Peleus. But that prayer
Hast thou forgotten, favouring the folk
Of tyrannous Laomedon, whose kine
Thou keptest. He, a mortal, did despite
To thee, the deathless! O, thou art wit-bereft!
Thou favourest Troy, thy sufferings all forgot.
Thou wretch, and doth thy false heart know not this,
What man is an offence, and meriteth
Suffering, and who is honoured of the Gods?
Ever Achilles showed us reverence--yea,
Was of our race. Ha, but the punishment
Of Troy, I ween, shall not be lighter, though
Aeacus' son have fallen; for his son
Right soon shall come from Scyros to the war
To help the Argive men, no less in might
Than was his sire, a bane to many a foe.
But thou--thou for the Trojans dost not care,
But for his valour enviedst Peleus' son,
Seeing he was the mightest of all men.

Thou fool! how wilt thou meet the Nereid's eyes,
When she shall stand in Zeus' hall midst the Gods,
Who praised thee once, and loved as her own son?"

So Hera spake, in bitterness of soul
Upbraiding, but he answered her not a word,
Of reverence for his mighty Father's bride;
Nor could he lift his eyes to meet her eyes,
But sat abashed, aloof from all the Gods
Eternal, while in unforgiving wrath
Scowled on him all the Immortals who maintained
The Danaans' cause; but such as fain would bring
Triumph to Troy, these with exultant hearts
Extolled him, hiding it from Hera's eyes,
Before whose wrath all Heaven-abiders shrank.

But Peleus' son the while forgat not yet
War's fury: still in his invincible limbs
The hot blood throbbed, and still he longed for fight.
Was none of all the Trojans dared draw nigh
The stricken hero, but at distance stood,
As round a wounded lion hunters stand
Mid forest-brakes afraid, and, though the shaft
Stands in his heart, yet faileth not in him
His royal courage, but with terrible glare
Roll his fierce eyes, and roar his grimly jaws;
So wrath and anguish of his deadly hurt
To fury stung Peleides' soul; but aye
His strength ebbed through the god-envenomed wound.
Yet leapt he up, and rushed upon the foe,
And flashed the lightning of his lance; it slew
The goodly Orythaon, comrade stout
Of Hector, through his temples crashing clear:

His helm stayed not the long lance fury-sped
Which leapt therethrough, and won within the bones
The heart of the brain, and spilt his lusty life.
Then stabbed he 'neath the brow Hipponous
Even to the eye-roots, that the eyeball fell
To earth: his soul to Hades flitted forth.
Then through the jaw he pierced Alcathous,
And shore away his tongue: in dust he fell
Gasping his life out, and the spear-head shot
Out through his ear. These, as they rushed on him,
That hero slew; but many a fleer's life
He spilt, for in his heart still leapt the blood.

But when his limbs grew chill, and ebbed away
His spirit, leaning on his spear he stood,
While still the Trojans fled in huddled rout
Of panic, and he shouted unto them:
"Trojan and Dardan cravens, ye shall not
Even in my death, escape my merciless spear,
But unto mine Avenging Spirits ye
Shall pay--ay, one and all--destruction's debt!"

He spake; they heard and quailed: as mid the hills
Fawns tremble at a lion's deep-mouthed roar,
And terror-stricken flee the monster, so
The ranks of Trojan chariot-lords, the lines
Of battle-helpers drawn from alien lands,
Quailed at the last shout of Achilles, deemed
That he was woundless yet. But 'neath the weight
Of doom his aweless heart, his mighty limbs,
At last were overborne. Down midst the dead
He fell, as fails a beetling mountain-cliff.
Earth rang beneath him: clanged with a thundercrash

His arms, as Peleus' son the princely fell.
And still his foes with most exceeding dread
Stared at him, even as, when some murderous beast
Lies slain by shepherds, tremble still the sheep
Eyeing him, as beside the fold he lies,
And shrinking, as they pass him, far aloof
And, even as he were living, fear him dead;
So feared they him, Achilles now no more.

Yet Paris strove to kindle those faint hearts;
For his own heart exulted, and he hoped,
Now Peleus' son, the Danaans' strength, had fallen,
Wholly to quench the Argive battle-fire:
"Friends, if ye help me truly and loyally,
Let us this day die, slain by Argive men,
Or live, and hale to Troy with Hector's steeds
In triumph Peleus' son thus fallen dead,
The steeds that, grieving, yearning for their lord
To fight have borne me since my brother died.
Might we with these but hale Achilles slain,
Glory were this for Hector's horses, yea,
For Hector--if in Hades men have sense
Of righteous retribution. This man aye
Devised but mischief for the sons of Troy;
And now Troy's daughters with exultant hearts
From all the city streets shall gather round,
As pantheresses wroth for stolen cubs,
Or lionesses, might stand around a man
Whose craft in hunting vexed them while he lived.
So round Achilles--a dead corpse at last!--
In hurrying throngs Troy's daughters then shall come
In unforgiving, unforgetting hate,
For parents wroth, for husbands slain, for sons,

For noble kinsmen. Most of all shall joy
My father, and the ancient men, whose feet
Unwillingly are chained within the walls
By eld, if we shall hale him through our gates,
And give our foe to fowls of the air for meat."

Then they, which feared him theretofore, in haste
Closed round the corpse of strong-heart Aeacus' son,
Glaucus, Aeneas, battle-fain Agenor,
And other cunning men in deadly fight,
Eager to hale him thence to Ilium
The god-built burg. But Aias failed him not.
Swiftly that godlike man bestrode the dead:
Back from the corpse his long lance thrust them all.
Yet ceased they not from onslaught; thronging round,
Still with swift rushes fought they for the prize,
One following other, like to long-lipped bees
Which hover round their hive in swarms on swarms
To drive a man thence; but he, recking naught
Of all their fury, carveth out the combs
Of nectarous honey: harassed sore are they
By smoke-reek and the robber; spite of all
Ever they dart against him; naught cares he;
So naught of all their onsets Aias recked;
But first he stabbed Agelaus in the breast,
And slew that son of Maion: Thestor next:
Ocythous he smote, Agestratus,
Aganippus, Zorus, Nessus, Erymas
The war-renowned, who came from Lycia-land
With mighty-hearted Glaucus, from his home
In Melanippion on the mountain-ridge,
Athena's fane, which Massikyton fronts
Anigh Chelidonia's headland, dreaded sore

Of scared seafarers, when its lowering crags
Must needs be doubled. For his death the blood
Of famed Hippolochus' son was horror-chilled;
For this was his dear friend. With one swift thrust
He pierced the sevenfold hides of Aias' shield,
Yet touched his flesh not; stayed the spear-head was
By those thick hides and by the corset-plate
Which lapped his battle-tireless limbs. But still
From that stern conflict Glaucus drew not back,
Burning to vanquish Aias, Aeacus' son,
And in his folly vaunting threatened him:
"Aias, men name thee mightiest man of all
The Argives, hold thee in passing-high esteem
Even as Achilles: therefore thou, I wot,
By that dead warrior dead this day shalt lie!"

So hurled he forth a vain word, knowing not
How far in might above him was the man
Whom his spear threatened. Battle-bider Aias
Darkly and scornfully glaring on him, said
"Thou craven wretch, and knowest thou not this,
How much was Hector mightier than thou
In war-craft? yet before my might, my spear,
He shrank. Ay, with his valour was there blent
Discretion. Thou thy thoughts are deathward set,
Who dar'st defy me to the battle, me,
A mightier far than thou! Thou canst not say
That friendship of our fathers thee shall screen;
Nor me thy gifts shall wile to let thee pass
Scatheless from war, as once did Tydeus' son.
Though thou didst 'scape his fury, will not I
Suffer thee to return alive from war.
Ha, in thy many helpers dost thou trust

Who with thee, like so many worthless flies,
Flit round the noble Achilles' corpse? To these
Death and black doom shall my swift onset deal."

Then on the Trojans this way and that he turned,
As mid long forest-glens a lion turns
On hounds, and Trojans many and Lycians slew
That came for honour hungry, till he stood
Mid a wide ring of flinchers; like a shoal
Of darting fish when sails into their midst
Dolphin or shark, a huge sea-fosterling;
So shrank they from the might of Telamon's son,
As aye he charged amidst the rout. But still
Swarmed fighters up, till round Achilles' corse
To right, to left, lay in the dust the slain
Countless, as boars around a lion at bay;
And evermore the strife waxed deadlier.
Then too Hippolochus' war-wise son was slain
By Aias of the heart of fire. He fell
Backward upon Achilles, even as falls
A sapling on a sturdy mountain-oak;
So quelled by the spear on Peleus' son he fell.
But for his rescue Anchises' stalwart son
Strove hard, with all his comrades battle-fain,
And haled the corse forth, and to sorrowing friends
Gave it, to bear to Ilium's hallowed burg.
Himself to spoil Achilles still fought on,
Till warrior Aias pierced him with the spear
Through the right forearm. Swiftly leapt he back
From murderous war, and hasted thence to Troy.
There for his healing cunning leeches wrought,
Who stanched the blood-rush, and laid on the gash
Balms, such as salve war-stricken warriors' pangs.

But Aias still fought on: here, there he slew
With thrusts like lightning-flashes. His great heart
Ached sorely for his mighty cousin slain.
And now the warrior-king Laertes' son
Fought at his side: before him blenched the foe,
As he smote down Peisander's fleetfoot son,
The warrior Maenalus, who left his home
In far-renowned Abydos: down on him
He hurled Atymnius, the goodly son
Whom Pegasis the bright-haired Nymph had borne
To strong Emathion by Granicus' stream.
Dead by his side he laid Orestius' son,
Proteus, who dwelt 'neath lofty Ida's folds.
Ah, never did his mother welcome home
That son from war, Panaceia beauty-famed!
He fell by Odysseus' hands, who spilt the lives
Of many more whom his death-hungering spear
Reached in that fight around the mighty dead.
Yet Alcon, son of Megacles battle-swift,
Hard by Odysseus' right knee drave the spear
Home, and about the glittering greave the blood
Dark-crimson welled. He recked not of the wound,
But was unto his smiter sudden death;
For clear through his shield he stabbed him with his spear
Amidst his battle-fury: to the earth
Backward he dashed him by his giant might
And strength of hand: clashed round him in the dust
His armour, and his corslet was distained
With crimson life-blood. Forth from flesh and shield
The hero plucked the spear of death: the soul
Followed the lance-head from the body forth,
And life forsook its mortal mansion. Then
Rushed on his comrades, in his wound's despite,

Odysseus, nor from that stern battle-toil
Refrained him. And by this a mingled host
Of Danaans eager-hearted fought around
The mighty dead, and many and many a foe
Slew they with those smooth-shafted ashen spears.
Even as the winds strew down upon the ground
The flying leaves, when through the forest-glades
Sweep the wild gusts, as waneth autumn-tide,
And the old year is dying; so the spears
Of dauntless Danaans strewed the earth with slain,
For loyal to dead Achilles were they all,
And loyal to hero Aias to the death.
For like black Doom he blasted the ranks of Troy.
Then against Aias Paris strained his bow;
But he was ware thereof, and sped a stone
Swift to the archer's head: that bolt of death
Crashed through his crested helm, and darkness closed
Round him. In dust down fell he: naught availed
His shafts their eager lord, this way and that
Scattered in dust: empty his quiver lay,
Flew from his hand the bow. In haste his friends
Upcaught him from the earth, and Hector's steeds
Hurried him thence to Troy, scarce drawing breath,
And moaning in his pain. Nor left his men
The weapons of their lord, but gathered up
All from the plain, and bare them to the prince;
While Aias after him sent a wrathful shout:
"Dog, thou hast 'scaped the heavy hand of death
To-day! But swiftly thy last hour shall come
By some strong Argive's hands, or by mine own,
But now have I a nobler task in hand,
From murder's grip to rescue Achilles' corse."
Then turned he on the foe, hurling swift doom

On such as fought around Peleides yet.
'These saw how many yielded up the ghost
Neath his strong hands, and, with hearts failing them
For fear, against him could they stand no more.
As rascal vultures were they, which the swoop
Of an eagle, king of birds, scares far away
From carcasses of sheep that wolves have torn;
So this way, that way scattered they before
The hurtling stones, the sword, the might of Aias.
In utter panic from the war they fled,
In huddled rout, like starlings from the swoop
Of a death-dealing hawk, when, fleeing bane,
One drives against another, as they dart
All terror-huddled in tumultuous flight.
So from the war to Priam's burg they fled
Wretchedly clad with terror as a cloak,
Quailing from mighty Aias' battle-shout,
As with hands dripping blood-gouts he pursued.
Yea, all, one after other, had he slain,
Had they not streamed through city-gates flung wide
Hard-panting, pierced to the very heart with fear.
Pent therewithin he left them, as a shepherd
Leaves folded sheep, and strode back o'er the plain;
Yet never touched he with his feet the ground,
But aye he trod on dead men, arms, and blood;
For countless corpses lay o'er that wide stretch
Even from broad-wayed Troy to Hellespont,
Bodies of strong men slain, the spoil of Doom.
As when the dense stalks of sun-ripened corn
Fall 'neath the reapers' hands, and the long swaths,
Heavy with full ears, overspread the field,
And joys the heart of him who oversees
The toil, lord of the harvest; even so,

By baleful havoc overmastered, lay
All round face-downward men remembering not
The death-denouncing war-shout. But the sons
Of fair Achaea left their slaughtered foes
In dust and blood unstripped of arms awhile
Till they should lay upon the pyre the son
Of Peleus, who in battle-shock had been
Their banner of victory, charging in his might.
So the kings drew him from that stricken field
Straining beneath the weight of giant limbs,
And with all loving care they bore him on,
And laid him in his tent before the ships.
And round him gathered that great host, and wailed
Heart-anguished him who had been the Achaeans' strength,
And now, forgotten all the splendour of spears,
Lay mid the tents by moaning Hellespont,
In stature more than human, even as lay
Tityos, who sought to force Queen Leto, when
She fared to Pytho: swiftly in his wrath
Apollo shot, and laid him low, who seemed
Invincible: in a foul lake of gore
There lay he, covering many a rood of ground,
On the broad earth, his mother; and she moaned
Over her son, of blessed Gods abhorred;
But Lady Leto laughed. So grand of mould
There in the foemen's land lay Aeacus' son,
For joy to Trojans, but for endless grief
To Achaean men lamenting. Moaned the air
With sighing from the abysses of the sea;
And passing heavy grew the hearts of all,
Thinking: "Now shall we perish by the hands
Of Trojans!" Then by those dark ships they thought
Of white-haired fathers left in halls afar,

Of wives new-wedded, who by couches cold
Mourned, waiting, waiting, with their tender babes
For husbands unreturning; and they groaned
In bitterness of soul. A passion of grief
Came o'er their hearts; they fell upon their faces
On the deep sand flung down, and wept as men
All comfortless round Peleus' mighty son,
And clutched and plucked out by the roots their hair,
And east upon their heads defiling sand.
Their cry was like the cry that goeth up
From folk that after battle by their walls
Are slaughtered, when their maddened foes set fire
To a great city, and slay in heaps on heaps
Her people, and make spoil of all her wealth;
So wild and high they wailed beside the sea,
Because the Danaans' champion, Aeacus' son,
Lay, grand in death, by a God's arrow slain,
As Ares lay, when She of the Mighty Father
With that huge stone down dashed him on Troy's plain.

Ceaselessly wailed the Myrmidons Achilles,
A ring of mourners round the kingly dead,
That kind heart, friend alike to each and all,
To no man arrogant nor hard of mood,
But ever tempering strength with courtesy.

Then Aias first, deep-groaning, uttered forth
His yearning o'er his father's brother's son
God-stricken--ay, no man had smitten him
Of all upon the wide-wayed earth that dwell!
Him glorious Aias heavy-hearted mourned,
Now wandering to the tent of Peleus' son,
Now cast down all his length, a giant form,

On the sea-sands; and thus lamented he:
"Achilles, shield and sword of Argive men,
Thou hast died in Troy, from Phthia's plains afar,
Smitten unwares by that accursed shaft,
Such thing as weakling dastards aim in fight!
For none who trusts in wielding the great shield,
None who for war can skill to set the helm
Upon his brows, and sway the spear in grip,
And cleave the brass about the breasts of foes,
Warreth with arrows, shrinking from the fray.
Not man to man he met thee, whoso smote;
Else woundless never had he 'scaped thy lance!
But haply Zeus purposed to ruin all,
And maketh all our toil and travail vain--
Ay, now will grant the Trojans victory
Who from Achaea now hath reft her shield!
Ah me! how shall old Peleus in his halls
Take up the burden of a mighty grief
Now in his joyless age! His heart shall break
At the mere rumour of it. Better so,
Thus in a moment to forget all pain.
But if these evil tidings slay him not,
Ah, laden with sore sorrow eld shall come
Upon him, eating out his heart with grief
By a lone hearth Peleus so passing dear
Once to the Blessed! But the Gods vouchsafe
No perfect happiness to hapless men."

So he in grief lamented Peleus' son.
Then ancient Phoenix made heart-stricken moan,
Clasping the noble form of Aeacus' seed,
And in wild anguish wailed the wise of heart:
"Thou art reft from me, dear child, and cureless pain

Hast left to me! Oh that upon my face
The veiling earth had fallen, ere I saw
Thy bitter doom! No pang more terrible
Hath ever stabbed mine heart no, not that hour
Of exile, when I fled from fatherland
And noble parents, fleeing Hellas through,
Till Peleus welcomed me with gifts, and lord
Of his Dolopians made me. In his arms
Thee through his halls one day he bare, and set
Upon my knees, and bade me foster thee,
His babe, with all love, as mine own dear child:
I hearkened to him: blithely didst thou cling
About mine heart, and, babbling wordless speech,
Didst call me `father' oft, and didst bedew
My breast and tunic with thy baby lips.
Ofttimes with soul that laughed for glee I held
Thee in mine arms; for mine heart whispered me
`This fosterling through life shall care for thee,
Staff of thine age shall be.' And that mine hope
Was for a little while fulfilled; but now
Thou hast vanished into darkness, and to me
Is left long heart-ache wild with all regret.
Ah, might my sorrow slay me, ere the tale
To noble Peleus come! When on his ears
Falleth the heavy tidings, he shall weep
And wail without surcease. Most piteous grief
We twain for thy sake shall inherit aye,
Thy sire and I, who, ere our day of doom,
Mourning shall go down to the grave for thee--
Ay, better this than life unholpen of thee!"

So moaned his ever-swelling tide of grief.
And Atreus' son beside him mourned and wept

With heart on fire with inly smouldering pain:
"Thou hast perished, chiefest of the Danaan men,
Hast perished, and hast left the Achaean host
Fenceless! Now thou art fallen, are they left
An easier prey to foes. Thou hast given joy
To Trojans by thy fall, who dreaded thee
As sheep a lion. These with eager hearts
Even to the ships will bring the battle now.
Zeus, Father, thou too with deceitful words
Beguilest mortals! Thou didst promise me
That Priam's burg should be destroyed; but now
That promise given dost thou not fulfil,
But thou didst cheat mine heart: I shall not win
The war's goal, now Achilles is no more."

So did he cry heart-anguished. Mourned all round
Wails multitudinous for Peleus' son:
The dark ships echoed back the voice of grief,
And sighed and sobbed the immeasurable air.
And as when long sea-rollers, onward driven
By a great wind, heave up far out at sea,
And strandward sweep with terrible rush, and aye
Headland and beach with shattered spray are scourged,
And roar unceasing; so a dread sound rose
Of moaning of the Danaans round the corse,
Ceaselessly wailing Peleus' aweless son.

And on their mourning soon black night had come,
But spake unto Atreides Neleus' son,
Nestor, whose own heart bare its load of grief
Remembering his own son Antilochus:
"O mighty Agamemnon, sceptre-lord
Of Argives, from wide-shrilling lamentation

Refrain we for this day. None shall withhold
Hereafter these from all their heart's desire
Of weeping and lamenting many days.
But now go to, from aweless Aeacus' son
Wash we the foul blood-gouts, and lay we him
Upon a couch: unseemly it is to shame
The dead by leaving them untended long."

So counselled Neleus' son, the passing-wise.
Then hasted he his men, and bade them set
Caldrons of cold spring-water o'er the flames,
And wash the corse, and clothe in vesture fair,
Sea-purple, which his mother gave her son
At his first sailing against Troy. With speed
They did their lord's command: with loving care,
All service meetly rendered, on a couch
Laid they the mighty fallen, Peleus' son.

The Trito-born, the passing-wise, beheld
And pitied him, and showered upon his head
Ambrosia, which hath virtue aye to keep
Taintless, men say, the flesh of warriors slain.
Like softly-breathing sleeper dewy-fresh
She made him: over that dead face she drew
A stern frown, even as when he lay, with wrath
Darkening his grim face, clasping his slain friend
Patroclus; and she made his frame to be
More massive, like a war-god to behold.
And wonder seized the Argives, as they thronged
And saw the image of a living man,
Where all the stately length of Peleus' son
Lay on the couch, and seemed as though he slept.

Around him all the woeful captive-maids,
Whom he had taken for a prey, what time
He had ravaged hallowed Lemnos, and had scaled
The towered crags of Thebes, Eetion's town,
Wailed, as they stood and rent their fair young flesh,
And smote their breasts, and from their hearts bemoaned
That lord of gentleness and courtesy,
Who honoured even the daughters of his foes.
And stricken most of all with heart-sick pain
Briseis, hero Achilles' couchmate, bowed
Over the dead, and tore her fair young flesh
With ruthless fingers, shrieking: her soft breast
Was ridged with gory weals, so cruelly
She smote it thou hadst said that crimson blood
Had dripped on milk. Yet, in her griefs despite,
Her winsome loveliness shone out, and grace
Hung like a veil about her, as she wailed:
"Woe for this grief passing all griefs beside!
Never on me came anguish like to this
Not when my brethren died, my fatherland
Was wasted--like this anguish for thy death!
Thou wast my day, my sunlight, my sweet life,
Mine hope of good, my strong defence from harm,
Dearer than all my beauty--yea, more dear
Than my lost parents! Thou wast all in all
To me, thou only, captive though I be.
Thou tookest from me every bondmaid's task
And like a wife didst hold me. Ah, but now
Me shall some new Achaean master bear
To fertile Sparta, or to thirsty Argos.
The bitter cup of thraldom shall I drain,
Severed, ah me, from thee! Oh that the earth
Had veiled my dead face ere I saw thy doom!"

The Fall of Troy

So for slain Peleus' son did she lament
With woeful handmaids and heart-anguished Greeks,
Mourning a king, a husband. Never dried
Her tears were: ever to the earth they streamed
Like sunless water trickling from a rock
While rime and snow yet mantle o'er the earth
Above it; yet the frost melts down before
The east-wind and the flame-shafts of the sun.

Now came the sound of that upringing wail
To Nereus' Daughters, dwellers in the depths
Unfathomed. With sore anguish all their hearts
Were smitten: piteously they moaned: their cry
Shivered along the waves of Hellespont.
Then with dark mantles overpalled they sped
Swiftly to where the Argive men were thronged.
As rushed their troop up silver paths of sea,
The flood disported round them as they came.
With one wild cry they floated up; it rang,
A sound as when fleet-flying cranes forebode
A great storm. Moaned the monsters of the deep
Plaintively round that train of mourners. Fast
On sped they to their goal, with awesome cry
Wailing the while their sister's mighty son.
Swiftly from Helicon the Muses came
Heart-burdened with undying grief, for love
And honour to the Nereid starry-eyed.

Then Zeus with courage filled the Argive men,
That-eyes of flesh might undismayed behold
That glorious gathering of Goddesses.
Then those Divine Ones round Achilles' corse
Pealed forth with one voice from immortal lips

A lamentation. Rang again the shores
Of Hellespont. As rain upon the earth
Their tears fell round the dead man, Aeacus' son;
For out of depths of sorrow rose their moan.
And all the armour, yea, the tents, the ships
Of that great sorrowing multitude were wet
With tears from ever-welling springs of grief.
His mother cast her on him, clasping him,
And kissed her son's lips, crying through her tears:
"Now let the rosy-vestured Dawn in heaven
Exult! Now let broad-flowing Axius
Exult, and for Asteropaeus dead
Put by his wrath! Let Priam's seed be glad
But I unto Olympus will ascend,
And at the feet of everlasting Zeus
Will cast me, bitterly planning that he gave
Me, an unwilling bride, unto a man--
A man whom joyless eld soon overtook,
To whom the Fates are near, with death for gift.
Yet not so much for his lot do I grieve
As for Achilles; for Zeus promised me
To make him glorious in the Aeacid halls,
In recompense for the bridal I so loathed
That into wild wind now I changed me, now
To water, now in fashion as a bird
I was, now as the blast of flame; nor might
A mortal win me for his bride, who seemed
All shapes in turn that earth and heaven contain,
Until the Olympian pledged him to bestow
A godlike son on me, a lord of war.
Yea, in a manner this did he fulfil
Faithfully; for my son was mightiest
Of men. But Zeus made brief his span of life

Unto my sorrow. Therefore up to heaven
Will I: to Zeus's mansion will I go
And wail my son, and will put Zeus in mind
Of all my travail for him and his sons
In their sore stress, and sting his soul with shame."

So in her wild lament the Sea-queen cried.
But now to Thetis spake Calliope,
She in whose heart was steadfast wisdom throned:
"From lamentation, Thetis, now forbear,
And do not, in the frenzy of thy grief
For thy lost son, provoke to wrath the Lord
Of Gods and men. Lo, even sons of Zeus,
The Thunder-king, have perished, overborne
By evil fate. Immortal though I be,
Mine own son Orpheus died, whose magic song
Drew all the forest-trees to follow him,
And every craggy rock and river-stream,
And blasts of winds shrill-piping stormy-breathed,
And birds that dart through air on rushing wings.
Yet I endured mine heavy sorrow: Gods
Ought not with anguished grief to vex their souls.
Therefore make end of sorrow-stricken wail
For thy brave child; for to the sons of earth
Minstrels shall chant his glory and his might,
By mine and by my sisters' inspiration,
Unto the end of time. Let not thy soul
Be crushed by dark grief, nor do thou lament
Like those frail mortal women. Know'st thou not
That round all men which dwell upon the earth
Hovereth irresistible deadly Fate,
Who recks not even of the Gods? Such power
She only hath for heritage. Yea, she

Soon shall destroy gold-wealthy Priam's town,
And Trojans many and Argives doom to death,
Whomso she will. No God can stay her hand."

So in her wisdom spake Calliope.
Then plunged the sun down into Ocean's stream,
And sable-vestured Night came floating up
O'er the wide firmament, and brought her boon
Of sleep to sorrowing mortals. On the sands
There slept they, all the Achaean host, with heads
Bowed 'neath the burden of calamity.
But upon Thetis sleep laid not his hand:
Still with the deathless Nereids by the sea
She sate; on either side the Muses spake
One after other comfortable words
To make that sorrowing heart forget its pain.

But when with a triumphant laugh the Dawn
Soared up the sky, and her most radiant light
Shed over all the Trojans and their king,
Then, sorrowing sorely for Achilles still,
The Danaans woke to weep. Day after day,
For many days they wept. Around them moaned
Far-stretching beaches of the sea, and mourned
Great Nereus for his daughter Thetis' sake;
And mourned with him the other Sea-gods all
For dead Achilles. Then the Argives gave
The corpse of great Peleides to the flame.
A pyre of countless tree-trunks built they up
Which, all with one mind toiling, from the heights
Of Ida they brought down; for Atreus' sons
Sped on the work, and charged them to bring thence
Wood without measure, that consumed with speed

The Fall of Troy

Might be Achilles' body. All around
Piled they about the pyre much battle-gear
Of strong men slain; and slew and cast thereon
Full many goodly sons of Trojan men,
And snorting steeds, and mighty bulls withal,
And sheep and fatling swine thereon they cast.
And wailing captive maids from coffers brought
Mantles untold; all cast they on the pyre:
Gold heaped they there and amber. All their hair
The Myrmidons shore, and shrouded with the same
The body of their king. Briseis laid
Her own shorn tresses on the corpse, her gift,
Her last, unto her lord. Great jars of oil
Full many poured they out thereon, with jars
Of honey and of wine, rich blood of the grape
That breathed an odour as of nectar, yea,
Cast incense-breathing perfumes manifold
Marvellous sweet, the precious things put forth
By earth, and treasures of the sea divine.

Then, when all things were set in readiness
About the pyre, all, footmen, charioteers,
Compassed that woeful bale, clashing their arms,
While, from the viewless heights Olympian, Zeus
Rained down ambrosia on dead Aeacus' son.
For honour to the Goddess, Nereus' child,
He sent to Aeolus Hermes, bidding him
Summon the sacred might of his swift winds,
For that the corpse of Aeacus' son must now
Be burned. With speed he went, and Aeolus
Refused not: the tempestuous North in haste
He summoned, and the wild blast of the West;
And to Troy sped they on their whirlwind wings.

Fast in mad onrush, fast across the deep
They darted; roared beneath them as they flew
The sea, the land; above crashed thunder-voiced
Clouds headlong hurtling through the firmament.
Then by decree of Zeus down on the pyre
Of slain Achilles, like a charging host
Swooped they; upleapt the Fire-god's madding breath:
Uprose a long wail from the Myrmidons.
Then, though with whirlwind rushes toiled the winds,
All day, all night, they needs must fan the flames
Ere that death-pyre burned out. Up to the heavens
Vast-volumed rolled the smoke. The huge tree-trunks
Groaned, writhing, bursting, in the heat, and dropped
The dark-grey ash all round. So when the winds
Had tirelessly fulfilled their mighty task,
Back to their cave they rode cloud-charioted.

Then, when the fire had last of all consumed
That hero-king, when all the steeds, the men
Slain round the pyre had first been ravined up,
With all the costly offerings laid around
The mighty dead by Achaia's weeping sons,
The glowing embers did the Myrmidons quench
With wine. Then clear to be discerned were seen
His bones; for nowise like the rest were they,
But like an ancient Giant's; none beside
With these were blent; for bulls and steeds, and sons
Of Troy, with all that mingled hecatomb,
Lay in a wide ring round his corse, and he
Amidst them, flame-devoured, lay there alone.
So his companions groaning gathered up
His bones, and in a silver casket laid
Massy and deep, and banded and bestarred

With flashing gold; and Nereus' daughters shed
Ambrosia over them, and precious nards
For honour to Achilles: fat of kine
And amber honey poured they over all.
A golden vase his mother gave, the gift
In old time of the Wine-god, glorious work
Of the craft-master Fire-god, in the which
They laid the casket that enclosed the bones
Of mighty-souled Achilles. All around
The Argives heaped a barrow, a giant sign,
Upon a foreland's uttermost end, beside
The Hellespont's deep waters, wailing loud
Farewells unto the Myrmidons' hero-king.

Nor stayed the immortal steeds of Aeacus' son
Tearless beside the ships; they also mourned
Their slain king: sorely loth were they to abide
Longer mid mortal men or Argive steeds
Bearing a burden of consuming grief;
But fain were they to soar through air, afar
From wretched men, over the Ocean's streams,
Over the Sea-queen's caverns, unto where
Divine Podarge bare that storm-foot twain
Begotten of the West-wind clarion-voiced
Yea, and they had accomplished their desire,
But the Gods' purpose held them back, until
From Scyros' isle Achilles' fleetfoot son
Should come. Him waited they to welcome, when
He came unto the war-host; for the Fates,
Daughters of holy Chaos, at their birth
Had spun the life-threads of those deathless foals,
Even to serve Poseidon first, and next
Peleus the dauntless king, Achilles then

The invincible, and, after these, the fourth,
The mighty-hearted Neoptolemus,
Whom after death to the Elysian Plain
They were to bear, unto the Blessed Land,
By Zeus' decree. For which cause, though their hearts
Were pierced with bitter anguish, they abode
Still by the ships, with spirits sorrowing
For their old lord, and yearning for the new.

Then from the surge of heavy-plunging seas
Rose the Earth-shaker. No man saw his feet
Pace up the strand, but suddenly he stood
Beside the Nereid Goddesses, and spake
To Thetis, yet for Achilles bowed with grief:
"Refrain from endless mourning for thy son.
Not with the dead shall he abide, but dwell
With Gods, as doth the might of Herakles,
And Dionysus ever fair. Not him
Dread doom shall prison in darkness evermore,
Nor Hades keep him. To the light of Zeus
Soon shall he rise; and I will give to him
A holy island for my gift: it lies
Within the Euxine Sea: there evermore
A God thy son shall be. The tribes that dwell
Around shall as mine own self honour him
With incense and with steam of sacrifice.
Hush thy laments, vex not thine heart with grief."

Then like a wind-breath had he passed away
Over the sea, when that consoling word
Was spoken; and a little in her breast
Revived the spirit of Thetis: and the God
Brought this to pass thereafter. All the host

Moved moaning thence, and came unto the ships
That brought them o'er from Hellas. Then returned
To Helicon the Muses: 'neath the sea,
Wailing the dear dead, Nereus' Daughters sank,

BOOK IV

How in the Funeral Games of Achilles heroes contended.

    Nor did the hapless Trojans leave unwept
The warrior-king Hippolochus' hero-son,
But laid, in front of the Dardanian gate,
Upon the pyre that captain war-renowned.
But him Apollo's self caught swiftly up
Out of the blazing fire, and to the winds
Gave him, to bear away to Lycia-land;
And fast and far they bare him, 'neath the glens
Of high Telandrus, to a lovely glade;
And for a monument above his grave
Upheaved a granite rock. The Nymphs therefrom
Made gush the hallowed water of a stream
For ever flowing, which the tribes of men
Still call fair-fleeting Glaucus. This the gods
Wrought for an honour to the Lycian king.

    But for Achilles still the Argives mourned
Beside the swift ships: heart-sick were they all
With dolorous pain and grief. Each yearned for him
As for a son; no eye in that wide host
Was tearless. But the Trojans with great joy

Exulted, seeing their sorrow from afar,
And the great fire that spake their foe consumed.
And thus a vaunting voice amidst them cried:
"Now hath Cronion from his heaven vouchsafed
A joy past hope unto our longing eyes,
To see Achilles fallen before Troy.
Now he is smitten down, the glorious hosts
Of Troy, I trow, shall win a breathing-space
From blood of death and from the murderous fray.
Ever his heart devised the Trojans' bane;
In his hands maddened aye the spear of doom
With gore besprent, and none of us that faced
Him in the fight beheld another dawn.
But now, I wot, Achaea's valorous sons
Shall flee unto their galleys shapely-prowed,
Since slain Achilles lies. Ah that the might
Of Hector still were here, that he might slay
The Argives one and all amidst their tents!"

So in unbridled joy a Trojan cried;
But one more wise and prudent answered him:
"Thou deemest that yon murderous Danaan host
Will straightway get them to the ships, to flee
Over the misty sea. Nay, still their lust
Is hot for fight: us will they nowise fear,
Still are there left strong battle-eager men,
As Aias, as Tydeides, Atreus' sons:
Though dead Achilles be, I still fear these.
Oh that Apollo Silverbow would end them!
Then in that day were given to our prayers
A breathing-space from war and ghastly death."

In heaven was dole among the Immortal Ones,

Even all that helped the stalwart Danaans' cause.
In clouds like mountains piled they veiled their heads
For grief of soul. But glad those others were
Who fain would speed Troy to a happy goal.
Then unto Cronos' Son great Hera spake:
"Zeus, Lightning-father, wherefore helpest thou
Troy, all forgetful of the fair-haired bride
Whom once to Peleus thou didst give to wife
Midst Pelion's glens? Thyself didst bring to pass
Those spousals of a Goddess: on that day
All we Immortals feasted there, and gave
Gifts passing-fair. All this dost thou forget,
And hast devised for Hellas heaviest woe."

So spake she; but Zeus answered not a word;
For pondering there he sat with burdened breast,
Thinking how soon the Argives should destroy
The city of Priam, thinking how himself
Would visit on the victors ruin dread
In war and on the great sea thunder-voiced.
Such thoughts were his, ere long to be fulfilled.

Now sank the sun to Ocean's fathomless flood:
O'er the dim land the infinite darkness stole,
Wherein men gain a little rest from toil.
Then by the ships, despite their sorrow, supped
The Argives, for ye cannot thrust aside
Hunger's importunate craving, when it comes
Upon the breast, but straightway heavy and faint
Lithe limbs become; nor is there remedy
Until one satisfy this clamorous guest
Therefore these ate the meat of eventide
In grief for Achilles' hard necessity

Constrained them all. And, when they had broken bread,
Sweet sleep came on them, loosening from their frames
Care's heavy chain, and quickening strength anew

But when the starry Bears had eastward turned
Their heads, expectant of the uprushing light
Of Helios, and when woke the Queen of Dawn,
Then rose from sleep the stalwart Argive men
Purposing for the Trojans death and doom.
Stirred were they like the roughly-ridging sea
Icarian, or as sudden-rippling corn
In harvest field, what time the rushing wings
Of the cloud-gathering West sweep over it;
So upon Hellespont's strand the folk were stirred.
And to those eager hearts cried Tydeus' son:
"If we be battle-biders, friends, indeed,
More fiercely fight we now the hated foe,
Lest they take heart because Achilles lives
No longer. Come, with armour, car, and steed
Let us beset them. Glory waits our toil?"

But battle-eager Aias answering spake
"Brave be thy words, and nowise idle talk,
Kindling the dauntless Argive men, whose hearts
Before were battle-eager, to the fight
Against the Trojan men, O Tydeus' son.
But we must needs abide amidst the ships
Till Goddess Thetis come forth of the sea;
For that her heart is purposed to set here
Fair athlete-prizes for the funeral-games.
This yesterday she told me, ere she plunged
Into sea-depths, yea, spake to me apart
From other Danaans; and, I trow, by this

Her haste hath brought her nigh. Yon Trojan men,
Though Peleus' son hath died, shall have small heart
For battle, while myself am yet alive,
And thou, and noble Atreus' son, the king."

So spake the mighty son of Telamon,
But knew not that a dark and bitter doom
For him should follow hard upon those games
By Fate's contrivance. Answered Tydeus' son
"O friend, if Thetis comes indeed this day
With goodly gifts for her son's funeral-games,
Then bide we by the ships, and keep we here
All others. Meet it is to do the will
Of the Immortals: yea, to Achilles too,
Though the Immortals willed it not, ourselves
Must render honour grateful to the dead."

So spake the battle-eager Tydeus' son.
And lo, the Bride of Peleus gliding came
Forth of the sea, like the still breath of dawn,
And suddenly was with the Argive throng
Where eager-faced they waited, some, that looked
Soon to contend in that great athlete-strife,
And some, to joy in seeing the mighty strive.
Amidst that gathering Thetis sable-stoled
Set down her prizes, and she summoned forth
Achaea's champions: at her best they came.

But first amidst them all rose Neleus' son,
Not as desiring in the strife of fists
To toil, nor strain of wrestling; for his arms
And all his sinews were with grievous eld
Outworn, but still his heart and brain were strong.

Of all the Achaeans none could match himself
Against him in the folkmote's war of words;
Yea, even Laertes' glorious son to him
Ever gave place when men for speech were met;
Nor he alone, but even the kingliest
Of Argives, Agamemnon, lord of spears.
Now in their midst he sang the gracious Queen
Of Nereids, sang how she in willsomeness
Of beauty was of all the Sea-maids chief.
Well-pleased she hearkened. Yet again he sang,
Singing of Peleus' Bridal of Delight,
Which all the blest Immortals brought to pass
By Pelion's crests; sang of the ambrosial feast
When the swift Hours brought in immortal hands
Meats not of earth, and heaped in golden maunds;
Sang how the silver tables were set forth
In haste by Themis blithely laughing; sang
How breathed Hephaestus purest flame of fire;
Sang how the Nymphs in golden chalices
Mingled ambrosia; sang the ravishing dance
Twined by the Graces' feet; sang of the chant
The Muses raised, and how its spell enthralled
All mountains, rivers, all the forest brood;
How raptured was the infinite firmament,
Cheiron's fair caverns, yea, the very Gods.

Such noble strain did Neleus' son pour out
Into the Argives' eager ears; and they
Hearkened with ravished souls. Then in their midst
He sang once more the imperishable deeds
Of princely Achilles. All the mighty throng
Acclaimed him with delight. From that beginning
With fitly chosen words did he extol

The glorious hero; how he voyaged and smote
Twelve cities; how he marched o'er leagues on leagues
Of land, and spoiled eleven; how he slew
Telephus and Eetion's might renowned
In Thebe; how his spear laid Cyenus low,
Poseidon's son, and godlike Polydorus,
Troilus the goodly, princely Asteropaeus;
And how he dyed with blood the river-streams
Of Xanthus, and with countless corpses choked
His murmuring flow, when from the limbs he tore
Lycaon's life beside the sounding river;
And how he smote down Hector; how he slew
Penthesileia, and the godlike son
Of splendour-throned Dawn;--all this he sang
To Argives which already knew the tale;
Sang of his giant mould, how no man's strength
In fight could stand against him, nor in games
Where strong men strive for mastery, where the swift
Contend with flying feet or hurrying wheels
Of chariots, nor in combat panoplied;
And how in goodlihead he far outshone
All Danaans, and how his bodily might
Was measureless in the stormy clash of war.
Last, he prayed Heaven that he might see a son
Like that great sire from sea-washed Scyros come.

That noble song acclaiming Argives praised;
Yea, silver-looted Thetis smiled, and gave
The singer fleetfoot horses, given of old
Beside Caicus' mouth by Telephus
To Achilles, when he healed the torturing wound
With that same spear wherewith himself had pierced
Telephus' thigh, and thrust the point clear through.

These Nestor Neleus' son to his comrades gave,
And, glorying in their godlike lord, they led
The steeds unto his ships. Then Thetis set
Amidst the athlete-ring ten kine, to be
Her prizes for the footrace, and by each
Ran a fair suckling calf. These the bold might
Of Peleus' tireless son had driven down
From slopes of Ida, prizes of his spear.

To strive for these rose up two victory-fain,
Teucer the first, the son of Telamon,
And Aias, of the Locrian archers chief.
These twain with swift hands girded them about
With loin-cloths, reverencing the Goddess-bride
Of Peleus, and the Sea-maids, who with her
Came to behold the Argives' athlete-sport.
And Atreus' son, lord of all Argive men,
Showed them the turning-goal of that swift course.
Then these the Queen of Rivalry spurred on,
As from the starting-line like falcons swift
They sped away. Long doubtful was the race:
Now, as the Argives gazed, would Aias' friends
Shout, now rang out the answering cheer from friends
Of Teucer. But when in their eager speed
Close on the end they were, then Teucer's feet
Were trammelled by unearthly powers: some god
Or demon dashed his foot against the stock
Of a deep-rooted tamarisk. Sorely wrenched
Was his left ankle: round the joint upswelled
The veins high-ridged. A great shout rang from all
That watched the contest. Aias darted past
Exultant: ran his Locrian folk to hail
Their lord, with sudden joy in all their souls.

Then to his ships they drave the kine, and cast
Fodder before them. Eager-helpful friends
Led Teucer halting thence. The leeches drew
Blood from his foot: then over it they laid
Soft-shredded linen ointment-smeared, and swathed
With smooth bands round, and charmed away the pain.

Then swiftly rose two mighty-hearted ones
Eager to match their strength in wrestling strain,
The son of Tydeus and the giant Aias.
Into the midst they strode, and marvelling gazed
The Argives on men shapen like to gods.
Then grappled they, like lions famine-stung
Fighting amidst the mountains o'er a stag,
Whose strength is even-balanced; no whit less
Is one than other in their deadly rage;
So these long time in might were even-matched,
Till Aias locked his strong hands round the son
Of Tydeus, straining hard to break his back;
But he, with wrestling-craft and strength combined,
Shifted his hip 'neath Telamon's son, and heaved
The giant up; with a side-twist wrenched free
From Aias' ankle-lock his thigh, and so
With one huge shoulder-heave to earth he threw
That mighty champion, and himself came down
Astride him: then a mighty shout went up.
But battle-stormer Aias, chafed in mind,
Sprang up, hot-eager to essay again
That grim encounter. From his terrible hands
He dashed the dust, and challenged furiously
With a great voice Tydeides: not a whit
That other quailed, but rushed to close with him.
Rolled up the dust in clouds from 'neath their feet:

Hurtling they met like battling mountain-bulls
That clash to prove their dauntless strength, and spurn
The dust, while with their roaring all the hills
Re-echo: in their desperate fury these
Dash their strong heads together, straining long
Against each other with their massive strength,
Hard-panting in the fierce rage of their strife,
While from their mouths drip foam-flakes to the ground;
So strained they twain with grapple of brawny hands.
'Neath that hard grip their backs and sinewy necks
Cracked, even as when in mountain-glades the trees
Dash storm-tormented boughs together. Oft
Tydeides clutched at Aias' brawny thighs,
But could not stir his steadfast-rooted feet.
Oft Aias hurled his whole weight on him, bowed
His shoulders backward, strove to press him down;
And to new grips their hands were shifting aye.
All round the gazing people shouted, some
Cheering on glorious Tydeus' son, and some
The might of Aias. Then the giant swung
The shoulders of his foe to right, to left;
Then gripped him 'neath the waist; with one fierce heave
And giant effort hurled him like a stone
To earth. The floor of Troyland rang again
As fell Tydeides: shouted all the folk.
Yet leapt he up all eager to contend
With giant Aias for the third last fall:
But Nestor rose and spake unto the twain:
"From grapple of wrestling, noble sons, forbear;
For all we know that ye be mightiest
Of Argives since the great Achilles died."

Then these from toil refrained, and from their brows
Wiped with their hands the plenteous-streaming sweat:
They kissed each other, and forgat their strife.
Then Thetis, queen of Goddesses, gave to them
Four handmaids; and those strong and aweless ones
Marvelled beholding them, for these surpassed
All captive-maids in beauty and household-skill,
Save only lovely-tressed Briseis. These
Achilles captive brought from Lesbos' Isle,
And in their service joyed. The first was made
Stewardess of the feast and lady of meats;
The second to the feasters poured the wine;
The third shed water on their hands thereafter;
The fourth bare all away, the banquet done.
These Tydeus' son and giant Aias shared,
And, parted two and two, unto their ships
Sent they those fair and serviceable ones.

Next, for the play of fists Idomeneus rose,
For cunning was he in all athlete-lore;
But none came forth to meet him, yielding all
To him, the elder-born, with reverent awe.
So in their midst gave Thetis unto him
A chariot and fleet steeds, which theretofore
Mighty Patroclus from the ranks of Troy
Drave, when he slew Sarpedon, seed of Zeus,
These to his henchmen gave Idomeneus
To drive unto the ships: himself remained
Still sitting in the glorious athlete-ring.
Then Phoenix to the stalwart Argives cried:
"Now to Idomeneus the Gods have given
A fair prize uncontested, free of toil
Of mighty arms and shoulders, honouring

The elder-born with bloodless victory.
But lo, ye younger men, another prize
Awaiteth the swift play of cunning hands.
Step forth then: gladden great Peleides' soul."

He spake, they heard; but each on other looked,
And, loth to essay the contest, all sat still,
Till Neleus' son rebuked those laggard souls:
"Friends, it were shame that men should shun the play
Of clenched hands, who in that noble sport
Have skill, wherein young men delight, which links
Glory to toil. Ah that my thews were strong
As when we held King Pelias' funeral-feast,
I and Acastus, kinsmen joining hands,
When I with godlike Polydeuces stood
In gauntlet-strife, in even-balanced fray,
And when Ancaeus in the wrestlers' ring
Mightier than all beside, yet feared and shrank
From me, and dared not strive with me that day,
For that ere then amidst the Epeian men--
No battle-blenchers they!--I had vanquished him,
For all his might, and dashed him to the dust
By dead Amaryncus' tomb, and thousands round
Sat marvelling at my prowess and my strength.
Therefore against me not a second time
Raised he his hands, strong wrestler though he were;
And so I won an uncontested prize.
But now old age is on me, and many griefs.
Therefore I bid you, whom it well beseems,
To win the prize; for glory crowns the youth
Who bears away the meed of athlete-strife."

Stirred by his gallant chiding, a brave man
Rose, son of haughty godlike Panopeus,
The man who framed the Horse, the bane of Troy,
Not long thereafter. None dared meet him now
In play of fists, albeit in deadly craft
Of war, when Ares rusheth through the field,
He was not cunning. But for strife of hands
The fair prize uncontested had been won
By stout Epeius--yea, he was at point
To bear it thence unto the Achaean ships;
But one strode forth to meet him, Theseus' son,
The spearman Acamas, the mighty of heart,
Bearing already on his swift hands girt
The hard hide-gauntlets, which Evenor's son
Agelaus on his prince's hands had drawn
With courage-kindling words. The comrades then
Of Panopeus' princely son for Epeius raised
A heartening cheer. He like a lion stood
Forth in the midst, his strong hands gauntleted
With bull's hide hard as horn. Loud rang the cheers
From side to side of that great throng, to fire
The courage of the mighty ones to clash
Hands in the gory play. Sooth, little spur
Needed they for their eagerness for fight.
But, ere they closed, they flashed out proving blows
To wot if still, as theretofore, their arms
Were limber and lithe, unclogged by toil of war;
Then faced each other, and upraised their hands
With ever-watching eyes, and short quick steps
A-tiptoe, and with ever-shifting feet,
Each still eluding other's crushing might.
Then with a rush they closed like thunder-clouds
Hurled on each other by the tempest-blast,

Flashing forth lightnings, while the welkin thrills
As clash the clouds and hollow roar the winds;
So 'neath the hard hide-gauntlets clashed their jaws.
Down streamed the blood, and from their brows the sweat
Blood-streaked made on the flushed cheeks crimson bars.
Fierce without pause they fought, and never flagged
Epeius, but threw all his stormy strength
Into his onrush. Yet did Theseus' son
Never lose heart, but baffled the straight blows
Of those strong hands, and by his fighting-craft
Flinging them right and left, leapt in, brought home
A blow to his eyebrow, cutting to the bone.
Even then with counter-stroke Epeius reached
Acamas' temple, and hurled him to the ground.
Swift he sprang up, and on his stalwart foe
Rushed, smote his head: as he rushed in again,
The other, slightly swerving, sent his left
Clean to his brow; his right, with all his might
Behind it, to his nose. Yet Acamas still
Warded and struck with all the manifold shifts
Of fighting-craft. But now the Achaeans all
Bade stop the fight, though eager still were both
To strive for coveted victory. Then came
Their henchmen, and the gory gauntlets loosed
In haste from those strong hands. Now drew they breath
From that great labour, as they bathed their brows
With sponges myriad-pored. Comrades and friends
With pleading words then drew them face to face,
And prayed, "In friendship straight forget your wrath."
So to their comrades' suasion hearkened they;
For wise men ever bear a placable mind.
They kissed each other, and their hearts forgat
That bitter strife. Then Thetis sable-stoled

Gave to their glad hands two great silver bowls
The which Euneus, Jason's warrior son
In sea-washed Lemnos to Achilles gave
To ransom strong Lycaon from his hands.
These had Hephaestus fashioned for his gift
To glorious Dionysus, when he brought
His bride divine to Olympus, Minos' child
Far-famed, whom in sea-washed Dia's isle
Theseus unwitting left. The Wine-god brimmed
With nectar these, and gave them to his son;
And Thoas at his death to Hypsipyle
With great possessions left them. She bequeathed
The bowls to her godlike son, who gave them up
Unto Achilles for Lycaon's life.
The one the son of lordly Theseus took,
And goodly Epeius sent to his ship with joy
The other. Then their bruises and their scars
Did Podaleirius tend with loving care.
First pressed he out black humours, then his hands
Deftly knit up the gashes: salves he laid
Thereover, given him by his sire of old,
Such as had virtue in one day to heal
The deadliest hurts, yea, seeming-cureless wounds.
Straight was the smart assuaged, and healed the scars
Upon their brows and 'neath their clustering hair

Then for the archery-test Oileus' son
Stood forth with Teucer, they which in the race
Erewhile contended. Far away from these
Agamemnon, lord of spears, set up a helm
Crested with plumes, and spake: "The master-shot
Is that which shears the hair-crest clean away."
Then straightway Aias shot his arrow first,

And smote the helm-ridge: sharply rang the brass.
Then Teucer second with most earnest heed
Shot: the swift shaft hath shorn the plume away.
Loud shouted all the people as they gazed,
And praised him without stint, for still his foot
Halted in pain, yet nowise marred his aim
When with his hands he sped the flying shaft.
Then Peleus' bride gave unto him the arms
Of godlike Troilus, the goodliest
Of all fair sons whom Hecuba had borne
In hallowed Troy; yet of his goodlihead
No joy she had; the prowess and the spear
Of fell Achilles reft his life from him.
As when a gardener with new-whetted scythe
Mows down, ere it may seed, a blade of corn
Or poppy, in a garden dewy-fresh
And blossom-flushed, which by a water-course
Crowdeth its blooms--mows it ere it may reach
Its goal of bringing offspring to the birth,
And with his scythe-sweep makes its life-work vain
And barren of all issue, nevermore
Now to be fostered by the dews of spring;
So did Peleides cut down Priam's son
The god-like beautiful, the beardless yet
And virgin of a bride, almost a child!
Yet the Destroyer Fate had lured him on
To war, upon the threshold of glad youth,
When youth is bold, and the heart feels no void.

Forthwith a bar of iron massy and long
From the swift-speeding hand did many essay
To hurl; but not an Argive could prevail
To cast that ponderous mass. Aias alone

Sped it from his strong hand, as in the time
Of harvest might a reaper fling from him
A dry oak-bough, when all the fields are parched.
And all men marvelled to behold how far
Flew from his hand the bronze which scarce two men
Hard-straining had uplifted from the ground.
Even this Antaeus' might was wont to hurl
Erstwhile, ere the strong hands of Hercules
O'ermastered him. This, with much spoil beside,
Hercules took, and kept it to make sport
For his invincible hand; but afterward
Gave it to valiant Peleus, who with him
Had smitten fair-towered Ilium's burg renowned;
And he to Achilles gave it, whose swift ships
Bare it to Troy, to put him aye in mind
Of his own father, as with eager will
He fought with stalwart Trojans, and to be
A worthy test wherewith to prove his strength.
Even this did Aias from his brawny hand
Fling far. So then the Nereid gave to him
The glorious arms from godlike Memnon stripped.
Marvelling the Argives gazed on them: they were
A giant's war-gear. Laughing a glad laugh
That man renowned received them: he alone
Could wear them on his brawny limbs; they seemed
As they had even been moulded to his frame.
The great bar thence he bore withal, to be
His joy when he was fain of athlete-toil.

Still sped the contests on; and many rose
Now for the leaping. Far beyond the marks
Of all the rest brave Agapenor sprang:
Loud shouted all for that victorious leap;

The Fall of Troy

And Thetis gave him the fair battle-gear
Of mighty Cycnus, who had smitten first
Protesilaus, then had reft the life
From many more, till Peleus' son slew him
First of the chiefs of grief-enshrouded Troy.

Next, in the javelin-cast Euryalus
Hurled far beyond all rivals, while the folk
Shouted aloud: no archer, so they deemed,
Could speed a winged shaft farther than his cast;
Therefore the Aeacid hero's mother gave
To him a deep wide silver oil-flask, ta'en
By Achilles in possession, when his spear
Slew Mynes, and he spoiled Lyrnessus' wealth.

Then fiery-hearted Aias eagerly
Rose, challenging to strife of hands and feet
The mightiest hero there; but marvelling
They marked his mighty thews, and no man dared
Confront him. Chilling dread had palsied all
Their courage: from their hearts they feared him, lest
His hands invincible should all to-break
His adversary's face, and naught but pain
Be that man's meed. But at the last all men
Made signs to battle-bider Euryalus,
For well they knew him skilled in fighting-craft;
But he too feared that giant, and he cried:
"Friends, any other Achaean, whom ye will,
Blithe will I face; but mighty Alas--no!
Far doth he overmatch me. He will rend
Mine heart, if in the onset anger rise
Within him: from his hands invincible,
I trow, I should not win to the ships alive."

Loud laughed they all: but glowed with triumph-joy
The heart of Aias. Gleaming talents twain
Of silver he from Thetis' hands received,
His uncontested prize. His stately height
Called to her mind her dear son, and she sighed.

They which had skill in chariot-driving then
Rose at the contest's summons eagerly:
Menelaus first, Eurypylus bold in fight,
Eumelus, Thoas, godlike Polypoetes
Harnessed their steeds, and led them to the cars
All panting for the joy of victory.
Then rode they in a glittering chariot rank
Out to one place, to a stretch of sand, and stood
Ranged at the starting-line. The reins they grasped
In strong hands quickly, while the chariot-steeds
Shoulder to shoulder fretted, all afire
To take the lead at starting, pawed the sand,
Pricked ears, and o'er their frontlets flung the foam.
With sudden-stiffened sinews those car-lords
Lashed with their whips the tempest-footed steeds;
Then swift as Harpies sprang they forth; they strained
Furiously at the harness, onward whirling
The chariots bounding ever from the earth.
Thou couldst not see a wheel-track, no, nor print
Of hoof upon the sand--they verily flew.
Up from the plain the dust-clouds to the sky
Soared, like the smoke of burning, or a mist
Rolled round the mountain-forelands by the might
Of the dark South-wind or the West, when wakes
A tempest, when the hill-sides stream with rain.
Burst to the front Eumelus' steeds: behind

Close pressed the team of godlike Thoas: shouts
Still answered shouts that cheered each chariot, while
Onward they swept across the wide-wayed plain.

((LACUNA))

"From hallowed Elis, when he had achieved
A mighty triumph, in that he outstripped
The swift ear of Oenomaus evil-souled,
The ruthless slayer of youths who sought to wed
His daughter Hippodameia passing-wise.
Yet even he, for all his chariot-lore,
Had no such fleetfoot steeds as Atreus' son--
Far slower!--the wind is in the feet of these."

So spake he, giving glory to the might
Of those good steeds, and to Atreides' self;
And filled with joy was Menelaus' soul.
Straightway his henchmen from the yoke-band loosed
The panting team, and all those chariot-lords,
Who in the race had striven, now unyoked
Their tempest-footed steeds. Podaleirius then
Hasted to spread salves over all the wounds
Of Thoas and Eurypylus, gashes scored
Upon their frames when from the cars they fell
But Menelaus with exceeding joy
Of victory glowed, when Thetis lovely-tressed
Gave him a golden cup, the chief possession
Once of Eetion the godlike; ere
Achilles spoiled the far-famed burg of Thebes.

Then horsemen riding upon horses came
Down to the course: they grasped in hand the whip

And bounding from the earth bestrode their steeds,
The while with foaming mouths the coursers champed
The bits, and pawed the ground, and fretted aye
To dash into the course. Forth from the line
Swiftly they darted, eager for the strife,
Wild as the blasts of roaring Boreas
Or shouting Notus, when with hurricane-swoop
He heaves the wide sea high, when in the east
Uprises the disastrous Altar-star
Bringing calamity to seafarers;
So swift they rushed, spurning with flying feet
The deep dust on the plain. The riders cried
Each to his steed, and ever plied the lash
And shook the reins about the clashing bits.
On strained the horses: from the people rose
A shouting like the roaring of a sea.
On, on across the level plain they flew;
And now the flashing-footed Argive steed
By Sthenelus bestridden, had won the race,
But from the course he swerved, and o'er the plain
Once and again rushed wide; nor Capaneus' son,
Good horseman though he were, could turn him back
By rein or whip, because that steed was strange
Still to the race-course; yet of lineage
Noble was he, for in his veins the blood
Of swift Arion ran, the foal begotten
By the loud-piping West-wind on a Harpy,
The fleetest of all earth-born steeds, whose feet
Could race against his father's swiftest blasts.
Him did the Blessed to Adrastus give:
And from him sprang the steed of Sthenelus,
Which Tydeus' son had given unto his friend
In hallowed Troyland. Filled with confidence

In those swift feet his rider led him forth
Unto the contest of the steeds that day,
Looking his horsemanship should surely win
Renown: yet victory gladdened not his heart
In that great struggle for Achilles' prizes;
Nay, swift albeit he was, the King of Men
By skill outraced him. Shouted all the folk,
"Glory to Agamemnon!" Yet they acclaimed
The steed of valiant Sthenelus and his lord,
For that the fiery flying of his feet
Still won him second place, albeit oft
Wide of the course he swerved. Then Thetis gave
To Atreus' son, while laughed his lips for joy,
God-sprung Polydorus' breastplate silver-wrought.
To Sthenelus Asteropaeus' massy helm,
Two lances, and a taslet strong, she gave.
Yea, and to all the riders who that day
Came at Achilles' funeral-feast to strive
She gave gifts. But the son of the old war-lord,
Laertes, inly grieved to be withheld
From contests of the strong, how fain soe'er,
By that sore wound which Alcon dealt to him
In the grim fight around dead Aeacas' son.

BOOK V

How the Arms of Achilles were cause of madness and death unto Aias.

So when all other contests had an end,
Thetis the Goddess laid down in the midst
Great-souled Achilles' arms divinely wrought;
And all around flashed out the cunning work
Wherewith the Fire-god overchased the shield
Fashioned for Aeacus' son, the dauntless-souled.

Inwrought upon that labour of a God
Were first high heaven and cloudland, and beneath
Lay earth and sea: the winds, the clouds were there,
The moon and sun, each in its several place;
There too were all the stars that, fixed in heaven,
Are borne in its eternal circlings round.
Above and through all was the infinite air
Where to and fro flit birds of slender beak:
Thou hadst said they lived, and floated on the breeze.
Here Tethys' all-embracing arms were wrought,
And Ocean's fathomless flow. The outrushing flood
Of rivers crying to the echoing hills
All round, to right, to left, rolled o'er the land.

Round it rose league-long mountain-ridges, haunts
Of terrible lions and foul jackals: there
Fierce bears and panthers prowled; with these were seen
Wild boars that whetted deadly-clashing tusks
In grimly-frothing jaws. There hunters sped
After the hounds: beaters with stone and dart,
To the life portrayed, toiled in the woodland sport.

And there were man-devouring wars, and all
Horrors of fight: slain men were falling down
Mid horse-hoofs; and the likeness of a plain
Blood-drenched was on that shield invincible.
Panic was there, and Dread, and ghastly Enyo
With limbs all gore-bespattered hideously,
And deadly Strife, and the Avenging Spirits
Fierce-hearted--she, still goading warriors on
To the onset they, outbreathing breath of fire.
Around them hovered the relentless Fates;
Beside them Battle incarnate onward pressed
Yelling, and from their limbs streamed blood and sweat.
There were the ruthless Gorgons: through their hair
Horribly serpents coiled with flickering tongues.
A measureless marvel was that cunning work
Of things that made men shudder to behold
Seeming as though they verily lived and moved.

And while here all war's marvels were portrayed,
Yonder were all the works of lovely peace.
The myriad tribes of much-enduring men
Dwelt in fair cities. Justice watched o'er all.
To diverse toils they set their hands; the fields
Were harvest-laden; earth her increase bore.

Most steeply rose on that god-laboured work
The rugged flanks of holy Honour's mount,
And there upon a palm-tree throned she sat
Exalted, and her hands reached up to heaven.
All round her, paths broken by many rocks
Thwarted the climbers' feet; by those steep tracks
Daunted ye saw returning many folk:
Few won by sweat of toil the sacred height.

And there were reapers moving down long swaths
Swinging the whetted sickles: 'neath their hands
The hot work sped to its close. Hard after these
Many sheaf-binders followed, and the work
Grew passing great. With yoke-bands on their necks
Oxen were there, whereof some drew the wains
Heaped high with full-eared sheaves, and further on
Were others ploughing, and the glebe showed black
Behind them. Youths with ever-busy goads
Followed: a world of toil was there portrayed.

And there a banquet was, with pipe and harp,
Dances of maids, and flashing feet of boys,
All in swift movement, like to living souls.

Hard by the dance and its sweet winsomeness
Out of the sea was rising lovely-crowned
Cypris, foam-blossoms still upon her hair;
And round her hovered smiling witchingly
Desire, and danced the Graces lovely-tressed.

And there were lordly Nereus' Daughters shown
Leading their sister up from the wide sea
To her espousals with the warrior-king.

And round her all the Immortals banqueted
On Pelion's ridge far-stretching. All about
Lush dewy watermeads there were, bestarred
With flowers innumerable, grassy groves,
And springs with clear transparent water bright.

There ships with sighing sheets swept o'er the sea,
Some beating up to windward, some that sped
Before a following wind, and round them heaved
The melancholy surge. Seared shipmen rushed
This way and that, adread for tempest-gusts,
Hauling the white sails in, to 'scape the death--
It all seemed real--some tugging at the oars,
While the dark sea on either side the ship
Grew hoary 'neath the swiftly-plashing blades.

And there triumphant the Earth-shaker rode
Amid sea-monsters' stormy-footed steeds
Drew him, and seemed alive, as o'er the deep
They raced, oft smitten by the golden whip.
Around their path of flight the waves fell smooth,
And all before them was unrippled calm.
Dolphins on either hand about their king
Swarmed, in wild rapture of homage bowing backs,
And seemed like live things o'er the hazy sea
Swimming, albeit all of silver wrought.

Marvels of untold craft were imaged there
By cunning-souled Hephaestus' deathless hands
Upon the shield. And Ocean's fathomless flood
Clasped like a garland all the outer rim,
And compassed all the strong shield's curious work.

And therebeside the massy helmet lay.
Zeus in his wrath was set upon the crest
Throned on heaven's dome; the Immortals all around
Fierce-battling with the Titans fought for Zeus.
Already were their foes enwrapped with flame,
For thick and fast as snowflakes poured from heaven
The thunderbolts: the might of Zeus was roused,
And burning giants seemed to breathe out flames.

And therebeside the fair strong corslet lay,
Unpierceable, which clasped Peleides once:
There were the greaves close-lapping, light alone
To Achilles; massy of mould and huge they were.

And hard by flashed the sword whose edge and point
No mail could turn, with golden belt, and sheath
Of silver, and with haft of ivory:
Brightest amid those wondrous arms it shone.
Stretched on the earth thereby was that dread spear,
Long as the tall-tressed pines of Pelion,
Still breathing out the reek of Hector's blood.

Then mid the Argives Thetis sable-stoled
In her deep sorrow for Achilles spake;
"Now all the athlete-prizes have been won
Which I set forth in sorrow for my child.
Now let that mightiest of the Argives come
Who rescued from the foe my dead: to him
These glorious and immortal arms I give
Which even the blessed Deathless joyed to see."

Then rose in rivalry, each claiming them,
Laertes' seed and godlike Telamon's son,

Aias, the mightiest far of Danaan men:
He seemed the star that in the glittering sky
Outshines the host of heaven, Hesperus,
So splendid by Peleides' arms he stood;
"And let these judge," he cried, "Idomeneus,
Nestor, and kingly-counselled Agamemnon,"
For these, he weened, would sureliest know the truth
Of deeds wrought in that glorious battle-toil.
"To these I also trust most utterly,"
Odysseus said, "for prudent of their wit
Be these, and princeliest of all Danaan men."

But to Idomeneus and Atreus' son
Spake Nestor apart, and willingly they heard:
"Friends, a great woe and unendurable
This day the careless Gods have laid on us,
In that into this lamentable strife
Aias the mighty hath been thrust by them
Against Odysseus passing-wise. For he,
To whichsoe'er God gives the victor's glory--
O yea, he shall rejoice! But he that loseth--
All for the grief in all the Danaans' hearts
For him! And ours shall be the deepest grief
Of all; for that man will not in the war
Stand by us as of old. A sorrowful day
It shall be for us, whichsoe'er of these
Shall break into fierce anger, seeing they
Are of our heroes chiefest, this in war,
And that in counsel. Hearken then to me,
Seeing that I am older far than ye,
Not by a few years only: with mine age
Is prudence joined, for I have suffered and wrought
Much; and in counsel ever the old man,

Who knoweth much, excelleth younger men.
Therefore let us ordain to judge this cause
'Twixt godlike Aias and war-fain Odysseus,
Our Trojan captives. They shall say whom most
Our foes dread, and who saved Peleides' corse
From that most deadly fight. Lo, in our midst
Be many spear-won Trojans, thralls of Fate;
And these will pass true judgment on these twain,
To neither showing favour, since they hate
Alike all authors of their misery."

He spake: replied Agamemnon lord of spears:
"Ancient, there is none other in our midst
Wiser than thou, of Danaans young or old,
In that thou say'st that unforgiving wrath
Will burn in him to whom the Gods herein
Deny the victory; for these which strive
Are both our chiefest. Therefore mine heart too
Is set on this, that to the thralls of war
This judgment we commit: the loser then
Shall against Troy devise his deadly work
Of vengeance, and shall not be wroth with us."

He spake, and these three, being of one mind,
In hearing of all men refused to judge
Judgment so thankless: they would none of it.
Therefore they set the high-born sons of Troy
There in the midst, spear-thralls although they were,
To give just judgment in the warriors' strife.
Then in hot anger Aias rose, and spake:
"Odysseus, frantic soul, why hath a God
Deluded thee, to make thee hold thyself
My peer in might invincible? Dar'st thou say

That thou, when slain Achilles lay in dust,
When round him swarmed the Trojans, didst bear back
That furious throng, when I amidst them hurled
Death, and thou coweredst away? Thy dam
Bare thee a craven and a weakling wretch
Frail in comparison of me, as is
A cur beside a lion thunder-voiced!
No battle-biding heart is in thy breast,
But wiles and treachery be all thy care.
Hast thou forgotten how thou didst shrink back
From faring with Achaea's gathered host
To Ilium's holy burg, till Atreus' sons
Forced thee, the cowering craven, how loth soe'er,
To follow them--would God thou hadst never come!
For by thy counsel left we in Lemnos' isle
Groaning in agony Poeas' son renowned.
And not for him alone was ruin devised
Of thee; for godlike Palamedes too
Didst thou contrive destruction--ha, he was
Alike in battle and council better than thou!
And now thou dar'st to rise up against me,
Neither remembering my kindness, nor
Having respect unto the mightier man
Who rescued thee erewhile, when thou didst quaff
In fight before the onset of thy foes,
When thou, forsaken of all Greeks beside,
 Midst tumult of the fray, wast fleeing too!
Oh that in that great fight Zeus' self had stayed
My dauntless might with thunder from his heaven!
Then with their two-edged swords the Trojan men
Had hewn thee limb from limb, and to their dogs
Had cast thy carrion! Then thou hadst not presumed
To meet me, trusting in thy trickeries!

    Wretch, wherefore, if thou vauntest thee in might
    Beyond all others, hast thou set thy ships
    In the line's centre, screened from foes, nor dared
    As I, on the far wing to draw them up?
    Because thou wast afraid! Not thou it was
    Who savedst from devouring fire the ships;
    But I with heart unquailing there stood fast
    Facing the fire and Hector ay, even he
    Gave back before me everywhere in fight.
    Thou--thou didst fear him aye with deadly fear!
    Oh, had this our contention been but set
    Amidst that very battle, when the roar
    Of conflict rose around Achilles slain!
    Then had thine own eyes seen me bearing forth
    Out from the battle's heart and fury of foes
    That goodly armour and its hero lord
    Unto the tents. But here thou canst but trust
    In cunning speech, and covetest a place
    Amongst the mighty! Thou--thou hast not strength
    To wear Achilles' arms invincible,
    Nor sway his massy spear in thy weak hands!
    But I they are verily moulded to my frame:
    Yea, seemly it is I wear those glorious arms,
    Who shall not shame a God's gifts passing fair.
    But wherefore for Achilles' glorious arms
    With words discourteous wrangling stand we here?
    Come, let us try in strife with brazen spears
    Who of us twain is best in murderous right!
    For silver-footed Thetis set in the midst
    This prize for prowess, not for pestilent words.
    In folkmote may men have some use for words:
    In pride of prowess I know me above thee far,
    And great Achilles' lineage is mine own."

He spake: with scornful glance and bitter speech
Odysseus the resourceful chode with him:
"Aias, unbridled tongue, why these vain words
To me? Thou hast called me pestilent, niddering,
And weakling: yet I boast me better far
Than thou in wit and speech, which things increase
The strength of men. Lo, how the craggy rock,
Adamantine though it seem, the hewers of stone
Amid the hills by wisdom undermine
Full lightly, and by wisdom shipmen cross
The thunderous-plunging sea, when mountain-high
It surgeth, and by craft do hunters quell
Strong lions, panthers, boars, yea, all the brood
Of wild things. Furious-hearted bulls are tamed
To bear the yoke-bands by device of men.
Yea, all things are by wit accomplished. Still
It is the man who knoweth that excels
The witless man alike in toils and counsels.
For my keen wit did Oeneus' valiant son
Choose me of all men with him to draw nigh
To Hector's watchmen: yea, and mighty deeds
We twain accomplished. I it was who brought
To Atreus' sons Peleides far-renowned,
Their battle-helper. Whensoe'er the host
Needeth some other champion, not for the sake
Of thine hands will he come, nor by the rede
Of other Argives: of Achaeans I
Alone will draw him with soft suasive words
To where strong men are warring. Mighty power
The tongue hath over men, when courtesy
Inspires it. Valour is a deedless thing;
And bulk and big assemblage of a man
Cometh to naught, by wisdom unattended.

But unto me the Immortals gave both strength
And wisdom, and unto the Argive host
Made me a blessing. Nor, as thou hast said,
Hast thou in time past saved me when in flight
From foes. I never fled, but steadfastly
Withstood the charge of all the Trojan host.
Furious the enemy came on like a flood
But I by might of hands cut short the thread
Of many lives. Herein thou sayest not true
Me in the fray thou didst not shield nor save,
But for thine own life roughtest, lest a spear
Should pierce thy back if thou shouldst turn to flee
From war. My ships? I drew them up mid-line,
Not dreading the battle-fury of any foe,
But to bring healing unto Atreus' sons
Of war's calamities: and thou didst set
Far from their help thy ships. Nay more, I seamed
With cruel stripes my body, and entered so
The Trojans' burg, that I might learn of them
All their devisings for this troublous war.
Nor ever I dreaded Hector's spear; myself
Rose mid the foremost, eager for the fight,
When, prowess-confident, he defied us all.
Yea, in the fight around Achilles, I
Slew foes far more than thou; 'twas I who saved
The dead king with this armour. Not a whit
I dread thy spear now, but my grievous hurt
With pain still vexeth me, the wound I gat
In fighting for these arms and their slain lord.
In me as in Achilles is Zeus' blood."

He spake; strong Aias answered him again.
"Most cunning and most pestilent of men,

The Fall of Troy

Nor I, nor any other Argive, saw
Thee toiling in that fray, when Trojans strove
Fiercely to hale away Achilles slain.
My might it was that with the spear unstrung
The knees of some in fight, and others thrilled
With panic as they pressed on ceaselessly.
Then fled they in dire straits, as geese or cranes
Flee from an eagle swooping as they feed
Along a grassy meadow; so, in dread
The Trojans shrinking backward from my spear
And lightening sword, fled into Ilium
To 'scape destruction. If thy might came there
Ever at all, not anywhere nigh me
With foes thou foughtest: somewhere far aloof
Mid other ranks thou toiledst, nowhere nigh
Achilles, where the one great battle raged."

He spake; replied Odysseus the shrewd heart:
"Aias, I hold myself no worse than thou
In wit or might, how goodly in outward show
Thou be soever. Nay, I am keener far
Of wit than thou in all the Argives' eyes.
In battle-prowess do I equal thee
Haply surpass; and this the Trojans know,
Who tremble when they see me from afar.
Aye, thou too know'st, and others know my strength
By that hard struggle in the wrestling-match,
When Peleus' son set glorious prizes forth
Beside the barrow of Patroclus slain."

So spake Laertes' son the world-renowned.
Then on that strife disastrous of the strong
The sons of Troy gave judgment. Victory

And those immortal arms awarded they
With one consent to Odysseus mighty in war.
Greatly his soul rejoiced; but one deep groan
Brake from the Greeks. Then Aias' noble might
Stood frozen stiff; and suddenly fell on him
Dark wilderment; all blood within his frame
Boiled, and his gall swelled, bursting forth in flood.
Against his liver heaved his bowels; his heart
With anguished pangs was thrilled; fierce stabbing throes
Shot through the filmy veil 'twixt bone and brain;
And darkness and confusion wrapped his mind.
With fixed eyes staring on the ground he stood
Still as a statue. Then his sorrowing friends
Closed round him, led him to the shapely ships,
Aye murmuring consolations. But his feet
Trod for the last time, with reluctant steps,
That path; and hard behind him followed Doom.

When to the ships beside the boundless sea
The Argives, faint for supper and for sleep,
Had passed, into the great deep Thetis plunged,
And all the Nereids with her. Round them swam
Sea-monsters many, children of the brine.

Against the wise Prometheus bitter-wroth
The Sea-maids were, remembering how that Zeus,
Moved by his prophecies, unto Peleus gave
Thetis to wife, a most unwilling bride.
Then cried in wrath to these Cymothoe:
"O that the pestilent prophet had endured
All pangs he merited, when, deep-burrowing,
The eagle tare his liver aye renewed!"

The Fall of Troy

So to the dark-haired Sea-maids cried the Nymph.
Then sank the sun: the onrush of the night
Shadowed the fields, the heavens were star-bestrewn;
And by the long-prowed ships the Argives slept
By ambrosial sleep o'ermastered, and by wine
The which from proud Idomeneus' realm of Crete:
The shipmen bare o'er foaming leagues of sea.

But Aias, wroth against the Argive men,
Would none of meat or drink, nor clasped him round
The arms of sleep. In fury he donned his mail,
He clutched his sword, thinking unspeakable thoughts;
For now he thought to set the ships aflame,
And slaughter all the Argives, now, to hew
With sudden onslaught of his terrible sword
Guileful Odysseus limb from limb. Such things
He purposed--nay, had soon accomplished all,
Had Pallas not with madness smitten him;
For over Odysseus, strong to endure, her heart
Yearned, as she called to mind the sacrifices
Offered to her of him continually.
Therefore she turned aside from Argive men
The might of Aias. As a terrible storm,
Whose wings are laden with dread hurricane-blasts,
Cometh with portents of heart-numbing fear
To shipmen, when the Pleiads, fleeing adread
From glorious Orion, plunge beneath
The stream of tireless Ocean, when the air
Is turmoil, and the sea is mad with storm;
So rushed he, whithersoe'er his feet might bear.
This way and that he ran, like some fierce beast
Which darteth down a rock-walled glen's ravines
With foaming jaws, and murderous intent

Against the hounds and huntsmen, who have torn
Out of the cave her cubs, and slain: she runs
This way and that, and roars, if mid the brakes
Haply she yet may see the dear ones lost;
Whom if a man meet in that maddened mood,
Straightway his darkest of all days hath dawned;
So ruthless-raving rushed he; blackly boiled
His heart, as caldron on the Fire-god's hearth
Maddens with ceaseless hissing o'er the flames
From blazing billets coiling round its sides,
At bidding of the toiler eager-souled
To singe the bristles of a huge-fed boar;
So was his great heart boiling in his breast.
Like a wild sea he raved, like tempest-blast,
Like the winged might of tireless flame amidst
The mountains maddened by a mighty wind,
When the wide-blazing forest crumbles down
In fervent heat. So Aias, his fierce heart
With agony stabbed, in maddened misery raved.
Foam frothed about his lips; a beast-like roar
Howled from his throat. About his shoulders clashed
His armour. They which saw him trembled, all
Cowed by the fearful shout of that one man.

From Ocean then uprose Dawn golden-reined:
Like a soft wind upfloated Sleep to heaven,
And there met Hera, even then returned
To Olympus back from Tethys, unto whom
But yester-morn she went. She clasped him round,
And kissed him, who had been her marriage-kin
Since at her prayer on Ida's crest he had lulled
To sleep Cronion, when his anger burned
Against the Argives. Straightway Hera passed

To Zeus's mansion, and Sleep swiftly flew
To Pasithea's couch. From slumber woke
All nations of the earth. But Aias, like
Orion the invincible, prowled on,
Still bearing murderous madness in his heart.
He rushed upon the sheep, like lion fierce
Whose savage heart is stung with hunger-pangs.
Here, there, he smote them, laid them dead in dust
Thick as the leaves which the strong North-wind's might
Strews, when the waning year to winter turns;
So on the sheep in fury Aias fell,
Deeming he dealt to Danaans evil doom.

Then to his brother Menelaus came,
And spake, but not in hearing of the rest:
"This day shall surely be a ruinous day
For all, since Aias thus is sense-distraught.
It may be he will set the ships aflame,
And slay us all amidst our tents, in wrath
For those lost arms. Would God that Thetis ne'er
Had set them for the prize of rivalry!
Would God Laertes' son had not presumed
In folly of soul to strive with a better man!
Fools were we all; and some malignant God
Beguiled us; for the one great war-defence
Left us, since Aeacus' son in battle fell,
Was Aias' mighty strength. And now the Gods
Will to our loss destroy him, bringing bane
On thee and me, that all we may fill up
The cup of doom, and pass to nothingness."

He spake; replied Agamemnon, lord of spears:
"Now nay, Menelaus, though thine heart he wrung,

Be thou not wroth with the resourceful king
Of Cephallenian folk, but with the Gods
Who plot our ruin. Blame not him, who oft
Hath been our blessing and our enemies' curse."

So heavy-hearted spake the Danaan kings.
But by the streams of Xanthus far away
'Neath tamarisks shepherds cowered to hide from death,
As when from a swift eagle cower hares
'Neath tangled copses, when with sharp fierce scream
This way and that with wings wide-shadowing
He wheeleth very nigh; so they here, there,
Quailed from the presence of that furious man.
At last above a slaughtered ram he stood,
And with a deadly laugh he cried to it:
"Lie there in dust; be meat for dogs and kites!
Achilles' glorious arms have saved not thee,
For which thy folly strove with a better man!
Lie there, thou cur! No wife shall fall on thee,
And clasp, and wail thee and her fatherless childs,
Nor shalt thou greet thy parents' longing eyes,
The staff of their old age! Far from thy land
Thy carrion dogs and vultures shall devour!"

So cried he, thinking that amidst the slain
Odysseus lay blood-boltered at his feet.
But in that moment from his mind and eyes
Athena tore away the nightmare-fiend
Of Madness havoc-breathing, and it passed
Thence swiftly to the rock-walled river Styx
Where dwell the winged Erinnyes, they which still
Visit with torments overweening men.

Then Aias saw those sheep upon the earth
Gasping in death; and sore amazed he stood,
For he divined that by the Blessed Ones
His senses had been cheated. All his limbs
Failed under him; his soul was anguished-thrilled:
He could not in his horror take one step
Forward nor backward. Like some towering rock
Fast-rooted mid the mountains, there he stood.
But when the wild rout of his thoughts had rallied,
He groaned in misery, and in anguish wailed:
"Ah me! why do the Gods abhor me so?
They have wrecked my mind, have with fell madness filled,
Making me slaughter all these innocent sheep!
Would God that on Odysseus' pestilent heart
Mine hands had so avenged me! Miscreant, he
Brought on me a fell curse! O may his soul
Suffer all torments that the Avenging Fiends
Devise for villains! On all other Greeks
May they bring murderous battle, woeful griefs,
And chiefly on Agamemnon, Atreus' son!
Not scatheless to the home may he return
So long desired! But why should I consort,
I, a brave man, with the abominable?
Perish the Argive host, perish my life,
Now unendurable! The brave no more
Hath his due guerdon, but the baser sort
Are honoured most and loved, as this Odysseus
Hath worship mid the Greeks: but utterly
Have they forgotten me and all my deeds,
All that I wrought and suffered in their cause."

So spake the brave son of strong Telamon,
Then thrust the sword of Hector through his throat.

Forth rushed the blood in torrent: in the dust
Outstretched he lay, like Typhon, when the bolts
Of Zeus had blasted him. Around him groaned
The dark earth as he fell upon her breast.

Then thronging came the Danaans, when they saw
Low laid in dust the hero; but ere then
None dared draw nigh him, but in deadly fear
They watched him from afar. Now hasted they
And flung themselves upon the dead, outstretched
Upon their faces: on their heads they cast
Dust, and their wailing went up to the sky.
As when men drive away the tender lambs
Out of the fleecy flock, to feast thereon,
And round the desolate pens the mothers leap
Ceaselessly bleating, so o'er Aias rang
That day a very great and bitter cry.
Wild echoes pealed from Ida forest-palled,
And from the plain, the ships, the boundless sea.

Then Teucer clasping him was minded too
To rush on bitter doom: howbeit the rest
Held from the sword his hand. Anguished he fell
Upon the dead, outpouring many a tear
More comfortlessly than the orphan babe
That wails beside the hearth, with ashes strewn
On head and shoulders, wails bereavement's day
That brings death to the mother who hath nursed
The fatherless child; so wailed he, ever wailed
His great death-stricken brother, creeping slow
Around the corpse, and uttering his lament:
"O Aias, mighty-souled, why was thine heart
Distraught, that thou shouldst deal unto thyself

Murder and bale? All, was it that the sons
Of Troy might win a breathing-space from woes,
Might come and slay the Greeks, now thou art not?
From these shall all the olden courage fail
When fast they fall in fight. Their shield from harm
Is broken now! For me, I have no will
To see mine home again, now thou art dead.
Nay, but I long here also now to die,
That so the earth may shroud me--me and thee
Not for my parents so much do I care,
If haply yet they live, if haply yet
Spared from the grave, in Salamis they dwell,
As for thee, O my glory and my crown!"

So cried he groaning sore; with answering moan
Queenly Tecmessa wailed, the princess-bride
Of noble Aias, captive of his spear,
Yet ta'en by him to wife, and household-queen
O'er all his substance, even all that wives
Won with a bride-price rule for wedded lords.
Clasped in his mighty arms, she bare to him
A son Eurysaces, in all things like
Unto his father, far as babe might be
Yet cradled in his tent. With bitter moan
Fell she on that dear corpse, all her fair form
Close-shrouded in her veil, and dust-defiled,
And from her anguished heart cried piteously:
"Alas for me, for me now thou art dead,
Not by the hands of foes in fight struck down,
But by thine own! On me is come a grief
Ever-abiding! Never had I looked
To see thy woeful death-day here by Troy.
Ah, visions shattered by rude hands of Fate!

Oh that the earth had yawned wide for my grave
Ere I beheld thy bitter doom! On me
No sharper, more heart-piercing pang hath come--
No, not when first from fatherland afar
And parents thou didst bear me, wailing sore
Mid other captives, when the day of bondage
Had come on me, a princess theretofore.
Not for that dear lost home so much I grieve,
Nor for my parents dead, as now for thee:
For all thine heart was kindness unto me
The hapless, and thou madest me thy wife,
One soul with thee; yea, and thou promisedst
To throne me queen of fair-towered Salamis,
When home we won from Troy. The Gods denied
Accomplishment thereof. And thou hast passed
Unto the Unseen Land: thou hast forgot
Me and thy child, who never shall make glad
His father's heart, shall never mount thy throne.
But him shall strangers make a wretched thrall:
For when the father is no more, the babe
Is ward of meaner men. A weary life
The orphan knows, and suffering cometh in
From every side upon him like a flood.
To me too thraldom's day shall doubtless come,
Now thou hast died, who wast my god on earth."

Then in all kindness Agamemnon spake:
"Princess, no man on earth shall make thee thrall,
While Teucer liveth yet, while yet I live.
Thou shalt have worship of us evermore
And honour as a Goddess, with thy son,
As though yet living were that godlike man,
Aias, who was the Achaeans' chiefest strength.

Ah that he had not laid this load of grief
On all, in dying by his own right hand!
For all the countless armies of his foes
Never availed to slay him in fair fight."

So spake he, grieved to the inmost heart. The folk
Woefully wafted all round. O'er Hellespont
Echoes of mourning rolled: the sighing air
Darkened around, a wide-spread sorrow-pall.
Yea, grief laid hold on wise Odysseus' self
For the great dead, and with remorseful soul
To anguish-stricken Argives thus he spake:
"O friends, there is no greater curse to men
Than wrath, which groweth till its bitter fruit
Is strife. Now wrath hath goaded Aias on
To this dire issue of the rage that filled
His soul against me. Would to God that ne'er
Yon Trojans in the strife for Achilles' arms
Had crowned me with that victory, for which
Strong Telamon's brave son, in agony
Of soul, thus perished by his own right hand!
Yet blame not me, I pray you, for his wrath:
Blame the dark dolorous Fate that struck him down.
For, had mine heart foreboded aught of this,
This desperation of a soul distraught,
Never for victory had I striven with him,
Nor had I suffered any Danaan else,
Though ne'er so eager, to contend with him.
Nay, I had taken up those arms divine
With mine own hands, and gladly given them
To him, ay, though himself desired it not.
But for such mighty grief and wrath in him
I had not looked, since not for a woman's sake

Nor for a city, nor possessions wide,
I then contended, but for Honour's meed,
Which alway is for all right-hearted men
The happy goal of all their rivalry.
But that great-hearted man was led astray
By Fate, the hateful fiend; for surely it is
Unworthy a man to be made passion's fool.
The wise man's part is, steadfast-souled to endure
All ills, and not to rage against his lot."

So spake Laertes' son, the far-renowned.
But when they all were weary of grief and groan,
Then to those sorrowing ones spake Neleus' son:
"O friends, the pitiless-hearted Fates have laid
Stroke after stroke of sorrow upon us,
Sorrow for Aias dead, for mighty Achilles,
For many an Argive, and for mine own son
Antilochus. Yet all unmeet it is
Day after day with passion of grief to wail
Men slain in battle: nay, we must forget
Laments, and turn us to the better task
Of rendering dues beseeming to the dead,
The dues of pyre, of tomb, of bones inurned.
No lamentations will awake the dead;
No note thereof he taketh, when the Fates,
The ruthless ones, have swallowed him in night."

So spake he words of cheer: the godlike kings
Gathered with heavy hearts around the dead,
And many hands upheaved the giant corpse,
And swiftly bare him to the ships, and there
Washed they away the blood that clotted lay
Dust-flecked on mighty limbs and armour: then

In linen swathed him round. From Ida's heights
Wood without measure did the young men bring,
And piled it round the corpse. Billets and logs
Yet more in a wide circle heaped they round;
And sheep they laid thereon, fair-woven vests,
And goodly kine, and speed-triumphant steeds,
And gleaming gold, and armour without stint,
From slain foes by that glorious hero stripped.
And lucent amber-drops they laid thereon,
Tears, say they, which the Daughters of the Sun,
The Lord of Omens, shed for Phaethon slain,
When by Eridanus' flood they mourned for him.
These, for undying honour to his son,
The God made amber, precious in men's eyes.
Even this the Argives on that broad-based pyre
Cast freely, honouring the mighty dead.
And round him, groaning heavily, they laid
Silver most fair and precious ivory,
And jars of oil, and whatsoe'er beside
They have who heap up goodly and glorious wealth.
Then thrust they in the strength of ravening flame,
And from the sea there breathed a wind, sent forth
By Thetis, to consume the giant frame
Of Aias. All the night and all the morn
Burned 'neath the urgent stress of that great wind
Beside the ships that giant form, as when
Enceladus by Zeus' levin was consumed
Beneath Thrinacia, when from all the isle
Smoke of his burning rose--or like as when
Hercules, trapped by Nessus' deadly guile,
Gave to devouring fire his living limbs,
What time he dared that awful deed, when groaned
All Oeta as he burned alive, and passed

His soul into the air, leaving the man
Far-famous, to be numbered with the Gods,
When earth closed o'er his toil-tried mortal part.
So huge amid the flames, all-armour clad,
Lay Aias, all the joy of fight forgot,
While a great multitude watching thronged the sands.
Glad were the Trojans, but the Achaeans grieved.

But when that goodly frame by ravening fire
Was all consumed, they quenched the pyre with wine;
They gathered up the bones, and reverently
Laid in a golden casket. Hard beside
Rhoeteium's headland heaped they up a mound
Measureless-high. Then scattered they amidst
The long ships, heavy-hearted for the man
Whom they had honoured even as Achilles.
Then black night, bearing unto all men sleep,
Upfloated: so they brake bread, and lay down
Waiting the Child of the Mist. Short was sleep,
Broken by fitful staring through the dark,
Haunted by dread lest in the night the foe
Should fall on them, now Telamon's son was dead.

BOOK VI

How came for the helping of Troy Eurypylus, Hercules' grandson.

Rose Dawn from Ocean and Tithonus' bed,
And climbed the steeps of heaven, scattering round
Flushed flakes of splendour; laughed all earth and air.
Then turned unto their labours, each to each,
Mortals, frail creatures daily dying. Then
Streamed to a folkmote all the Achaean men
At Menelaus' summons. When the host
Were gathered all, then in their midst he spake:
"Hearken my words, ye god-descended kings:
Mine heart within my breast is burdened sore
For men which perish, men that for my sake
Came to the bitter war, whose home-return
Parents and home shall welcome nevermore;
For Fate hath cut off thousands in their prime.
Oh that the heavy hand of death had fallen
On me, ere hitherward I gathered these!
But now hath God laid on me cureless pain
In seeing all these ills. Who could rejoice
Beholding strivings, struggles of despair?
Come, let us, which be yet alive, in haste
Flee in the ships, each to his several land,

Since Aias and Achilles both are dead.
I look not, now they are slain, that we the rest
Shall 'scape destruction; nay, but we shall fall
Before yon terrible Trojans for my sake
And shameless Helen's! Think not that I care
For her: for you I care, when I behold
Good men in battle slain. Away with her--
Her and her paltry paramour! The Gods
Stole all discretion out of her false heart
When she forsook mine home and marriage-bed.
Let Priam and the Trojans cherish her!
But let us straight return: 'twere better far
To flee from dolorous war than perish all."

So spake he but to try the Argive men.
Far other thoughts than these made his heart burn
With passionate desire to slay his foes,
To break the long walls of their city down
From their foundations, and to glut with blood
Ares, when Paris mid the slain should fall.
Fiercer is naught than passionate desire!
Thus as he pondered, sitting in his place,
Uprose Tydeides, shaker of the shield,
And chode in fiery speech with Menelaus:
"O coward Atreus' son, what craven fear
Hath gripped thee, that thou speakest so to us
As might a weakling child or woman speak?
Not unto thee Achaea's noblest sons
Will hearken, ere Troy's coronal of towers
Be wholly dashed to the dust: for unto men
Valour is high renown, and flight is shame!
If any man shall hearken to the words
Of this thy counsel, I will smite from him

His head with sharp blue steel, and hurl it down
For soaring kites to feast on. Up! all ye
Who care to enkindle men to battle: rouse
Our warriors all throughout the fleet to whet
The spear, to burnish corslet, helm and shield;
And cause both man and horse, all which be keen
In fight, to break their fast. Then in yon plain
Who is the stronger Ares shall decide."

So speaking, in his place he sat him down;
Then rose up Thestor's son, and in the midst,
Where meet it is to speak, stood forth and cried:
"Hear me, ye sons of battle-biding Greeks:
Ye know I have the spirit of prophecy.
Erewhile I said that ye in the tenth year
Should lay waste towered Ilium: this the Gods
Are even now fulfilling; victory lies
At the Argives' very feet. Come, let us send
Tydeides and Odysseus battle-staunch
With speed to Scyros overseas, by prayers
Hither to bring Achilles' hero son:
A light of victory shall he be to us."

So spake wise Thestius' son, and all the folk
Shouted for joy; for all their hearts and hopes
Yearned to see Calchas' prophecy fulfilled.
Then to the Argives spake Laertes' son:
"Friends, it befits not to say many words
This day to you, in sorrow's weariness.
I know that wearied men can find no joy
In speech or song, though the Pierides,
The immortal Muses, love it. At such time
Few words do men desire. But now, this thing

That pleaseth all the Achaean host, will I
Accomplish, so Tydeides fare with me;
For, if we twain go, we shall surely bring,
Won by our words, war-fain Achilles' son,
Yea, though his mother, weeping sore, should strive
Within her halls to keep him; for mine heart
Trusts that he is a hero's valorous son."

Then out spake Menelaus earnestly:
"Odysseus, the strong Argives' help at need,
If mighty-souled Achilles' valiant son
From Scyros by thy suasion come to aid
Us who yearn for him, and some Heavenly One
Grant victory to our prayers, and I win home
To Hellas, I will give to him to wife
My noble child Hermione, with gifts
Many and goodly for her marriage-dower
With a glad heart. I trow he shall not scorn
Either his bride or high-born sire-in-law."

With a great shout the Danaans hailed his words.
Then was the throng dispersed, and to the ships
They scattered hungering for the morning meat
Which strengtheneth man's heart. So when they ceased
From eating, and desire was satisfied,
Then with the wise Odysseus Tydeus' son
Drew down a swift ship to the boundless sea,
And victual and all tackling cast therein.
Then stepped they aboard, and with them twenty men,
Men skilled to row when winds were contrary,
Or when the unrippled sea slept 'neath a calm.
They smote the brine, and flashed the boiling foam:
On leapt the ship; a watery way was cleft

About the oars that sweating rowers tugged.
As when hard-toiling oxen, 'neath the yoke
Straining, drag on a massy-timbered wain,
While creaks the circling axle 'neath its load,
And from their weary necks and shoulders streams
Down to the ground the sweat abundantly;
So at the stiff oars toiled those stalwart men,
And fast they laid behind them leagues of sea.
Gazed after them the Achaeans as they went,
Then turned to whet their deadly darts and spears,
The weapons of their warfare. In their town
The aweless Trojans armed themselves the while
War-eager, praying to the Gods to grant
Respite from slaughter, breathing-space from toil.

To these, while sorely thus they yearned, the Gods
Brought present help in trouble, even the seed
Of mighty Hercules, Eurypylus.
A great host followed him, in battle skilled,
All that by long Caicus' outflow dwelt,
Full of triumphant trust in their strong spears.
Round them rejoicing thronged the sons of Troy:
As when tame geese within a pen gaze up
On him who casts them corn, and round his feet
Throng hissing uncouth love, and his heart warms
As he looks down on them; so thronged the sons
Of Troy, as on fierce-heart Eurypylus
They gazed; and gladdened was his aweless soul
To see those throngs: from porchways women looked
Wide-eyed with wonder on the godlike man.
Above all men he towered as on he strode,
As looks a lion when amid the hills
He comes on jackals. Paris welcomed him,

As Hector honouring him, his cousin he,
Being of one blood with him, who was born Of
Astyoche, King Priam's sister fair
Whom Telephus embraced in his strong arms,
Telephus, whom to aweless Hercules
Auge the bright-haired bare in secret love.
That babe, a suckling craving for the breast,
A swift hind fostered, giving him the teat
As to her own fawn in all love; for Zeus
So willed it, in whose eyes it was not meet
That Hercules' child should perish wretchedly.
His glorious son with glad heart Paris led
Unto his palace through the wide-wayed burg
Beside Assaracus' tomb and stately halls
Of Hector, and Tritonis' holy fane.
Hard by his mansion stood, and therebeside
The stainless altar of Home-warder Zeus
Rose. As they went, he lovingly questioned him
Of brethren, parents, and of marriage-kin;
And all he craved to know Eurypylus told.
So communed they, on-pacing side by side.
Then came they to a palace great and rich:
There goddess-like sat Helen, clothed upon
With beauty of the Graces. Maidens four
About her plied their tasks: others apart
Within that goodly bower wrought the works
Beseeming handmaids. Helen marvelling gazed
Upon Eurypylus, on Helen he.
Then these in converse each with other spake
In that all-odorous bower. The handmaids brought
And set beside their lady high-seats twain;
And Paris sat him down, and at his side
Eurypylus. That hero's host encamped

Without the city, where the Trojan guards
Kept watch. Their armour laid they on the earth;
Their steeds, yet breathing battle, stood thereby,
And cribs were heaped with horses' provender.

Upfloated night, and darkened earth and air;
Then feasted they before that cliff-like wall,
Ceteian men and Trojans: babel of talk
Rose from the feasters: all around the glow
Of blazing campfires lighted up the tents:
Pealed out the pipe's sweet voice, and hautboys rang
With their clear-shrilling reeds; the witching strain
Of lyres was rippling round. From far away
The Argives gazed and marvelled, seeing the plain
Aglare with many fires, and hearing notes
Of flutes and lyres, neighing of chariot-steeds
And pipes, the shepherd's and the banquet's joy.
Therefore they bade their fellows each in turn
Keep watch and ward about the tents till dawn,
Lest those proud Trojans feasting by their walls
Should fall on them, and set the ships aflame.

Within the halls of Paris all this while
With kings and princes Telephus' hero son
Feasted; and Priam and the sons of Troy
Each after each prayed him to play the man
Against the Argives, and in bitter doom
To lay them low; and blithe he promised all.
So when they had supped, each hied him to his home;
But there Eurypylus laid him down to rest
Full nigh the feast-hall, in the stately bower
Where Paris theretofore himself had slept
With Helen world-renowned. A bower it was

Most wondrous fair, the goodliest of them all.
There lay he down; but otherwhere their rest
Took they, till rose the bright-throned Queen of Morn.
Up sprang with dawn the son of Telephus,
And passed to the host with all those other kings
In Troy abiding. Straightway did the folk
All battle-eager don their warrior-gear,
Burning to strike in forefront of the fight.
And now Eurypylus clad his mighty limbs
In armour that like levin-flashes gleamed;
Upon his shield by cunning hands were wrought
All the great labours of strong Hercules.

Thereon were seen two serpents flickering
Black tongues from grimly jaws: they seemed in act
To dart; but Hercules' hands to right and left--
Albeit a babe's hands--now were throttling them;
For aweless was his spirit. As Zeus' strength
From the beginning was his strength. The seed
Of Heaven-abiders never deedless is
Nor helpless, but hath boundless prowess, yea,
Even when in the womb unborn it lies.

Nemea's mighty lion there was seen
Strangled in the strong arms of Hercules,
His grim jaws dashed about with bloody foam:
He seemed in verity gasping out his life.

Thereby was wrought the Hydra many-necked
Flickering its dread tongues. Of its fearful heads
Some severed lay on earth, but many more
Were budding from its necks, while Hercules
And Iolaus, dauntless-hearted twain,

The Fall of Troy

Toiled hard; the one with lightning sickle-sweeps
Lopped the fierce heads, his fellow seared each neck
With glowing iron; the monster so was slain.

Thereby was wrought the mighty tameless Boar
With foaming jaws; real seemed the pictured thing,
As by Aleides' giant strength the brute
Was to Eurystheus living borne on high.

There fashioned was the fleetfoot stag which laid
The vineyards waste of hapless husbandmen.
The Hero's hands held fast its golden horns,
The while it snorted breath of ravening fire.

Thereon were seen the fierce Stymphalian Birds,
Some arrow-smitten dying in the dust,
Some through the grey air darting in swift flight.
At this, at that one--hot in haste he seemed--
Hercules sped the arrows of his wrath.

Augeias' monstrous stable there was wrought
With cunning craft on that invincible targe;
And Hercules was turning through the same
The deep flow of Alpheius' stream divine,
While wondering Nymphs looked down on every hand
Upon that mighty work. Elsewhere portrayed
Was the Fire-breathing Bull: the Hero's grip
On his strong horns wrenched round the massive neck:
The straining muscles on his arm stood out:
The huge beast seemed to bellow. Next thereto
Wrought on the shield was one in beauty arrayed
As of a Goddess, even Hippolyta.
The hero by the hair was dragging her

From her swift steed, with fierce resolve to wrest
With his strong hands the Girdle Marvellous
From the Amazon Queen, while quailing shrank away
The Maids of War. There in the Thracian land
Were Diomedes' grim man-eating steeds:
These at their gruesome mangers had he slain,
And dead they lay with their fiend-hearted lord.

There lay the bulk of giant Geryon
Dead mid his kine. His gory heads were cast
In dust, dashed down by that resistless club.
Before him slain lay that most murderous hound
Orthros, in furious might like Cerberus
His brother-hound: a herdman lay thereby,
Eurytion, all bedabbled with his blood.

There were the Golden Apples wrought, that gleamed
In the Hesperides' garden undefiled:
All round the fearful Serpent's dead coils lay,
And shrank the Maids aghast from Zeus' bold son.

And there, a dread sight even for Gods to see,
Was Cerberus, whom the Loathly Worm had borne
To Typho in a craggy cavern's gloom
Close on the borders of Eternal Night,
A hideous monster, warder of the Gate
Of Hades, Home of Wailing, jailer-hound
Of dead folk in the shadowy Gulf of Doom.
But lightly Zeus' son with his crashing blows
Tamed him, and haled him from the cataract flood
Of Styx, with heavy-drooping head, and dragged
The Dog sore loth to the strange upper air
All dauntlessly. And there, at the world's end,

The Fall of Troy

Were Caucasus' long glens, where Hercules,
Rending Prometheus' chains, and hurling them
This way and that with fragments of the rock
Whereinto they were riveted, set free
The mighty Titan. Arrow-smitten lay
The Eagle of the Torment therebeside.

There stormed the wild rout of the Centaurs round
The hall of Pholus: goaded on by Strife
And wine, with Hercules the monsters fought.
Amidst the pine-trunks stricken to death they lay
Still grasping those strange weapons in dead hands,
While some with stems long-shafted still fought on
In fury, and refrained not from the strife;
And all their heads, gashed in the pitiless fight,
Were drenched with gore--the whole scene seemed to live--
With blood the wine was mingled: meats and bowls
And tables in one ruin shattered lay.

There by Evenus' torrent, in fierce wrath
For his sweet bride, he laid with the arrow low
Nessus in mid-flight. There withal was wrought
Antaeus' brawny strength, who challenged him
To wrestling-strife; he in those sinewy arms
Raised high above the earth, was crushed to death.

There where swift Hellespont meets the outer sea,
Lay the sea-monster slain by his ruthless shafts,
While from Hesione he rent her chains.

Of bold Alcides many a deed beside
Shone on the broad shield of Eurypylus.
He seemed the War-god, as from rank to rank

He sped; rejoiced the Trojans following him,
Seeing his arms, and him clothed with the might
Of Gods; and Paris hailed him to the fray:
"Glad am I for thy coming, for mine heart
Trusts that the Argives all shall wretchedly
Be with their ships destroyed; for such a man
Mid Greeks or Trojans never have I seen.
Now, by the strength and fury of Hercules--
To whom in stature, might, and goodlihead
Most like thou art I pray thee, have in mind
Him, and resolve to match his deeds with thine.
Be the strong shield of Trojans hard-bestead:
Win us a breathing-space. Thou only, I trow,
From perishing Troy canst thrust the dark doom back."

With kindling words he spake. That hero cried:
"Great-hearted Paris, like the Blessed Ones
In goodlihead, this lieth foreordained
On the Gods' knees, who in the fight shall fall,
And who outlive it. I, as honour bids,
And as my strength sufficeth, will not flinch
From Troy's defence. I swear to turn from fight
Never, except in victory or death."

Gallantly spake he: with exceeding joy
Rejoiced the Trojans. Champions then he chose,
Alexander and Aeneas fiery-souled,
Polydamas, Pammon, and Deiphobus,
And Aethicus, of Paphlagonian men
The staunchest man to stem the tide of war;
These chose he, cunning all in battle-toil,
To meet the foe in forefront of the fight.
Swiftly they strode before that warrior-throng

Then from the city cheering charged. The host
Followed them in their thousands, as when bees
Follow by bands their leaders from the hives,
With loud hum on a spring day pouring forth.
So to the fight the warriors followed these;
And, as they charged, the thunder-tramp of men
And steeds, and clang of armour, rang to heaven.
As when a rushing mighty wind stirs up
The barren sea-plain from its nethermost floor,
And darkling to the strand roll roaring waves
Belching sea-tangle from the bursting surf,
And wild sounds rise from beaches harvestless;
So, as they charged, the wide earth rang again.

Now from their rampart forth the Argives poured
Round godlike Agamemnon. Rang their shouts
Cheering each other on to face the fight,
And not to cower beside the ships in dread
Of onset-shouts of battle-eager foes.
They met those charging hosts with hearts as light
As calves bear, when they leap to meet the kine
Down faring from hill-pastures in the spring
Unto the steading, when the fields are green
With corn-blades, when the earth is glad with flowers,
And bowls are brimmed with milk of kine and ewes,
And multitudinous lowing far and near
Uprises as the mothers meet their young,
And in their midst the herdman joys; so great
Was the uproar that rose when met the fronts
Of battle: dread it rang on either hand.
Hard-strained was then the fight: incarnate
Strife Stalked through the midst, with Slaughter ghastly-faced.
Crashed bull-hide shields, and spears, and helmet-crests

Meeting: the brass flashed out like leaping flames.
Bristled the battle with the lances; earth
Ran red with blood, as slaughtered heroes fell
And horses, mid a tangle of shattered ears,
Some yet with spear-wounds gasping, while on them
Others were falling. Through the air upshrieked
An awful indistinguishable roar;
For on both hosts fell iron-hearted Strife.
Here were men hurling cruel jagged stones,
There speeding arrows and new-whetted darts,
There with the axe or twibill hewing hard,
Slashing with swords, and thrusting out with spears:
Their mad hands clutched all manner of tools of death.

At first the Argives bore the ranks of Troy
Backward a little; but they rallied, charged,
Leapt on the foe, and drenched the field with blood.
Like a black hurricane rushed Eurypylus
Cheering his men on, hewing Argives down
Awelessly: measureless might was lent to him
By Zeus, for a grace to glorious Hercules.
Nireus, a man in beauty like the Gods,
His spear long-shafted stabbed beneath the ribs,
Down on the plain he fell, forth streamed the blood
Drenching his splendid arms, drenching the form
Glorious of mould, and his thick-clustering hair.
There mid the slain in dust and blood he lay,
Like a young lusty olive-sapling, which
A river rushing down in roaring flood,
Tearing its banks away, and cleaving wide
A chasm-channel, hath disrooted; low
It lieth heavy-blossomed; so lay then
The goodly form, the grace of loveliness

Of Nireus on earth's breast. But o'er the slain
Loud rang the taunting of Eurypylus:
"Lie there in dust! Thy beauty marvellous
Naught hath availed thee! I have plucked thee away
From life, to which thou wast so fain to cling.
Rash fool, who didst defy a mightier man
Unknowing! Beauty is no match for strength!"

He spake, and leapt upon the slain to strip
His goodly arms: but now against him came
Machaon wroth for Nireus, by his side
Doom-overtaken. With his spear he drave
At his right shoulder: strong albeit he was,
He touched him, and blood spurted from the gash.
Yet, ere he might leap back from grapple of death,
Even as a lion or fierce mountain-boar
Maddens mid thronging huntsmen, furious-fain
To rend the man whose hand first wounded him;
So fierce Eurypylus on Machaon rushed.
The long lance shot out swiftly, and pierced him through
On the right haunch; yet would he not give back,
Nor flinch from the onset, fast though flowed the blood.
In haste he snatched a huge stone from the ground,
And dashed it on the head of Telephus' son;
But his helm warded him from death or harm
Then waxed Eurypylus more hotly wroth
With that strong warrior, and in fury of soul
Clear through Machaon's breast he drave his spear,
And through the midriff passed the gory point.
He fell, as falls beneath a lion's jaws
A bull, and round him clashed his glancing arms.
Swiftly Eurypylus plucked the lance of death
Out of the wound, and vaunting cried aloud:

"Wretch, wisdom was not bound up in thine heart,
That thou, a weakling, didst come forth to fight
A mightier. Therefore art thou in the toils
Of Doom. Much profit shall be thine, when kites
Devour the flesh of thee in battle slain!
Ha, dost thou hope still to return, to 'scape
Mine hands? A leech art thou, and soothing salves
Thou knowest, and by these didst haply hope
To flee the evil day! Not thine own sire,
On the wind's wings descending from Olympus,
Should save thy life, not though between thy lips
He should pour nectar and ambrosia!"

Faint-breathing answered him the dying man:
"Eurypylus, thine own weird is to live
Not long: Fate is at point to meet thee here
On Troy's plain, and to still thine impious tongue."

So passed his spirit into Hades' halls.
Then to the dead man spake his conqueror:
"Now on the earth lie thou. What shall betide
Hereafter, care I not--yea, though this day
Death's doom stand by my feet: no man may live
For ever: each man's fate is foreordained."

Stabbing the corpse he spake. Then shouted loud
Teucer, at seeing Machaon in the dust.
Far thence he stood hard-toiling in the fight,
For on the centre sore the battle lay:
Foe after foe pressed on; yet not for this
Was Teucer heedless of the fallen brave,
Neither of Nireus lying hard thereby
Behind Machaon in the dust. He saw,

And with a great voice raised the rescue-cry:
"Charge, Argives! Flinch not from the charging foe!
For shame unspeakable shall cover us
If Trojan men hale back to Ilium
Noble Machaon and Nireus godlike-fair.
Come, with a good heart let us face the foe
To rescue these slain friends, or fall ourselves
Beside them. Duty bids that men defend
Friends, and to aliens leave them not a prey,
Not without sweat of toil is glory won!"

Then were the Danaans anguish-stung: the earth
All round them dyed they red with blood of slain,
As foe fought foe in even-balanced fight.
By this to Podaleirius tidings came
How that in dust his brother lay, struck down
By woeful death. Beside the ships he sat
Ministering to the hurts of men with spears
Stricken. In wrath for his brother's sake he rose,
He clad him in his armour; in his breast
Dread battle-prowess swelled. For conflict grim
He panted: boiled the mad blood round his heart
He leapt amidst the foemen; his swift hands
Swung the snake-headed javelin up, and hurled,
And slew with its winged speed Agamestor's son
Cleitus, a bright-haired Nymph had given him birth
Beside Parthenius, whose quiet stream
Fleets smooth as oil through green lands, till it pours
Its shining ripples to the Euxine sea.
Then by his warrior-brother laid he low
Lassus, whom Pronoe, fair as a goddess, bare
Beside Nymphaeus' stream, hard by a cave,
A wide and wondrous cave: sacred it is

Men say, unto the Nymphs, even all that haunt
The long-ridged Paphlagonian hills, and all
That by full-clustered Heracleia dwell.
That cave is like the work of gods, of stone
In manner marvellous moulded: through it flows
Cold water crystal-clear: in niches round
Stand bowls of stone upon the rugged rock,
Seeming as they were wrought by carvers' hands.
Statues of Wood-gods stand around, fair Nymphs,
Looms, distaffs, all such things as mortal craft
Fashioneth. Wondrous seem they unto men
Which pass into that hallowed cave. It hath,
Up-leading and down-leading, doorways twain,
Facing, the one, the wild North's shrilling blasts,
And one the dank rain-burdened South. By this
Do mortals pass beneath the Nymphs' wide cave;
But that is the Immortals' path: no man
May tread it, for a chasm deep and wide
Down-reaching unto Hades, yawns between.
This track the Blest Gods may alone behold.
So died a host on either side that warred
Over Machaon and Aglaia's son.
But at the last through desperate wrestle of fight
The Danaans rescued them: yet few were they
Which bare them to the ships: by bitter stress
Of conflict were the more part compassed round,
And needs must still abide the battle's brunt.
But when full many had filled the measure up
Of fate, mid tumult, blood and agony,
Then to their ships did many Argives flee
Pressed by Eurypylus hard, an avalanche
Of havoc. Yet a few abode the strife
Round Aias and the Atreidae rallying;

And haply these had perished all, beset
By throngs on throngs of foes on every hand,
Had not Oileus' son stabbed with his spear
'Twixt shoulder and breast war-wise Polydamas;
Forth gushed the blood, and he recoiled a space.
Then Menelaus pierced Deiphobus
By the right breast, that with swift feet he fled.
And many of that slaughter-breathing throng
Were slain by Agamemnon: furiously
He rushed on godlike Aethicus with the spear;
But he shrank from the forefront back mid friends.

Now when Eurypylus the battle-stay
Marked how the ranks of Troy gave back from fight,
He turned him from the host that he had chased
Even to the ships, and rushed with eagle-swoop
On Atreus' strong sons and Oileus' seed
Stout-hearted, who was passing fleet of foot
And in fight peerless. Swiftly he charged on these
Grasping his spear long-shafted: at Iris side
Charged Paris, charged Aeneas stout of heart,
Who hurled a stone exceeding huge, that crashed
On Aias' helmet: dashed to the dust he was,
Yet gave not up the ghost, whose day of doom
Was fate-ordained amidst Caphaerus' rocks
On the home-voyage. Now his valiant men
Out of the foes' hands snatched him, bare him thence,
Scarce drawing breath, to the Achaean ships.
And now the Atreid kings, the war-renowned,
Were left alone, and murder-breathing foes
Encompassed them, and hurled from every side
Whate'er their hands might find the deadly shaft
Some showered, some the stone, the javelin some.

They in the midst aye turned this way and that,
As boars or lions compassed round with pales
On that day when kings gather to the sport
The people, and have penned the mighty beasts
Within the toils of death; but these, although
With walls ringed round, yet tear with tusk and fang
What luckless thrall soever draweth near.
So these death-compassed heroes slew their foes
Ever as they pressed on. Yet had their might
Availed not for defence, for all their will,
Had Teucer and Idomeneus strong of heart
Come not to help, with Thoas, Meriones,
And godlike Thrasymedes, they which shrank
Erewhile before Eurypylus yea, had fled
Unto the ships to 'scape the crushing doom,
But that, in fear for Atreus' sons, they rallied
Against Eurypylus: deadly waxed the fight.

Then Teucer with a mighty spear-thrust smote
Aeneas' shield, yet wounded not his flesh,
For the great fourfold buckler warded him;
Yet feared he, and recoiled a little space.
Leapt Meriones upon Laophoon
The son of Paeon, born by Axius' flood
Of bright-haired Cleomede. Unto Troy
With noble Asteropaeus had he come
To aid her folk: him Meriones' keen spear
Stabbed 'neath the navel, and the lance-head tore
His bowels forth; swift sped his soul away
Into the Shadow-land. Alcimedes,
The warrior-friend of Aias, Oileus' son,
Shot mid the press of Trojans; for he sped
With taunting shout a sharp stone from a sling

Into their battle's heart. They quailed in fear
Before the hum and onrush of the bolt.
Fate winged its flight to the bold charioteer
Of Pammon, Hippasus' son: his brow it smote
While yet he grasped the reins, and flung him stunned
Down from the chariot-seat before the wheels.
The rushing war-wain whirled his wretched form
'Twixt tyres and heels of onward-leaping steeds,
And awful death in that hour swallowed him
When whip and reins had flown from his nerveless hands.
Then grief thrilled Pammon: hard necessity
Made him both chariot-lord and charioteer.
Now to his doom and death-day had he bowed,
Had not a Trojan through that gory strife
Leapt, grasped the reins, and saved the prince, when now
His strength failed 'neath the murderous hands of foes.

As godlike Acamas charged, the stalwart son
Of Nestor thrust the spear above his knee,
And with that wound sore anguish came on him:
Back from the fight he drew; the deadly strife
He left unto his comrades: quenched was now
His battle-lust. Eurypylus' henchman smote
Echemmon, Thoas' friend, amidst the fray
Beneath the shoulder: nigh his heart the spear
Passed bitter-biting: o'er his limbs brake out
Mingled with blood cold sweat of agony.
He turned to flee; Eurypylus' giant might
Chased, caught him, shearing his heel-tendons through:
There, where the blow fell, his reluctant feet
Stayed, and the spirit left his mortal frame.
Thoas pricked Paris with quick-thrusting spear
On the right thigh: backward a space he ran

For his death-speeding bow, which had been left
To rearward of the fight. Idomeneus
Upheaved a stone, huge as his hands could swing,
And dashed it on Eurypylus' arm: to earth
Fell his death-dealing spear. Backward he stepped
To grasp another, since from out his hand
The first was smitten. So had Atreus' sons
A moment's breathing-space from stress of war.
But swiftly drew Eurypylus' henchmen near
Bearing a stubborn-shafted lance, wherewith
He brake the strength of many. In stormy might
Then charged he on the foe: whomso he met
He slew, and spread wide havoc through their ranks.

Now neither Atreus' sons might steadfast stand,
Nor any valiant Danaan beside,
For ruinous panic suddenly gripped the hearts
Of all; for on them all Eurypylus rushed
Flashing death in their faces, chased them, slew,
Cried to the Trojans and to his chariot-lords:
"Friends, be of good heart! To these Danaans
Let us deal slaughter and doom's darkness now!
Lo, how like scared sheep back to the ships they flee!
Forget not your death-dealing battle-lore,
O ye that from your youth are men of war!"

Then charged they on the Argives as one man;
And these in utter panic turned and fled
The bitter battle, those hard after them
Followed, as white-fanged hounds hold deer in chase
Up the long forest-glens. Full many in dust
They dashed down, howsoe'er they longed to escape.
The slaughter grim and great of that wild fray.

Eurypylus hath slain Bucolion,
Nesus, and Chromion and Antiphus;
Twain in Mycenae dwelt, a goodly land;
In Lacedaemon twain. Men of renown
Albeit they were, he slew them. Then he smote
A host unnumbered of the common throng.
My strength should not suffice to sing their fate,
How fain soever, though within my breast
Were iron lungs. Aeneas slew withal
Antimachus and Pheres, twain which left
Crete with Idomeneus. Agenor smote
Molus the princely,--with king Sthenelus
He came from Argos,--hurled from far behind
A dart new-whetted, as he fled from fight,
Piercing his right leg, and the eager shaft
Cut sheer through the broad sinew, shattering
The bones with anguished pain: and so his doom
Met him, to die a death of agony.
Then Paris' arrows laid proud Phorcys low,
And Mosynus, brethren both, from Salamis
Who came in Aias' ships, and nevermore
Saw the home-land. Cleolaus smote he next,
Meges' stout henchman; for the arrow struck
His left breast: deadly night enwrapped him round,
And his soul fleeted forth: his fainting heart
Still in his breast fluttering convulsively
Made the winged arrow shiver. Yet again
Did Paris shoot at bold Eetion.
Through his jaw leapt the sudden-flashing brass:
He groaned, and with his blood were mingled tears.
So ever man slew man, till all the space
Was heaped with Argives each on other cast.
Now had the Trojans burnt with fire the ships,

Had not night, trailing heavy-folded mist,
Uprisen. So Eurypylus drew back,
And Troy's sons with him, from the ships aloof
A little space, by Simois' outfall; there
Camped they exultant. But amidst the ships
Flung down upon the sands the Argives wailed
Heart-anguished for the slain, so many of whom
Dark fate had overtaken and laid in dust.

BOOK VII

How the Son of Achilles was brought to the War from the Isle of Scyros.

When heaven hid his stars, and Dawn awoke
Outspraying splendour, and night's darkness fled,
Then undismayed the Argives' warrior-sons
Marched forth without the ships to meet in fight
Eurypylus, save those that tarried still
To render to Machaon midst the ships
Death-dues, with Nireus--Nireus, who in grace
And goodlihead was like the Deathless Ones,
Yet was not strong in bodily might: the Gods
Grant not perfection in all things to men;
But evil still is blended with the good
By some strange fate: to Nireus' winsome grace
Was linked a weakling's prowess. Yet the Greeks
Slighted him not, but gave him all death-dues,
And mourned above his grave with no less grief
Than for Machaon, whom they honoured aye,
For his deep wisdom, as the immortal Gods.
One mound they swiftly heaped above these twain.

Then in the plain once more did murderous war
Madden: the multitudinous clash and cry

Rose, as the shields were shattered with huge stones,
Were pierced with lances. So they toiled in fight;
But all this while lay Podaleirius
Fasting in dust and groaning, leaving not
His brother's tomb; and oft his heart was moved
With his own hands to slay himself. And now
He clutched his sword, and now amidst his herbs
Sought for a deadly drug; and still his friends
Essayed to stay his hand and comfort him
With many pleadings. But he would not cease
From grieving: yea, his hands had spilt his life
There on his noble brother's new-made tomb,
But Nestor heard thereof, and sorrowed sore
In his affliction, and he came on him
As now he flung him on that woeful grave,
And now was casting dust upon his head,
Beating his breast, and on his brother's name
Crying, while thralls and comrades round their lord
Groaned, and affliction held them one and all.
Then gently spake he to that stricken one:
"Refrain from bitter moan and deadly grief,
My son. It is not for a wise man's honour
To wail, as doth a woman, o'er the fallen.
Thou shalt not bring him up to light again
Whose soul hath fleeted vanishing into air,
Whose body fire hath ravined up, whose bones
Earth has received. His end was worthy his life.
Endure thy sore grief, even as I endured,
Who lost a son, slain by the hands of foes,
A son not worse than thy Machaon, good
With spears in battle, good in counsel. None
Of all the youths so loved his sire as he
Loved me. He died for me yea, died to save

His father. Yet, when he was slain, did I
Endure to taste food, and to see the light,
Well knowing that all men must tread one path
Hades-ward, and before all lies one goal,
Death's mournful goal. A mortal man must bear
All joys, all griefs, that God vouchsafes to send."

Made answer that heart-stricken one, while still
Wet were his cheeks with ever-flowing tears:
"Father, mine heart is bowed 'neath crushing grief
For a brother passing wise, who fostered me
Even as a son. When to the heavens had passed
Our father, in his arms he cradled me:
Gladly he taught me all his healing lore;
We shared one table; in one bed we lay:
We had all things in common these, and love.
My grief cannot forget, nor I desire,
Now he is dead, to see the light of life."

Then spake the old man to that stricken one:
"To all men Fate assigns one same sad lot,
Bereavement: earth shall cover all alike,
Albeit we tread not the same path of life,
And none the path he chooseth; for on high
Good things and bad lie on the knees of
Gods Unnumbered, indistinguishably blent.
These no Immortal seeth; they are veiled
In mystic cloud-folds. Only Fate puts forth
Her hands thereto, nor looks at what she takes,
But casts them from Olympus down to earth.
This way and that they are wafted, as it were
By gusts of wind. The good man oft is whelmed
In suffering: wealth undeserved is heaped

On the vile person. Blind is each man's life;
Therefore he never walketh surely; oft
He stumbleth: ever devious is his path,
Now sloping down to sorrow, mounting now
To bliss. All-happy is no living man
From the beginning to the end, but still
The good and evil clash. Our life is short;
Beseems not then in grief to live. Hope on,
Still hope for better days: chain not to woe
Thine heart. There is a saying among men
That to the heavens unperishing mount the souls
Of good men, and to nether darkness sink
Souls of the wicked. Both to God and man
Dear was thy brother, good to brother-men,
And son of an Immortal. Sure am I
That to the company of Gods shall he
Ascend, by intercession of thy sire."

Then raised he that reluctant mourner up
With comfortable words. From that dark grave
He drew him, backward gazing oft with groans.
To the ships they came, where Greeks and Trojan men
Had bitter travail of rekindled war.

Eurypylus there, in dauntless spirit like
The War-god, with mad-raging spear and hands
Resistless, smote down hosts of foes: the earth
Was clogged with dead men slain on either side.
On strode he midst the corpses, awelessly
He fought, with blood-bespattered hands and feet;
Never a moment from grim strife he ceased.
Peneleos the mighty-hearted came
Against him in the pitiless fray: he fell

The Fall of Troy

Before Eurypylus' spear: yea, many more
Fell round him. Ceased not those destroying hands,
But wrathful on the Argives still he pressed,
As when of old on Pholoe's long-ridged heights
Upon the Centaurs terrible Hercules rushed
Storming in might, and slew them, passing-swift
And strong and battle-cunning though they were;
So rushed he on, so smote he down the array,
One after other, of the Danaan spears.
Heaps upon heaps, here, there, in throngs they fell
Strewn in the dust. As when a river in flood
Comes thundering down, banks crumble on either side
To drifting sand: on seaward rolls the surge
Tossing wild crests, while cliffs on every hand
Ring crashing echoes, as their brows break down
Beneath long-leaping roaring waterfalls,
And dikes are swept away; so fell in dust
The war-famed Argives by Eurypylus slain,
Such as he overtook in that red rout.
Some few escaped, whom strength of fleeing feet
Delivered. Yet in that sore strait they drew
Peneleos from the shrieking tumult forth,
And bare to the ships, though with swift feet themselves
Were fleeing from ghastly death, from pitiless doom.
Behind the rampart of the ships they fled
In huddled rout: they had no heart to stand
Before Eurypylus, for Hercules,
To crown with glory his son's stalwart son,
Thrilled them with panic. There behind their wall
They cowered, as goats to leeward of a hill
Shrink from the wild cold rushing of the wind
That bringeth snow and heavy sleet and haft.
No longing for the pasture tempteth them

Over the brow to step, and face the blast,
But huddling screened by rock-wall and ravine
They abide the storm, and crop the scanty grass
Under dim copses thronging, till the gusts
Of that ill wind shall lull: so, by their towers
Screened, did the trembling Danaans abide
Telephus' mighty son. Yea, he had burnt
The ships, and all that host had he destroyed,
Had not Athena at the last inspired
The Argive men with courage. Ceaselessly
From the high rampart hurled they at the foe
With bitter-biting darts, and slew them fast;
And all the walls were splashed with reeking gore,
And aye went up a moan of smitten men.

So fought they: nightlong, daylong fought they on,
Ceteians, Trojans, battle-biding Greeks,
Fought, now before the ships, and now again
Round the steep wall, with fury unutterable.
Yet even so for two days did they cease
From murderous fight; for to Eurypylus came
A Danaan embassage, saying, "From the war
Forbear we, while we give unto the flames
The battle-slain." So hearkened he to them:
From ruin-wreaking strife forebore the hosts;
And so their dead they buried, who in dust
Had fallen. Chiefly the Achaeans mourned
Peneleos; o'er the mighty dead they heaped
A barrow broad and high, a sign for men
Of days to be. But in a several place
The multitude of heroes slain they laid,
Mourning with stricken hearts. On one great pyre
They burnt them all, and buried in one grave.

So likewise far from thence the sons of Troy
Buried their slain. Yet murderous Strife slept not,
But roused again Eurypylus' dauntless might
To meet the foe. He turned not from the ships,
But there abode, and fanned the fury of war.

Meanwhile the black ship on to Scyros ran;
And those twain found before his palace-gate
Achilles' son, now hurling dart and lance,
Now in his chariot driving fleetfoot steeds.
Glad were they to behold him practising
The deeds of war, albeit his heart was sad
For his slain sire, of whom had tidings come
Ere this. With reverent eyes of awe they went
To meet him, for that goodly form and face
Seemed even as very Achilles unto them.
But he, or ever they had spoken, cried:
"All hail, ye strangers, unto this mine home
Say whence ye are, and who, and what the need
That hither brings you over barren seas."

So spake he, and Odysseus answered him:
"Friends are we of Achilles lord of war,
To whom of Deidameia thou wast born--
Yea, when we look on thee we seem to see
That Hero's self; and like the Immortal Ones
Was he. Of Ithaca am I: this man
Of Argos, nurse of horses--if perchance
Thou hast heard the name of Tydeus' warrior son
Or of the wise Odysseus. Lo, I stand
Before thee, sent by voice of prophecy.
I pray thee, pity us: come thou to Troy
And help us. Only so unto the war

An end shall be. Gifts beyond words to thee
The Achaean kings shall give: yea, I myself
Will give to thee thy godlike father's arms,
And great shall be thy joy in bearing them;
For these be like no mortal's battle-gear,
But splendid as the very War-god's arms.
Over their marvellous blazonry hath gold
Been lavished; yea, in heaven Hephaestus' self
Rejoiced in fashioning that work divine,
The which thine eyes shall marvel to behold;
For earth and heaven and sea upon the shield
Are wrought, and in its wondrous compass are
Creatures that seem to live and move--a wonder
Even to the Immortals. Never man
Hath seen their like, nor any man hath worn,
Save thy sire only, whom the Achaeans all
Honoured as Zeus himself. I chiefliest
From mine heart loved him, and when he was slain,
To many a foe I dealt a ruthless doom,
And through them all bare back to the ships his corse.
Therefore his glorious arms did Thetis give
To me. These, though I prize them well, to thee
Will I give gladly when thou com'st to Troy.
Yea also, when we have smitten Priam's towns
And unto Hellas in our ships return,
Shall Menelaus give thee, an thou wilt,
His princess-child to wife, of love for thee,
And with his bright-haired daughter shall bestow
Rich dower of gold and treasure, even all
That meet is to attend a wealthy king."

So spake he, and replied Achilles' son:
"If bidden of oracles the Achaean men

Summon me, let us with to-morrow's dawn
Fare forth upon the broad depths of the sea,
If so to longing Danaans I may prove
A light of help. Now pass we to mine halls,
And to such guest-fare as befits to set
Before the stranger. For my marriage-day--
To this the Gods in time to come shall see."

Then hall-ward led he them, and with glad hearts
They followed. To the forecourt when they came
Of that great mansion, found they there the Queen
Deidameia in her sorrow of soul
Grief-wasted, as when snow from mountain-sides
Before the sun and east-wind wastes away;
So pined she for that princely hero slain.
Then came to her amidst her grief the kings,
And greeted her in courteous wise. Her son
Drew near and told their lineage and their names;
But that for which they came he left untold
Until the morrow, lest unto her woe
There should be added grief and floods of tears,
And lest her prayers should hold him from the path
Whereon his heart was set. Straight feasted these,
And comforted their hearts with sleep, even all
Which dwelt in sea-ringed Scyros, nightlong lulled
By long low thunder of the girdling deep,
Of waves Aegean breaking on her shores.
But not on Deidameia fell the hands
Of kindly sleep. She bore in mind the names
Of crafty Odysseus and of Diomede
The godlike, how these twain had widowed her
Of battle-fain Achilles, how their words
Had won his aweless heart to fare with them

To meet the war-cry where stern Fate met him,
Shattered his hope of home-return, and laid
Measureless grief on Peleus and on her.
Therefore an awful dread oppressed her soul
Lest her son too to tumult of the war
Should speed, and grief be added to her grief.

Dawn climbed the wide-arched heaven, straightway they
Rose from their beds. Then Deidameia knew;
And on her son's broad breast she cast herself,
And bitterly wailed: her cry thrilled through the air,
As when a cow loud-lowing mid the hills
Seeks through the glens her calf, and all around
Echo long ridges of the mountain-steep;
So on all sides from dim recesses rang
The hall; and in her misery she cried:
"Child, wherefore is thy soul now on the wing
To follow strangers unto Ilium
The fount of tears, where perish many in fight,
Yea, cunning men in war and battle grim?
And thou art but a youth, and hast not learnt
The ways of war, which save men in the day
Of peril. Hearken thou to me, abide
Here in thine home, lest evil tidings come
From Troy unto my ears, that thou in fight
Hast perished; for mine heart saith, never thou
Hitherward shalt from battle-toil return.
Not even thy sire escaped the doom of death--
He, mightier than thou, mightier than all
Heroes on earth, yea, and a Goddess' son--
But was in battle slain, all through the wiles
And crafty counsels of these very men
Who now to woeful war be kindling thee.

The Fall of Troy

Therefore mine heart is full of shuddering fear
Lest, son, my lot should be to live bereaved
Of thee, and to endure dishonour and pain,
For never heavier blow on woman falls
Than when her lord hath perished, and her sons
Die also, and her house is left to her
Desolate. Straightway evil men remove
Her landmarks, yea, and rob her of her all,
Setting the right at naught. There is no lot
More woeful and more helpless than is hers
Who is left a widow in a desolate home."

Loud-wailing spake she; but her son replied:
"Be of good cheer, my mother; put from thee
Evil foreboding. No man is in war
Beyond his destiny slain. If my weird be
To die in my country's cause, then let me die
When I have done deeds worthy of my sire."

Then to his side old Lycomedes came,
And to his battle-eager grandson spake:
"O valiant-hearted son, so like thy sire,
I know thee strong and valorous; yet, O yet
For thee I fear the bitter war; I fear
The terrible sea-surge. Shipmen evermore
Hang on destruction's brink. Beware, my child,
Perils of waters when thou sailest back
From Troy or other shores, such as beset
Full oftentimes the voyagers that ride
The long sea-ridges, when the sun hath left
The Archer-star, and meets the misty Goat,
When the wild blasts drive on the lowering storm,
Or when Orion to the darkling west

Slopes, into Ocean's river sinking slow.
Beware the time of equal days and nights,
When blasts that o'er the sea's abysses rush,
None knoweth whence in fury of battle clash.
Beware the Pleiads' setting, when the sea
Maddens beneath their power nor these alone,
But other stars, terrors of hapless men,
As o'er the wide sea-gulf they set or rise."

Then kissed he him, nor sought to stay the feet
Of him who panted for the clamour of war,
Who smiled for pleasure and for eagerness
To haste to the ship. Yet were his hurrying feet
Stayed by his mother's pleading and her tears
Still in those halls awhile. As some swift horse
Is reined in by his rider, when he strains
Unto the race-course, and he neighs, and champs
The curbing bit, dashing his chest with foam,
And his feet eager for the course are still
Never, his restless hooves are clattering aye;
His mane is a stormy cloud, he tosses high
His head with snortings, and his lord is glad;
So reined his mother back the glorious son
Of battle-stay Achilles, so his feet
Were restless, so the mother's loving pride
Joyed in her son, despite her heart-sick pain.

A thousand times he kissed her, then at last
Left her alone with her own grief and moan
There in her father's halls. As o'er her nest
A swallow in her anguish cries aloud
For her lost nestlings which, mid piteous shrieks,
A fearful serpent hath devoured, and wrung

The loving mother's heart; and now above
That empty cradle spreads her wings, and now
Flies round its porchway fashioned cunningly
Lamenting piteously her little ones:
So for her child Deidameia mourned.
Now on her son's bed did she cast herself,
Crying aloud, against his door-post now
She leaned, and wept: now laid she in her lap
Those childhood's toys yet treasured in her bower,
Wherein his babe-heart joyed long years agone.
She saw a dart there left behind of him,
And kissed it o'er and o'er yea, whatso else
Her weeping eyes beheld that was her son's.

Naught heard he of her moans unutterable,
But was afar, fast striding to the ship.
He seemed, as his feet swiftly bare him on,
Like some all-radiant star; and at his side
With Tydeus' son war-wise Odysseus went,
And with them twenty gallant-hearted men,
Whom Deidameia chose as trustiest
Of all her household, and unto her son
Gave them for henchmen swift to do his will.
And these attended Achilles' valiant son,
As through the city to the ship he sped.
On, with glad laughter, in their midst he strode;
And Thetis and the Nereids joyed thereat.
Yea, glad was even the Raven-haired, the Lord
Of all the sea, beholding that brave son
Of princely Achilles, marking how he longed
For battle. Beardless boy albeit he was,
His prowess and his might were inward spurs
To him. He hasted forth his fatherland

Like to the War-god, when to gory strife
He speedeth, wroth with foes, when maddeneth
His heart, and grim his frown is, and his eyes
Flash levin-flame around him, and his face
Is clothed with glory of beauty terror-blent,
As on he rusheth: quail the very Gods.
So seemed Achilles' goodly son; and prayers
Went up through all the city unto Heaven
To bring their noble prince safe back from war;
And the Gods hearkened to them. High he towered
Above all stateliest men which followed him.

So came they to the heavy-plunging sea,
And found the rowers in the smooth-wrought ship
Handling the tackle, fixing mast and sail.
Straightway they went aboard: the shipmen cast
The hawsers loose, and heaved the anchor-stones,
The strength and stay of ships in time of need.
Then did the Sea-queen's lord grant voyage fair
To these with gracious mind; for his heart yearned
O'er the Achaeans, by the Trojan men
And mighty-souled Eurypylus hard-bestead.
On either side of Neoptolemus sat
Those heroes, gladdening his soul with tales
Of his sire's mighty deeds--of all he wrought
In sea-raids, and in valiant Telephus' land,
And how he smote round Priam's burg the men
Of Troy, for glory unto Atreus' sons.
His heart glowed, fain to grasp his heritage,
His aweless father's honour and renown.

In her bower, sorrowing for her son the while,
Deidameia poured forth sighs and tears.

The Fall of Troy

With agony of soul her very heart
Melted in her, as over coals doth lead
Or wax, and never did her moaning cease,
As o'er the wide sea her gaze followed him.
Ay, for her son a mother fretteth still,
Though it be to a feast that he hath gone,
By a friend bidden forth. But soon the sail
Of that good ship far-fleeting o'er the blue
Grew faint and fainter--melted in sea-haze.
But still she sighed, still daylong made her moan.

On ran the ship before a following wind,
Seeming to skim the myriad-surging sea,
And crashed the dark wave either side the prow:
Swiftly across the abyss unplumbed she sped.
Night's darkness fell about her, but the breeze
Held, and the steersman's hand was sure. O'er gulfs
Of brine she flew, till Dawn divine rose up
To climb the sky. Then sighted they the peaks
Of Ida, Chrysa next, and Smintheus' fane,
Then the Sigean strand, and then the tomb
Of Aeacus' son. Yet would Laertes' seed,
The man discreet of soul, not point it out
To Neoptolemus, lest the tide of grief
Too high should swell within his breast. They passed
Calydnae's isles, left Tenedos behind;
And now was seen the fane of Eleus,
Where stands Protesilaus' tomb, beneath
The shade of towery elms; when, soaring high
Above the plain, their topmost boughs discern
Troy, straightway wither all their highest sprays.
Nigh Ilium now the ship by wind and oar
Was brought: they saw the long strand fringed with keels

Of Argives, who endured sore travail of war
Even then about the wall, the which themselves
Had reared to screen the ships and men in stress
Of battle. Even now Eurypylus' hands
To earth were like to dash it and destroy;
But the quick eyes of Tydeus' strong son marked
How rained the darts and stones on that long wall.
Forth of the ship he sprang, and shouted loud
With all the strength of his undaunted breast:
"Friends, on the Argive men is heaped this day
Sore travail! Let us don our flashing arms
With speed, and to yon battle-turmoil haste.
For now upon our towers the warrior sons
Of Troy press hard--yea, haply will they tear
The long walls down, and burn the ships with fire,
And so the souls that long for home-return
Shall win it never; nay, ourselves shall fall
Before our due time, and shall lie in graves
In Troyland, far from children and from wives."

All as one man down from the ship they leapt;
For trembling seized on all for that grim sight--
On all save aweless Neoptolemus
Whose might was like his father's: lust of war
Swept o'er him. To Odysseus' tent in haste
They sped, for close it lay to where the ship
Touched land. About its walls was hung great store
Of change of armour, of wise Odysseus some,
And rescued some from gallant comrades slain.
Then did the brave man put on goodly arms;
But they in whose breasts faintlier beat their hearts
Must don the worser. Odysseus stood arrayed
In those which came with him from Ithaca:

To Diomede he gave fair battle-gear
Stripped in time past from mighty Socus slain.
But in his father's arms Achilles' son
Clad him and lo, he seemed Achilles' self!
Light on his limbs and lapping close they lay--
So cunning was Hephaestus' workmanship--
Which for another had been a giant's arms.
The massive helmet cumbered not his brows;
Yea, the great Pelian spear-shaft burdened not
His hand, but lightly swung he up on high
The heavy and tall lance thirsting still for blood.

Of many Argives which beheld him then
Might none draw nigh to him, how fain soe'er,
So fast were they in that grim grapple locked
Of the wild war that raged all down the wall.
But as when shipmen, under a desolate isle
Mid the wide sea by stress of weather bound,
Chafe, while afar from men the adverse blasts
Prison them many a day; they pace the deck
With sinking hearts, while scantier grows their store
Of food; they weary till a fair wind sings;
So joyed the Achaean host, which theretofore
Were heavy of heart, when Neoptolemus came,
Joyed in the hope of breathing-space from toil.
Then like the aweless lion's flashed his eyes,
Which mid the mountains leaps in furious mood
To meet the hunters that draw nigh his cave,
Thinking to steal his cubs, there left alone
In a dark-shadowed glen but from a height
The beast hath spied, and on the spoilers leaps
With grim jaws terribly roaring; even so
That glorious child of Aeacus' aweless son

Against the Trojan warriors burned in wrath.
Thither his eagle-swoop descended first
Where loudest from the plain uproared the fight,
There weakest, he divined, must be the wall,
The battlements lowest, since the surge of foes
Brake heaviest there. Charged at his side the rest
Breathing the battle-spirit. There they found
Eurypylus mighty of heart and all his men
Scaling a tower, exultant in the hope
Of tearing down the walls, of slaughtering
The Argives in one holocaust. No mind
The Gods had to accomplish their desire!
But now Odysseus, Diomede the strong,
Leonteus, and Neoptolemus, as a God
In strength and beauty, hailed their javelins down,
And thrust them from the wall. As dogs and shepherds
By shouting and hard fighting drive away
Strong lions from a steading, rushing forth
From all sides, and the brutes with glaring eyes
Pace to and fro; with savage lust for blood
Of calves and kine their jaws are slavering;
Yet must their onrush give back from the hounds
And fearless onset of the shepherd folk;
[So from these new defenders shrank the foe]
A little, far as one may hurl a stone
Exceeding great; for still Eurypylus
Suffered them not to flee far from the ships,
But cheered them on to bide the brunt, until
The ships be won, and all the Argives slain;
For Zeus with measureless might thrilled all his frame.
Then seized he a rugged stone and huge, and leapt
And hurled it full against the high-built wall.
It crashed, and terribly boomed that rampart steep

To its foundations. Terror gripped the Greeks,
As though that wall had crumbled down in dust;
Yet from the deadly conflict flinched they not,
But stood fast, like to jackals or to wolves
Bold robbers of the sheep--when mid the hills
Hunter and hound would drive them forth their caves,
Being grimly purposed there to slay their whelps.
Yet these, albeit tormented by the darts,
Flee not, but for their cubs' sake bide and fight;
So for the ships' sake they abode and fought,
And for their own lives. But Eurypylus
Afront of all the ships stood, taunting them:
"Coward and dastard souls! no darts of yours
Had given me pause, nor thrust back from your ships,
Had not your rampart stayed mine onset-rush.
Ye are like to dogs, that in a forest flinch
Before a lion! Skulking therewithin
Ye are fighting--nay, are shrinking back from death!
But if ye dare come forth on Trojan ground,
As once when ye were eager for the fray,
None shall from ghastly death deliver you:
Slain by mine hand ye all shall lie in dust!"

So did he shout a prophecy unfulfilled,
Nor heard Doom's chariot-wheels fast rolling near
Bearing swift death at Neoptolemus' hands,
Nor saw death gleaming from his glittering spear.
Ay, and that hero paused not now from fight,
But from the ramparts smote the Trojans aye.
From that death leaping from above they quailed
In tumult round Eurypylus: deadly fear
Gripped all their hearts. As little children cower
About a father's knees when thunder of Zeus

Crashes from cloud to cloud, when all the air
Shudders and groans, so did the sons of Troy,
With those Ceteians round their great king, cower
Ever as prince Neoptolemus hurled; for death
Rode upon all he cast, and bare his wrath
Straight rushing down upon the heads of foes.
Now in their hearts those wildered Trojans said
That once more they beheld Achilles' self
Gigantic in his armour. Yet they hid
That horror in their breasts, lest panic fear
Should pass from them to the Ceteian host
And king Eurypylus; so on every side
They wavered 'twixt the stress of their hard strait
And that blood-curdling dread, 'twixt shame and fear.
As when men treading a precipitous path
Look up, and see adown the mountain-slope
A torrent rushing on them, thundering down
The rocks, and dare not meet its clamorous flood,
But hurry shuddering on, with death in sight
Holding as naught the perils of the path;
So stayed the Trojans, spite of their desire
[To flee the imminent death that waited them]
Beneath the wall. Godlike Eurypylus
Aye cheered them on to fight. He trusted still
That this new mighty foe would weary at last
With toil of slaughter; but he wearied not.

That desperate battle-travail Pallas saw,
And left the halls of Heaven incense-sweet,
And flew o'er mountain-crests: her hurrying feet
Touched not the earth, borne by the air divine
In form of cloud-wreaths, swifter than the wind.
She came to Troy, she stayed her feet upon

Sigeum's windy ness, she looked forth thence
Over the ringing battle of dauntless men,
And gave the Achaeans glory. Achilles' son
Beyond the rest was filled with valour and strength
Which win renown for men in whom they meet.
Peerless was he in both: the blood of Zeus
Gave strength; to his father's valour was he heir;
So by those towers he smote down many a foe.
And as a fisher on the darkling sea,
To lure the fish to their destruction, takes
Within his boat the strength of fire; his breath
Kindles it to a flame, till round the boat
Glareth its splendour, and from the black sea
Dart up the fish all eager to behold
The radiance--for the last time; for the barbs
Of his three-pointed spear, as up they leap,
Slay them; his heart rejoices o'er the prey.
So that war-king Achilles' glorious son
Slew hosts of onward-rushing foes around
That wall of stone. Well fought the Achaeans all,
Here, there, adown the ramparts: rang again
The wide strand and the ships: the battered walls
Groaned ever. Men with weary ache of toil
Fainted on either side; sinews and might
Of strong men were unstrung. But o'er the son
Of battle-stay Achilles weariness
Crept not: his battle-eager spirit aye
Was tireless; never touched by palsying fear
He fought on, as with the triumphant strength
Of an ever-flowing river: though it roll
'Twixt blazing forests, though the madding blast
Roll stormy seas of flame, it feareth not,
For at its brink faint grows the fervent heat,

The strong flood turns its might to impotence;
So weariness nor fear could bow the knees
Of Hero Achilles' gallant-hearted son,
Still as he fought, still cheered his comrades on.
Of myriad shafts sped at him none might touch
His flesh, but even as snowflakes on a rock
Fell vainly ever: wholly screened was he
By broad shield and strong helmet, gifts of a God.
In these exulting did the Aeacid's son
Stride all along the wall, with ringing shouts
Cheering the dauntless Argives to the fray,
Being their mightiest far, bearing a soul
Insatiate of the awful onset-cry,
Burning with one strong purpose, to avenge
His father's death: the Myrmidons in their king
Exulted. Roared the battle round the wall.

Two sons he slew of Meges rich in gold,
Scion of Dymas--sons of high renown,
Cunning to hurl the dart, to drive the steed
In war, and deftly cast the lance afar,
Born at one birth beside Sangarius' banks
Of Periboea to him, Celtus one,
And Eubius the other. But not long
His boundless wealth enjoyed they, for the
Fates Span them a thread of life exceeding brief.
As on one day they saw the light, they died
On one day by the same hand. To the heart
Of one Neoptolemus sped a javelin; one
He smote down with a massy stone that crashed
Through his strong helmet, shattered all its ridge,
And dashed his brains to earth. Around them fell
Foes many, a host untold. The War-god's work

Waxed ever mightier till the eventide,
Till failed the light celestial; then the host
Of brave Eurypylus from the ships drew back
A little: they that held those leaguered towers
Had a short breathing-space; the sons of Troy
Had respite from the deadly-echoing strife,
From that hard rampart-battle. Verily all
The Argives had beside their ships been slain,
Had not Achilles' strong son on that day
Withstood the host of foes and their great chief
Eurypylus. Came to that young hero's side
Phoenix the old, and marvelling gazed on one
The image of Peleides. Tides of joy
And grief swept o'er him--grief, for memories
Of that swift-footed father--joy, for sight
Of such a son. He for sheer gladness wept;
For never without tears the tribes of men
Live--nay, not mid the transports of delight.
He clasped him round as father claspeth son
Whom, after long and troublous wanderings,
The Gods bring home to gladden a father's heart.
So kissed he Neoptolemus' head and breast,
Clasping him round, and cried in rapture of joy:
"Hail, goodly son of that Achilles whom
I nursed a little one in mine own arms
With a glad heart. By Heaven's high providence
Like a strong sapling waxed he in stature fast,
And daily I rejoiced to see his form
And prowess, my life's blessing, honouring him
As though he were the son of mine old age;
For like a father did he honour me.
I was indeed his father, he my son
In spirit: thou hadst deemed us of one blood

Who were in heart one: but of nobler mould
Was he by far, in form and strength a God.
Thou art wholly like him--yea, I seem to see
Alive amid the Argives him for whom
Sharp anguish shrouds me ever. I waste away
In sorrowful age--oh that the grave had closed
On me while yet he lived! How blest to be
By loving hands of kinsmen laid to rest!
Ah child, my sorrowing heart will nevermore
Forget him! Chide me not for this my grief.
But now, help thou the Myrmidons and Greeks
In their sore strait: wreak on the foe thy wrath
For thy brave sire. It shall be thy renown
To slay this war-insatiate Telephus' son;
For mightier art thou, and shalt prove, than he,
As was thy father than his wretched sire."

Made answer golden-haired Achilles' son:
"Ancient, our battle-prowess mighty Fate
And the o'ermastering War-god shall decide."

But, as he spake, he had fain on that same day
Forth of the gates have rushed in his sire's arms;
But night, which bringeth men release from toil,
Rose from the ocean veiled in sable pall.

With honour as of mighty Achilles' self
Him mid the ships the glad Greeks hailed, who had won
Courage from that his eager rush to war.
With princely presents did they honour him,
With priceless gifts, whereby is wealth increased;
For some gave gold and silver, handmaids some,
Brass without weight gave these, and iron those;

Others in deep jars brought the ruddy wine:
Yea, fleetfoot steeds they gave, and battle-gear,
And raiment woven fair by women's hands.
Glowed Neoptolemus' heart for joy of these.
A feast they made for him amidst the tents,
And there extolled Achilles' godlike son
With praise as of the immortal Heavenly Ones;
And joyful-voiced Agamemnon spake to him:
"Thou verily art the brave-souled Aeacid's son,
His very image thou in stalwart might,
In beauty, stature, courage, and in soul.
Mine heart burns in me seeing thee. I trust
Thine hands and spear shall smite yon hosts of foes,
Shall smite the city of Priam world-renowned--
So like thy sire thou art! Methinks I see
Himself beside the ships, as when his shout
Of wrath for dead Patroclus shook the ranks
Of Troy. But he is with the Immortal Ones,
Yet, bending from that heaven, sends thee to-day
To save the Argives on destruction's brink."

Answered Achilles' battle-eager son:
"Would I might meet him living yet, O King,
That so himself might see the son of his love
Not shaming his great father's name. I trust
So shall it be, if the Gods grant me life."

So spake he in wisdom and in modesty;
And all there marvelled at the godlike man.
But when with meat and wine their hearts were filled,
Then rose Achilles' battle-eager son,
And from the feast passed forth unto the tent
That was his sire's. Much armour of heroes slain

Lay there; and here and there were captive maids
Arraying that tent widowed of its lord,
As though its king lived. When that son beheld
Those Trojan arms and handmaid-thralls, he groaned,
By passionate longing for his father seized.
As when through dense oak-groves and tangled glens
Comes to the shadowed cave a lion's whelp
Whose grim sire by the hunters hath been slain,
And looketh all around that empty den,
And seeth heaps of bones of steeds and kine
Slain theretofore, and grieveth for his sire;
Even so the heart of brave Peleides' son
With grief was numbed. The handmaids marvelling gazed;
And fair Briseis' self, when she beheld
Achilles' son, was now right glad at heart,
And sorrowed now with memories of the dead.
Her soul was wildered all, as though indeed
There stood the aweless Aeacid living yet.

Meanwhile exultant Trojans camped aloof
Extolled Eurypylus the fierce and strong,
As erst they had praised Hector, when he smote
Their foes, defending Troy and all her wealth.
But when sweet sleep stole over mortal men,
Then sons of Troy and battle-biding Greeks
All slumber-heavy slept unsentinelled.

BOOK VIII

How Hercules' Grandson perished in fight with the Son of Achilles.

When from the far sea-line, where is the cave
Of Dawn, rose up the sun, and scattered light
Over the earth, then did the eager sons
Of Troy and of Achaea arm themselves
Athirst for battle: these Achilles' son
Cheered on to face the Trojans awelessly;
And those the giant strength of Telephus' seed
Kindled. He trusted to dash down the wall
To earth, and utterly destroy the ships
With ravening fire, and slay the Argive host.
Ah, but his hope was as the morning breeze
Delusive: hard beside him stood the Fates
Laughing to scorn his vain imaginings.

Then to the Myrmidons spake Achilles' son,
The aweless, to the fight enkindling them:
"Hear me, mine henchmen: take ye to your hearts
The spirit of war, that we may heal the wounds
Of Argos, and be ruin to her foes.
Let no man fear, for mighty prowess is
The child of courage; but fear slayeth strength

And spirit. Gird yourselves with strength for war;
Give foes no breathing-space, that they may say
That mid our ranks Achilles liveth yet."

Then clad he with his father's flashing arms
His shoulders. Then exulted Thetis' heart
When from the sea she saw the mighty strength
Of her son's son. Then forth with eagle-speed
Afront of that high wall he rushed, his ear
Drawn by the immortal horses of his sire.
As from the ocean-verge upsprings the sun
In glory, flashing fire far over earth--
Fire, when beside his radiant chariot-team
Races the red star Sirius, scatterer
Of woefullest diseases over men;
So flashed upon the eyes of Ilium's host
That battle-eager hero, Achilles' son.
Onward they whirled him, those immortal steeds,
The which, when now he longed to chase the foe
Back from the ships, Automedon, who wont
To rein them for his father, brought to him.
With joy that pair bore battleward their lord,
So like to Aeacus' son, their deathless hearts
Held him no worser than Achilles' self.
Laughing for glee the Argives gathered round
The might resistless of Neoptolemus,
Eager for fight as wasps [whose woodland bower
The axe] hath shaken, who dart swarming forth
Furious to sting the woodman: round their nest
Long eddying, they torment all passers by;
So streamed they forth from galley and from wall
Burning for fight, and that wide space was thronged,
And all the plain far blazed with armour-sheen,

As shone from heaven's vault the sun thereon.
As flees the cloud-rack through the welkin wide
Scourged onward by the North-wind's Titan blasts,
When winter-tide and snow are hard at hand,
And darkness overpalls the firmament;
So with their thronging squadrons was the earth
Covered before the ships. To heaven uprolled,
Dust hung on hovering wings' men's armour clashed;
Rattled a thousand chariots; horses neighed
On-rushing to the fray. Each warrior's prowess
Kindled him with its trumpet-call to war.

As leap the long sea-rollers, onward hurled
By two winds terribly o'er th' broad sea-flood
Roaring from viewless bournes, with whirlwind blasts
Crashing together, when a ruining storm
Maddens along the wide gulfs of the deep,
And moans the Sea-queen with her anguished waves
Which sweep from every hand, uptowering
Like precipiced mountains, while the bitter squall,
Ceaselessly veering, shrieks across the sea;
So clashed in strife those hosts from either hand
With mad rage. Strife incarnate spurred them on,
And their own prowess. Crashed together these
Like thunderclouds outlightening, thrilling the air.
With shattering trumpet-challenge, when the blasts
Are locked in frenzied wrestle, with mad breath
Rending the clouds, when Zeus is wroth with men
Who travail with iniquity, and flout
His law. So grappled they, as spear with spear
Clashed, shield with shield, and man on man was hurled.

And first Achilles' war-impetuous son

Struck down stout Melaneus and Alcidamas,
Sons of the war-lord Alexinomus,
Who dwelt in Caunus mountain-cradled, nigh
The clear lake shining at Tarbelus' feet
'Neath snow-capt Imbrus. Menes, fleetfoot son
Of King Cassandrus, slew he, born to him
By fair Creusa, where the lovely streams
Of Lindus meet the sea, beside the marches
Of battle-biding Carians, and the heights
Of Lycia the renowned. He slew withal
Morys the spearman, who from Phrygia came;
Polybus and Hippomedon by his side
He laid, this stabbed to the heart, that pierced between
Shoulder and neck: man after man he slew.
Earth groaned 'neath Trojan corpses; rank on rank
Crumbled before him, even as parched brakes
Sink down before the blast of ravening fire
When the north wind of latter summer blows;
So ruining squadrons fell before his charge.

Meanwhile Aeneas slew Aristolochus,
Crashing a great stone down on his head: it brake
Helmet and skull together, and fled his life.
Fleetfoot Eumaeus Diomede slew; he dwelt
In craggy Dardanus, where the bride-bed is
Whereon Anchises clasped the Queen of Love.
Agamemnon smote down Stratus: unto Thrace
Returned he not from war, but died far off
From his dear fatherland. And Meriones
Struck Chlemus down, Peisenor's son, the friend
Of god-like Glaucus, and his comrade leal,
Who by Limurus' outfall dwelt: the folk
Honoured him as their king, when reigned no more

Glaucus, in battle slain,--all who abode
Around Phoenice's towers, and by the crest
Of Massicytus, and Chimaera's glen.

So man slew man in fight; but more than all
Eurypylus hurled doom on many a foe.
First slew he battle-bider Eurytus,
Menoetius of the glancing taslet next,
Elephenor's godlike comrades. Fell with these
Harpalus, wise Odysseus' warrior-friend;
But in the fight afar that hero toiled,
And might not aid his fallen henchman: yet
Fierce Antiphus for that slain man was wroth,
And hurled his spear against Eurypylus,
Yet touched him not; the strong shaft glanced aside,
And pierced Meilanion battle-staunch, the son
Of Cleite lovely-faced, Erylaus' bride,
Who bare him where Caicus meets the sea.
Wroth for his comrade slain, Eurypylus
Rushed upon Antiphus, but terror-winged
He plunged amid his comrades; so the spear
Of the avenger slew him not, whose doom
Was one day wretchedly to be devoured
By the manslaying Cyclops: so it pleased
Stern Fate, I know not why. Elsewhither sped
Eurypylus; and aye as he rushed on
Fell 'neath his spear a multitude untold.
As tall trees, smitten by the strength of steel
In mountain-forest, fill the dark ravines,
Heaped on the earth confusedly, so fell
The Achaeans 'neath Eurypylus' flying spears--
Till heart-uplifted met him face to face
Achilles' son. The long spears in their hands

They twain swung up, each hot to smite his foe.
But first Eurypylus cried the challenge-cry;
"Who art thou? Whence hast come to brave me here?
To Hades merciless Fate is bearing thee;
For in grim fight hath none escaped mine hands;
But whoso, eager for the fray, have come
Hither, on all have I hurled anguished death.
By Xanthus' streams have dogs devoured their flesh
And gnawed their bones. Answer me, who art thou?
Whose be the steeds that bear thee exultant on?"

Answered Achilles' battle-eager son:
"Wherefore, when I am hurrying to the fray,
Dost thou, a foe, put question thus to me,
As might a friend, touching my lineage,
Which many know? Achilles' son am I,
Son of the man whose long spear smote thy sire,
And made him flee--yea, and the ruthless fates
Of death had seized him, but my father's self
Healed him upon the brink of woeful death.
The steeds which bear me were my godlike sire's;
These the West-wind begat, the Harpy bare:
Over the barren sea their feet can race
Skimming its crests: in speed they match the winds.
Since then thou know'st the lineage of my steeds
And mine, now put thou to the test the might
Of my strong spear, born on steep Pelion's crest,
Who hath left his father-stock and forest there."

He spake; and from the chariot sprang to earth
That glorious man: he swung the long spear up.
But in his brawny hand his foe hath seized
A monstrous stone: full at the golden shield

Of Neoptolemus he sped its flight;
But, no whir staggered by its whirlwind rush,
He like a giant mountain-foreland stood
Which all the banded fury of river-floods
Can stir not, rooted in the eternal hills;
So stood unshaken still Achilles' son.
Yet not for this Eurypylus' dauntless might
Shrank from Achilles' son invincible,
On-spurred by his own hardihood and by Fate.
Their hearts like caldrons seethed o'er fires of wrath,
Their glancing armour flashed about their limbs.
Like terrible lions each on other rushed,
Which fight amid the mountains famine-stung,
Writhing and leaping in the strain of strife
For a slain ox or stag, while all the glens
Ring with their conflict; so they grappled, so
Clashed they in pitiless strife. On either hand
Long lines of warriors Greek and Trojan toiled
In combat: round them roared up flames of war.
Like mighty rushing winds they hurled together
With eager spears for blood of life athirst.
Hard by them stood Enyo, spurred them on
Ceaselessly: never paused they from the strife.
Now hewed they each the other's shield, and now
Thrust at the greaves, now at the crested helms.
Reckless of wounds, in that grim toil pressed on
Those aweless heroes: Strife incarnate watched
And gloated o'er them. Ran the sweat in streams
From either: straining hard they stood their ground,
For both were of the seed of Blessed Ones.
From Heaven, with hearts at variance, Gods looked down;
For some gave glory to Achilles' son,
Some to Eurypylus the godlike. Still

They fought on, giving ground no more than rock.
Of granite mountains. Rang from side to side
Spear-smitten shields. At last the Pelian lance,
Sped onward by a mighty thrust, hath passed
Clear through Eurypylus' throat. Forth poured the blood
Torrent-like; through the portal of the wound
The soul from the body flew: darkness of death
Dropped o'er his eyes. To earth in clanging arms
He fell, like stately pine or silver fir
Uprooted by the fury of Boreas;
Such space of earth Eurypylus' giant frame
Covered in falling: rang again the floor
And plain of Troyland. Grey death-pallor swept
Over the corpse, and all the flush of life
Faded away. With a triumphant laugh
Shouted the mighty hero over him:
"Eurypylus, thou saidst thou wouldst destroy
The Danaan ships and men, wouldst slay us all
Wretchedly--but the Gods would not fulfil
Thy wish. For all thy might invincible,
My father's massy spear hath now subdued
Thee under me, that spear no man shall 'scape,
Though he be brass all through, who faceth me."

He spake, and tore the long lance from the corse,
While shrank the Trojans back in dread, at sight
Of that strong-hearted man. Straightway he stripped
The armour from the dead, for friends to bear
Fast to the ships Achaean. But himself
To the swift chariot and the tireless steeds
Sprang, and sped onward like a thunderbolt
That lightning-girdled leaps through the wide air
From Zeus's hands unconquerable--the bolt

The Fall of Troy

Before whose downrush all the Immortals quail
Save only Zeus. It rusheth down to earth,
It rendeth trees and rugged mountain-crags;
So rushed he on the Trojans, flashing doom
Before their eyes; dashed to the earth they fell
Before the charge of those immortal steeds:
The earth was heaped with slain, was dyed with gore.
As when in mountain-glens the unnumbered leaves
Down-streaming thick and fast hide all the ground,
So hosts of Troy untold on earth were strewn
By Neoptolemus and fierce-hearted Greeks,
Shed by whose hands the blood in torrents ran
'Neath feet of men and horses. Chariot-rails
Were dashed with blood-spray whirled up from the tyres.

Now had the Trojans fled within their gates
As calves that flee a lion, or as swine
Flee from a storm--but murderous Ares came,
Unmarked of other Gods, down from the heavens,
Eager to help the warrior sons of Troy.
Red-fire and Flame, Tumult and Panic-fear,
His car-steeds, bare him down into the fight,
The coursers which to roaring Boreas
Grim-eyed Erinnys bare, coursers that breathed
Life-blasting flame: groaned all the shivering air,
As battleward they sped. Swiftly he came
To Troy: loud rang the earth beneath the feet
Of that wild team. Into the battle's heart
Tossing his massy spear, he came; with a shout
He cheered the Trojans on to face the foe.
They heard, and marvelled at that wondrous cry,
Not seeing the God's immortal form, nor steeds,
Veiled in dense mist. But the wise prophet-soul

Of Helenus knew the voice divine that leapt
Unto the Trojans' ears, they knew not whence,
And with glad heart to the fleeing host he cried:
"O cravens, wherefore fear Achilles' son,
Though ne'er so brave? He is mortal even as we;
His strength is not as Ares' strength, who is come
A very present help in our sore need.
That was his shout far-pealing, bidding us
Fight on against the Argives. Let your hearts
Be strong, O friends: let courage fill your breasts.
No mightier battle-helper can draw nigh
To Troy than he. Who is of more avail
For war than Ares, when he aideth men
Hard-fighting? Lo, to our help he cometh now!
On to the fight! Cast to the winds your fears!"

They fled no more, they faced the Argive men,
As hounds, that mid the copses fled at first,
Turn them about to face and fight the wolf,
Spurred by the chiding of their shepherd-lord;
So turned the sons of Troy again to war,
Casting away their fear. Man leapt on man
Valiantly fighting; loud their armour clashed
Smitten with swords, with lances, and with darts.
Spears plunged into men's flesh: dread Ares drank
His fill of blood: struck down fell man on man,
As Greek and Trojan fought. In level poise
The battle-balance hung. As when young men
In hot haste prune a vineyard with the steel,
And each keeps pace with each in rivalry,
Since all in strength and age be equal-matched;
So did the awful scales of battle hang
Level: all Trojan hearts beat high, and firm

Stood they in trust on aweless Ares' might,
While the Greeks trusted in Achilles' son.
Ever they slew and slew: stalked through the midst
Deadly Enyo, her shoulders and her hands
Blood-splashed, while fearful sweat streamed from her limbs.
Revelling in equal fight, she aided none,
Lest Thetis' or the War-god's wrath be stirred.

Then Neoptolemus slew one far-renowned,
Perimedes, who had dwelt by Smintheus' grove;
Next Cestrus died, Phalerus battle-staunch,
Perilaus the strong, Menalcas lord of spears,
Whom Iphianassa bare by the haunted foot
Of Cilla to the cunning craftsman Medon.
In the home-land afar the sire abode,
And never kissed his son's returning head:
For that fair home and all his cunning works
Did far-off kinsmen wrangle o'er his grave.
Deiphobus slew Lycon battle-staunch:
The lance-head pierced him close above the groin,
And round the long spear all his bowels gushed out.
Aeneas smote down Dymas, who erewhile
In Aulis dwelt, and followed unto Troy
Arcesilaus, and saw never more
The dear home-land. Euryalus hurled a dart,
And through Astraeus' breast the death-winged point
Flew, shearing through the breathways of man's life;
And all that lay within was drenched with blood.
And hard thereby great-souled Agenor slew
Hippomenes, hero Teucer's comrade staunch,
With one swift thrust 'twixt shoulder and neck: his soul
Rushed forth in blood; death's night swept over him.
Grief for his comrade slain on Teucer fell;

He strained his bow, a swift-winged shaft he sped,
But smote him not, for slightly Agenor swerved.
Yet nigh him Deiophontes stood; the shaft
Into his left eye plunged, passed through the ball,
And out through his right ear, because the Fates
Whither they willed thrust on the bitter barbs.
Even as in agony he leapt full height,
Yet once again the archer's arrow hissed:
It pierced his throat, through the neck-sinews cleft
Unswerving, and his hard doom came on him.

So man to man dealt death; and joyed the Fates
And Doom, and fell Strife in her maddened glee
Shouted aloud, and Ares terribly
Shouted in answer, and with courage thrilled
The Trojans, and with panic fear the Greeks,
And shook their reeling squadrons. But one man
He scared not, even Achilles' son; he abode,
And fought undaunted, slaying foes on foes.
As when a young lad sweeps his hand around
Flies swarming over milk, and nigh the bowl
Here, there they lie, struck dead by that light touch,
And gleefully the child still plies the work;
So stern Achilles' glorious scion joyed
Over the slain, and recked not of the God
Who spurred the Trojans on: man after man
Tasted his vengeance of their charging host.
Even as a giant mountain-peak withstands
On-rushing hurricane-blasts, so he abode
Unquailing. Ares at his eager mood
Grew wroth, and would have cast his veil of cloud
Away, and met him face to face in fight,
But now Athena from Olympus swooped

The Fall of Troy

To forest-mantled Ida. Quaked the earth
And Xanthus' murmuring streams; so mightily
She shook them: terror-stricken were the souls
Of all the Nymphs, adread for Priam's town.
From her immortal armour flashed around
The hovering lightnings; fearful serpents breathed
Fire from her shield invincible; the crest
Of her great helmet swept the clouds. And now
She was at point to close in sudden fight
With Ares; but the mighty will of Zeus
Daunted them both, from high heaven thundering
His terrors. Ares drew back from the war,
For manifest to him was Zeus's wrath.
To wintry Thrace he passed; his haughty heart
Reeked no more of the Trojans. In the plain
Of Troy no more stayed Pallas; she was gone
To hallowed Athens. But the armies still
Strove in the deadly fray; and fainted now
The Trojans' prowess; but all battle-fain
The Argives pressed on these as they gave ground.
As winds chase ships that fly with straining sails
On to the outsea--as on forest-brakes
Leapeth the fury of flame--as swift hounds drive
Deer through the mountains, eager for the prey,
So did the Argives chase them: Achilles' son
Still cheered them on, still slew with that great spear
Whomso he overtook. On, on they fled
Till into stately-gated Troy they poured.

Then had the Argives a short breathing-space
From war, when they had penned the hosts of Troy
In Priam's burg, as shepherds pen up lambs
Upon a lonely steading. And, as when

After hard strain, a breathing-space is given
To oxen that, quick-panting 'neath the yoke,
Up a steep hill have dragged a load, so breathed
Awhile the Achaeans after toil in arms.
Then once more hot for the fray did they beset
The city-towers. But now with gates fast barred
The Trojans from the walls withstood the assault.
As when within their steading shepherd-folk
Abide the lowering tempest, when a day
Of storm hath dawned, with fury of lightnings, rain
And heavy-drifting snow, and dare not haste
Forth to the pasture, howsoever fain,
Till the great storm abate, and rivers, wide
With rushing floods, again be passable;
So trembling on their walls they abode the rage
Of foes against their ramparts surging fast.
And as when daws or starlings drop in clouds
Down on an orchard-close, full fain to feast
Upon its pleasant fruits, and take no heed
Of men that shout to scare them thence away,
Until the reckless hunger be appeased
That makes them bold; so poured round Priam's burg
The furious Danaans. Against the gates
They hurled themselves, they strove to batter down
The mighty-souled Earth-shaker's work divine.

Yet did tim Troyfolk not, despite their fear,
Flinch from the fight: they manned their towers, they toiled
Unresting: ever from the fair-built walls
Leapt arrows, stones, and fleet-winged javelins down
Amidst the thronging foes; for Phoebus thrilled
Their souls with steadfast hardihood. Fain was he
To save them still, though Hector was no more.

The Fall of Troy

Then Meriones shot forth a deadly shaft,
And smote Phylodamas, Polites' friend,
Beneath the jaw; the arrow pierced his throat.
Down fell he like a vulture, from a rock
By fowler's barbed arrow shot and slain;
So from the high tower swiftly down he fell:
His life fled; clanged his armour o'er the corpse.
With laughter of triumph stalwart Molus' son
A second arrow sped, with strong desire
To smite Polites, ill-starred Priam's son:
But with a swift side-swerve did he escape
The death, nor did the arrow touch his flesh.
As when a shipman, as his bark flies on
O'er sea-gulfs, spies amid the rushing tide
A rock, and to escape it swiftly puts
The helm about, and turns aside the ship
Even as he listeth, that a little strength
Averts a great disaster; so did he
Foresee and shun the deadly shaft of doom.

Ever they fought on; walls, towers, battlements
Were blood-besprent, wherever Trojans fell
Slain by the arrows of the stalwart Greeks.
Yet these escaped not scatheless; many of them
Dyed the earth red: aye waxed the havoc of death
As friends and foes were stricken. O'er the strife
Shouted for glee Enyo, sister of War.

Now had the Argives burst the gates, had breached
The walls of Troy, for boundless was their might;
But Ganymedes saw from heaven, and cried,
Anguished with fear for his own fatherland:
"O Father Zeus, if of thy seed I am,

If at thine best I left far-famed Troy
For immortality with deathless Gods,
O hear me now, whose soul is anguish-thrilled!
I cannot bear to see my fathers' town
In flames, my kindred in disastrous strife
Perishing: bitterer sorrow is there none!
Oh, if thine heart is fixed to do this thing,
Let me be far hence! Less shall be my grief
If I behold it not with these mine eyes.
That is the depth of horror and of shame
To see one's country wrecked by hands of foes."

With groans and tears so pleaded Ganymede.
Then Zeus himself with one vast pall of cloud
Veiled all the city of Priam world-renowned;
And all the murderous fight was drowned in mist,
And like a vanished phantom was the wall
In vapours heavy-hung no eye could pierce;
And all around crashed thunders, lightnings flamed
From heaven. The Danaans heard Zeus' clarion peal
Awe-struck; and Neleus' son cried unto them:
"Far-famous lords of Argives, all our strength
Palsied shall be, while Zeus protecteth thus
Our foes. A great tide of calamity
On us is rolling; haste we then to the ships;
Cease we awhile from bitter toil of strife,
Lest the fire of his wrath consume us all.
Submit we to his portents; needs must all
Obey him ever, who is mightier far
Than all strong Gods, all weakling sons of men.
On the presumptuous Titans once in wrath
He poured down fire from heaven: then burned all earth
Beneath, and Ocean's world-engirdling flood

Boiled from its depths, yea, to its utmost bounds:
Far-flowing mighty rivers were dried up:
Perished all broods of life-sustaining earth,
All fosterlings of the boundless sea, and all
Dwellers in rivers: smoke and ashes veiled
The air: earth fainted in the fervent heat.
Therefore this day I dread the might of Zeus.
Now, pass we to the ships, since for to-day
He helpeth Troy. To us too shall he grant
Glory hereafter; for the dawn on men,
Though whiles it frown, anon shall smile. Not yet,
But soon, shall Fate lead us to smite yon town,
If true indeed was Calchas' prophecy
Spoken aforetime to the assembled Greeks,
That in the tenth year Priam's burg should fall."

Then left they that far-famed town, and turned
From war, in awe of Zeus's threatenings,
Hearkening to one with ancient wisdom wise.
Yet they forgat not friends in battle slain,
But bare them from the field and buried them.
These the mist hid not, but the town alone
And its unscaleable wall, around which fell
Trojans and Argives many in battle slain.
So came they to the ships, and put from them
Their battle-gear, and strode into the waves
Of Hellespont fair-flowing, and washed away
All stain of dust and sweat and clotted gore.

The sun drave down his never-wearying steeds
Into the dark west: night streamed o'er the earth,
Bidding men cease from toil. The Argives then
Acclaimed Achilles' valiant son with praise

High as his father's. Mid triumphant mirth
He feasted in kings' tents: no battle-toil
Had wearied him; for Thetis from his limbs
Had charmed all ache of travail, making him
As one whom labour had no power to tire.
When his strong heart was satisfied with meat,
He passed to his father's tent, and over him
Sleep's dews were poured. The Greeks slept in the plain
Before the ships, by ever-changing guards
Watched; for they dreaded lest the host of Troy,
Or of her staunch allies, should kindle flame
Upon the ships, and from them all cut off
Their home-return. In Priam's burg the while
By gate and wall men watched and slept in turn,
Adread to hear the Argives' onset-shout.

BOOK IX

How from his long lone exile returned to the war Philoctetes.

When ended was night's darkness, and the Dawn
Rose from the world's verge, and the wide air glowed
With splendour, then did Argos' warrior-sons
Gaze o'er the plain; and lo, all cloudless-clear
Stood Ilium's towers. The marvel of yesterday
Seemed a strange dream. No thought the Trojans had
Of standing forth to fight without the wall.
A great fear held them thralls, the awful thought
That yet alive was Peleus' glorious son.
But to the King of Heaven Antenor cried:
"Zeus, Lord of Ida and the starry sky,
Hearken my prayer! Oh turn back from our town
That battle-eager murderous-hearted man,
Be he Achilles who hath not passed down
To Hades, or some other like to him.
For now in heaven-descended Priam's burg
By thousands are her people perishing:
No respite cometh from calamity:
Murder and havoc evermore increase.
O Father Zeus, thou carest not though we
Be slaughtered of our foes: thou helpest them,

Forgetting thy son, godlike Dardanus!
But, if this be the purpose of thine heart
That Argives shall destroy us wretchedly,
Now do it: draw not out our agony!"

In passionate prayer he cried; and Zeus from heaven
Hearkened, and hasted on the end of all,
Which else he had delayed. He granted him
This awful boon, that myriads of Troy's sons
Should with their children perish: but that prayer
He granted not, to turn Achilles' son
Back from the wide-wayed town; nay, all the more
He enkindled him to war, for he would now
Give grace and glory to the Nereid Queen.

So purposed he, of all Gods mightiest.
But now between the city and Hellespont
Were Greeks and Trojans burning men and steeds
In battle slain, while paused the murderous strife.
For Priam sent his herald Menoetes forth
To Agamemnon and the Achaean chiefs,
Asking a truce wherein to burn the dead;
And they, of reverence for the slain, gave ear;
For wrath pursueth not the dead. And when
They had lain their slain on those close-thronging pyres,
Then did the Argives to their tents return,
And unto Priam's gold-abounding halls
The Trojans, for Eurypylus sorrowing sore:
For even as Priam's sons they honoured him.
Therefore apart from all the other slain,
Before the Gate Dardanian--where the streams
Of eddying Xanthus down from Ida flow
Fed by the rains of heavens--they buried him.

The Fall of Troy

Aweless Achilles' son the while went forth
To his sire's huge tomb. Outpouring tears, he kissed
The tall memorial pillar of the dead,
And groaning clasped it round, and thus he cried:
"Hail, father! Though beneath the earth thou lie
In Hades' halls, I shall forget thee not.
Oh to have met thee living mid the host!
Then of each other had our souls had joy,
Then of her wealth had we spoiled Ilium.
But now, thou hast not seen thy child, nor I
Seen thee, who yearned to look on thee in life.
Yet, though thou be afar amidst the dead,
Thy spear, thy son, have made thy foes to quail;
And Danaans with exceeding joy behold
One like to thee in stature, fame and deeds."

He spake, and wiped the hot tears from his face;
And to his father's ships passed swiftly thence:
With him went Myrmidon warriors two and ten,
And white-haired Phoenix followed on with these
Woefully sighing for the glorious dead.

Night rose o'er earth, the stars flashed out in heaven;
So these brake bread, and slept till woke the Dawn.
Then the Greeks donned their armour: flashed afar
Its splendour up to the very firmament.
Forth of their gates in one great throng they poured,
Like snowflakes thick and fast, which drift adown
Heavily from the clouds in winter's cold;
So streamed they forth before the wall, and rose
Their dread shout: groaned the deep earth 'neath their tramp.

The Trojans heard that shout, and saw that host,
And marvelled. Crushed with fear were all their hearts
Foreboding doom; for like a huge cloud seemed
That throng of foes: with clashing arms they came:
Volumed and vast the dust rose 'neath their feet.
Then either did some God with hardihood thrill
Deiphobus' heart, and made it void of fear,
Or his own spirit spurred him on to fight,
To drive by thrust of spear that terrible host
Of foemen from the city of his birth.
So there in Troy he cried with heartening speech:
"O friends, be stout of heart to play the men!
Remember all the agonies that war
Brings in the end to them that yield to foes.
Ye wrestle not for Alexander alone,
Nor Helen, but for home, for your own lives,
For wives, for little ones, for parents grey,
For all the grace of life, for all ye have,
For this dear land--oh may she shroud me o'er
Slain in the battle, ere I see her lie
'Neath foemen's spears--my country! I know not
A bitterer pang than this for hapless men!
O be ye strong for battle! Forth to the fight
With me, and thrust this horror far away!
Think not Achilles liveth still to war
Against us: him the ravening fire consumed.
Some other Achaean was it who so late
Enkindled them to war. Oh, shame it were
If men who fight for fatherland should fear
Achilles' self, or any Greek beside!
Let us not flinch from war-toil! have we not
Endured much battle-travail heretofore?
What, know ye not that to men sorely tried

The Fall of Troy

Prosperity and joyance follow toil?
So after scourging winds and ruining storms
Zeus brings to men a morn of balmy air;
After disease new strength comes, after war
Peace: all things know Time's changeless law of change."

Then eager all for war they armed themselves
In haste. All through the town rang clangour of arms
As for grim fight strong men arrayed their limbs.
Here stood a wife, shuddering with dread of war,
Yet piling, as she wept, her husband's arms
Before his feet. There little children brought
To a father his war-gear with eager haste;
And now his heart was wrung to hear their sobs,
And now he smiled on those small ministers,
And stronger waxed his heart's resolve to fight
To the last gasp for these, the near and dear.
Yonder again, with hands that had not lost
Old cunning, a grey father for the fray
Girded a son, and murmured once and again:
"Dear boy, yield thou to no man in the war!"
And showed his son the old scars on his breast,
Proud memories of fights fought long ago.

So when they all stood mailed in battle-gear,
Forth of the gates they poured all eager-souled
For war. Against the chariots of the Greeks
Their chariots charged; their ranks of footmen pressed
To meet the footmen of the foe. The earth
Rang to the tramp of onset; pealed the cheer
From man to man; swift closed the fronts of war.
Loud clashed their arms all round; from either side
War-cries were mingled in one awful roar

Swift-winged full many a dart and arrow flew
From host to host; loud clanged the smitten shields
'Neath thrusting spears, 'neath javelin-point and sword:
Men hewed with battle-axes lightening down;
Crimson the armour ran with blood of men.
And all this while Troy's wives and daughters watched
From high walls that grim battle of the strong.
All trembled as they prayed for husbands, sons,
And brothers: white-haired sires amidst them sat,
And gazed, while anguished fear for sons devoured
Their hearts. But Helen in her bower abode
Amidst her maids, there held by utter shame.

So without pause before the wall they fought,
While Death exulted o'er them; deadly Strife
Shrieked out a long wild cry from host to host.
With blood of slain men dust became red mire:
Here, there, fast fell the warriors mid the fray.

Then slew Deiphobus the charioteer
Of Nestor, Hippasus' son: from that high car
Down fell he 'midst the dead; fear seized his lord
Lest, while his hands were cumbered with the reins,
He too by Priam's strong son might be slain.
Melanthius marked his plight: swiftly he sprang
Upon the car; he urged the horses on,
Shaking the reins, goading them with his spear,
Seeing the scourge was lost. But Priam's son
Left these, and plunged amid a throng of foes.
There upon many he brought the day of doom;
For like a ruining tempest on he stormed
Through reeling ranks. His mighty hand struck down
Foes numberless: the plain was heaped with dead.

The Fall of Troy

As when a woodman on the long-ridged hills
Plunges amid the forest-depths, and hews
With might and main, and fells sap-laden trees
To make him store of charcoal from the heaps
Of billets overturfed and set afire:
The trunks on all sides fallen strew the slopes,
While o'er his work the man exulteth; so
Before Deiphobus' swift death-dealing hands
In heaps the Achaeans each on other fell.
The charging lines of Troy swept over some;
Some fled to Xanthus' stream: Deiphobus chased
Into the flood yet more, and slew and slew.
As when on fish-abounding Hellespont's strand
The fishermen hard-straining drag a net
Forth of the depths to land; but, while it trails
Yet through the sea, one leaps amid the waves
Grasping in hand a sinuous-headed spear
To deal the sword-fish death, and here and there,
Fast as he meets them, slays them, and with blood
The waves are reddened; so were Xanthus' streams
Impurpled by his hands, and choked with dead.

Yet not without sore loss the Trojans fought;
For all this while Peleides' fierce-heart son
Of other ranks made havoc. Thetis gazed
Rejoicing in her son's son, with a joy
As great as was her grief for Achilles slain.
For a great host beneath his spear were hurled
Down to the dust, steeds, warriors slaughter-blent.
And still he chased, and still he slew: he smote
Amides war-renowned, who on his steed
Bore down on him, but of his horsemanship
Small profit won. The bright spear pierced him through

From navel unto spine, and all his bowels
Gushed out, and deadly Doom laid hold on him
Even as he fell beside his horse's feet.
Ascanius and Oenops next he slew;
Under the fifth rib of the one he drave
His spear, the other stabbed he 'neath the throat
Where a wound bringeth surest doom to man.
Whomso he met besides he slew--the names
What man could tell of all that by the hands
Of Neoptolemus died? Never his limbs
Waxed weary. As some brawny labourer,
With strong hands toiling in a fruitful field
The livelong day, rains down to earth the fruit
Of olives, swiftly beating with his pole,
And with the downfall covers all the ground,
So fast fell 'neath his hands the thronging foe.

Elsewhere did Agamemnon, Tydeus' son,
And other chieftains of the Danaans toil
With fury in the fight. Yet never quailed
The mighty men of Troy: with heart and soul
They also fought, and ever stayed from flight
Such as gave back. Yet many heeded not
Their chiefs, but fled, cowed by the Achaeans' might.

Now at the last Achilles' strong son marked
How fast beside Scamander's outfall Greeks
Were perishing. Those Troyward-fleeing foes
Whom he had followed slaying, left he now,
And bade Automedon thither drive, where hosts
Were falling of the Achaeans. Straightway he
Hearkened, and scourged the steeds immortal on
To that wild fray: bearing their lord they flew

Swiftly o'er battle-highways paved with death.

As Ares chariot-borne to murderous war
Fares forth, and round his onrush quakes the ground,
While on the God's breast clash celestial arms
Outflashing fire, so charged Achilles' son
Against Deiphobus. Clouds of dust upsoared
About his horses' feet. Automedon marked
The Trojan chief, and knew him. To his lord
Straightway he named that hero war-renowned:
"My king, this is Deiphobus' array--
The man who from thy father fled in fear.
Some God or fiend with courage fills him now."

Naught answered Neoptolemus, save to bid
Drive on the steeds yet faster, that with speed
He might avert grim death from perishing friends.
But when to each other now full nigh they drew,
Deiphobus, despite his battle-lust,
Stayed, as a ravening fire stays when it meets
Water. He marvelled, seeing Achilles' steeds
And that gigantic son, huge as his sire;
And his heart wavered, choosing now to flee,
And now to face that hero, man to man
As when a mountain boar from his young brood
Chases the jackals--then a lion leaps
From hidden ambush into view: the boar
Halts in his furious onset, loth to advance,
Loth to retreat, while foam his jaws about
His whetted tusks; so halted Priam's son
Car-steeds and car, perplexed, while quivered his hands
About the lance. Shouted Achilles' son:
"Ho, Priam's son, why thus so mad to smite

Those weaker Argives, who have feared thy wrath
And fled thine onset? So thou deem'st thyself
Far mightiest! If thine heart be brave indeed,
Of my spear now make trial in the strife."

On rushed he, as a lion against a stag,
Borne by the steeds and chariot of his sire.
And now full soon his lance had slain his foe,
Him and his charioteer--but Phoebus poured
A dense cloud round him from the viewless heights
Of heaven, and snatched him from the deadly fray,
And set him down in Troy, amid the rout
Of fleeing Trojans: so did Peleus' son
Stab but the empty air; and loud he cried:
"Dog, thou hast 'scaped my wrath! No might of thine
Saved thee, though ne'er so fain! Some God hath cast
Night's veil o'er thee, and snatched thee from thy death."

Then Cronos' Son dispersed that dense dark cloud:
Mist-like it thinned and vanished into air:
Straightway the plain and all the land were seen.
Then far away about the Scaean Gate
He saw the Trojans: seeming like his sire,
He sped against them; they at his coming quailed.
As shipmen tremble when a wild wave bears
Down on their bark, wind-heaved until it swings
Broad, mountain-high above them, when the sea
Is mad with tempest; so, as on he came,
Terror clad all those Trojans as a cloak,
The while he shouted, cheering on his men:
"Hear, friends!--fill full your hearts with dauntless strength,
The strength that well beseemeth mighty men
Who thirst to win them glorious victory,

The Fall of Troy

To win renown from battle's tumult! Come,
Brave hearts, now strive we even beyond our strength
Till we smite Troy's proud city, till we win
Our hearts' desire! Foul shame it were to abide
Long deedless here and strengthless, womanlike!
Ere I be called war-blencher, let me die!"

Then unto Ares' work their spirits flamed.
Down on the Trojans charged they: yea, and these
Fought with high courage, round their city now,
And now from wall and gate-towers. Never lulled
The rage of war, while Trojan hearts were hot
To hurl the foemen back, and the strong Greeks
To smite the town: grim havoc compassed all.

Then, eager for the Trojans' help, swooped down
Out of Olympus, cloaked about with clouds,
The son of Leto. Mighty rushing winds
Bare him in golden armour clad; and gleamed
With lightning-splendour of his descent the long
Highways of air. His quiver clashed; loud rang
The welkin; earth re-echoed, as he set
His tireless feet by Xanthus. Pealed his shout
Dreadly, with courage filling them of Troy,
Scaring their foes from biding the red fray.
But of all this the mighty Shaker of Earth
Was ware: he breathed into the fainting
Greeks Fierce valour, and the fight waxed murderous
Through those Immortals' clashing wills. Then died
Hosts numberless on either side. In wrath
Apollo thought to smite Achilles' son
In the same place where erst he smote his sire;
But birds of boding screamed to left, to stay

His mood, and other signs from heaven were sent;
Yet was his wrath not minded to obey
Those portents. Swiftly drew Earth-shaker nigh
In mist celestial cloaked: about his feet
Quaked the dark earth as came the Sea-king on.
Then, to stay Phoebus' hand, he cried to him:
"Refrain thy wrath: Achilles' giant son
Slay not! Olympus' Lord himself shall be
Wroth for his death, and bitter grief shall light
On me and all the Sea-gods, as erstwhile
For Achilles' sake. Nay, get thee back to heights
Celestial, lest thou kindle me to wrath,
And so I cleave a sudden chasm in earth,
And Ilium and all her walls go down
To darkness. Thine own soul were vexed thereat."

Then, overawed by the brother of his sire,
And fearing for Troy's fate and for her folk,
To heaven went back Apollo, to the sea
Poseidon. But the sons of men fought on,
And slew; and Strife incarnate gloating watched.

At last by Calchas' counsel Achaea's sons
Drew back to the ships, and put from them the thought
Of battle, seeing it was not foreordained
That Ilium should fall until the might
Of war-wise Philoctetes came to aid
The Achaean host. This had the prophet learnt.
From birds of prosperous omen, or had read
In hearts of victims. Wise in prophecy-lore
Was he, and like a God knew things to be.

Trusting in him, the sons of Atreus stayed

Awhile the war, and unto Lemnos, land
Of stately mansions, sent they Tydeus' son
And battle-staunch Odysseus oversea.
Fast by the Fire-god's city sped they on
Over the broad flood of the Aegean Sea
To vine-clad Lemnos, where in far-off days
The wives wreaked murderous vengeance on their lords,
In fierce wrath that they gave them not their due,
But couched beside the handmaid-thralls of Thrace,
The captives of their spears when they laid waste
The land of warrior Thracians. Then these wives,
Their hearts with fiery jealousy's fever filled,
Murdered in every home with merciless hands
Their husbands: no compassion would they show
To their own wedded lords--such madness shakes
The heart of man or woman, when it burns
With jealousy's fever, stung by torturing pangs.
So with souls filled with desperate hardihood
In one night did they slaughter all their lords;
And on a widowed nation rose the sun.

To hallowed Lemnos came those heroes twain;
They marked the rocky cave where lay the son
Of princely Poeas. Horror came on them
When they beheld the hero of their quest
Groaning with bitter pangs, on the hard earth
Lying, with many feathers round him strewn,
And others round his body, rudely sewn
Into a cloak, a screen from winter's cold.
For, oft as famine stung him, would he shoot
The shaft that missed no fowl his aim had doomed.
Their flesh he ate, their feathers vestured him.
And there lay herbs and healing leaves, the which,

Spread on his deadly wound, assuaged its pangs.
Wild tangled elf-locks hung about his head.
He seemed a wild beast, that hath set its foot,
Prowling by night, upon a hidden trap,
And so hath been constrained in agony
To bite with fierce teeth through the prisoned limb
Ere it could win back to its cave, and there
In hunger and torturing pains it languisheth.
So in that wide cave suffering crushed the man;
And all his frame was wasted: naught but skin
Covered his bones. Unwashen there he crouched
With famine-haggard cheeks, with sunken eyes
Glaring his misery 'neath cavernous brows.
Never his groaning ceased, for evermore
The ulcerous black wound, eating to the bone,
Festered with thrills of agonizing pain.
As when a beetling cliff, by seething seas
Aye buffeted, is carved and underscooped,
For all its stubborn strength, by tireless waves,
Till, scourged by winds and lashed by tempest-flails,
The sea into deep caves hath gnawed its base;
So greater 'neath his foot grew evermore
The festering wound, dealt when the envenomed fangs
Tare him of that fell water-snake, which men
Say dealeth ghastly wounds incurable,
When the hot sun hath parched it as it crawls
Over the sands; and so that mightiest man
Lay faint and wasted with his cureless pain;
And from the ulcerous wound aye streamed to earth
Fetid corruption fouling all the floor
Of that wide cave, a marvel to be heard
Of men unborn. Beside his stony bed
Lay a long quiver full of arrows, some

For hunting, some to smite his foes withal;
With deadly venom of that fell water-snake
Were these besmeared. Before it, nigh to his hand,
Lay the great bow, with curving tips of horn,
Wrought by the mighty hands of Hercules.

Now when that solitary spied these twain
Draw nigh his cave, he sprang to his bow, he laid
The deadly arrow on the string; for now
Fierce memory of his wrongs awoke against
These, who had left him years agone, in pain
Groaning upon the desolate sea-shore.
Yea, and his heart's stem will he had swiftly wrought,
But, even as upon that godlike twain
He gazed, Athena caused his bitter wrath
To melt away. Then drew they nigh to him
With looks of sad compassion, and sat down
On either hand beside him in the cave,
And of his deadly wound and grievous pangs
Asked; and he told them all his sufferings.
And they spake hope and comfort; and they said:
"Thy woeful wound, thine anguish, shall be healed,
If thou but come with us to Achaea's host--
The host that now is sorrowing after thee
With all its kings. And no man of them all
Was cause of thine affliction, but the Fates,
The cruel ones, whom none that walk the earth
Escape, but aye they visit hapless men
Unseen; and day by day with pitiless hearts
Now they afflict men, now again exalt
To honour--none knows why; for all the woes
And all the joys of men do these devise
After their pleasure." Hearkening he sat

To Odysseus and to godlike Diomede;
And all the hoarded wrath for olden wrongs
And all the torturing rage, melted away.

Straight to the strand dull-thundering and the ship,
Laughing for joy, they bare him with his bow.
There washed they all his body and that foul wound
With sponges, and with plenteous water bathed:
So was his soul refreshed. Then hasted they
And made meat ready for the famished man,
And in the galley supped with him. Then came
The balmy night, and sleep slid down on them.
Till rose the dawn they tarried by the strand
Of sea-girt Lemnos, but with dayspring cast
The hawsers loose, and heaved the anchor-stones
Out of the deep. Athena sent a breeze
Blowing behind the galley taper-prowed.
They strained the sail with either stern-sheet taut;
Seaward they pointed the stout-girdered ship;
O'er the broad flood she leapt before the wind;
Broken to right and left the dark wave sighed,
And seething all around was hoary foam,
While thronging dolphins raced on either hand
Flashing along the paths of silver sea.

Full soon to fish-fraught Hellespont they came
And the far-stretching ships. Glad were the Greeks
To see the longed-for faces. Forth the ship
With joy they stepped; and Poeas' valiant son
On those two heroes leaned thin wasted hands,
Who bare him painfully halting to the shore
Staying his weight upon their brawny arms.
As seems mid mountain-brakes an oak or pine

By strength of the woodcutter half hewn through,
Which for a little stands on what was left
Of the smooth trunk by him who hewed thereat
Hard by the roots, that its slow-smouldering wood
Might yield him pitch--now like to one in pain
It groans, in weakness borne down by the wind,
Yet is upstayed upon its leafy boughs
Which from the earth bear up its helpless weight;
So by pain unendurable bowed down
Leaned he on those brave heroes, and was borne
Unto the war-host. Men beheld, and all
Compassionated that great archer, crushed
By anguish of his hurt. But one drew near,
Podaleirius, godlike in his power to heal.
Swifter than thought he made him whole and sound;
For deftly on the wound he spread his salves,
Calling on his physician-father's name;
And soon the Achaeans shouted all for joy,
All praising with one voice Asclepius' son.
Lovingly then they bathed him, and with oil
Anointed. All his heaviness of cheer
And misery vanished by the Immortals' will;
And glad at heart were all that looked on him;
And from affliction he awoke to joy.
Over the bloodless face the flush of health
Glowed, and for wretched weakness mighty strength
Thrilled through him: goodly and great waxed all his limbs.
As when a field of corn revives again
Which erst had drooped, by rains of ruining storm
Down beaten flat, but by warm summer winds
Requickened, o'er the laboured land it smiles,
So Philoctetes' erstwhile wasted frame
Was all requickened:--in the galley's hold

He seemed to have left all cares that crushed his soul.

And Atreus' sons beheld him marvelling
As one re-risen from the dead: it seemed
The work of hands immortal. And indeed
So was it verily, as their hearts divined;
For 'twas the glorious Trito-born that shed
Stature and grace upon him. Suddenly
He seemed as when of old mid Argive men
He stood, before calamity struck him down.
Then unto wealthy Agamemnon's tent
Did all their mightiest men bring Poeas' son,
And set him chief in honour at the feast,
Extolling him. When all with meat and drink
Were filled, spake Agamemnon lord of spears:
"Dear friend, since by the will of Heaven our souls
Were once perverted, that in sea-girt Lemnos
We left thee, harbour not thine heart within
Fierce wrath for this: by the blest Gods constrained
We did it; and, I trow, the Immortals willed
To bring much evil on us, bereft of thee,
Who art of all men skilfullest to quell
With shafts of death all foes that face thee in fight.
For all the tangled paths of human life,
By land and sea, are by the will of Fate
Hid from our eyes, in many and devious tracks
Are cleft apart, in wandering mazes lost.
Along them men by Fortune's dooming drift
Like unto leaves that drive before the wind.
Oft on an evil path the good man's feet
Stumble, the brave finds not a prosperous path;
And none of earth-born men can shun the Fates,
And of his own will none can choose his way.

The Fall of Troy

So then doth it behove the wise of heart
Though on a troublous track the winds of fate
Sweep him away to suffer and be strong.
Since we were blinded then, and erred herein,
With rich gifts will we make amends to thee
Hereafter, when we take the stately towers
Of Troy: but now receive thou handmaids seven,
Fleet steeds two-score, victors in chariot-race,
And tripods twelve, wherein thine heart may joy
Through all thy days; and always in my tent
Shall royal honour at the feast be thine."

He spake, and gave the hero those fair gifts.
Then answered Poeas' mighty-hearted son;
"Friend, I forgive thee freely, and all beside
Whoso against me haply hath trangressed.
I know how good men's minds sometimes be warped:
Nor meet it is that one be obdurate
Ever, and nurse mean rancours: sternest wrath
Must yield anon unto the melting mood.
Now pass we to our rest; for better is sleep
Than feasting late, for him who longs to fight."

He spake, and rose, and came to his comrades' tent;
Then swiftly for their war-fain king they dight
The couch, while laughed their hearts for very joy.
Gladly he laid him down to sleep till dawn.

So passed the night divine, till flushed the hills
In the sun's light, and men awoke to toil.
Then all athirst for war the Argive men
'Gan whet the spear smooth-shafted, or the dart,
Or javelin, and they brake the bread of dawn,

And foddered all their horses. Then to these
Spake Poeas' son with battle-kindling speech:
"Up! let us make us ready for the war!
Let no man linger mid the galleys, ere
The glorious walls of Ilium stately-towered
Be shattered, and her palaces be burned!"

Then at his words each heart and spirit glowed:
They donned their armour, and they grasped their shields.
Forth of the ships in one huge mass they poured
Arrayed with bull-hide bucklers, ashen spears,
And gallant-crested helms. Through all their ranks
Shoulder to shoulder marched they: thou hadst seen
No gap 'twixt man and man as on they charged;
So close they thronged, so dense was their array.

BOOK X

How Paris was stricken to death, and in vain sought help of Oenone.

Now were the Trojans all without the town
Of Priam, armour-clad, with battle-cars
And chariot-steeds; for still they burnt their dead,
And still they feared lest the Achaean men
Should fall on them. They looked, and saw them come
With furious speed against the walls. In haste
They cast a hurried earth-mound o'er the slain,
For greatly trembled they to see their foes.
Then in their sore disquiet spake to them
Polydamas, a wise and prudent chief:
"Friends, unendurably against us now
Maddens the war. Go to, let us devise
How we may find deliverance from our strait.
Still bide the Danaans here, still gather strength:
Now therefore let us man our stately towers,
And thence withstand them, fighting night and day,
Until yon Danaans weary, and return
To Sparta, or, renownless lingering here
Beside the wall, lose heart. No strength of theirs
Shall breach the long walls, howsoe'er they strive,
For in the imperishable work of Gods

Weakness is none. Food, drink, we shall not lack,
For in King Priam's gold-abounding halls
Is stored abundant food, that shall suffice
For many more than we, through many years,
Though thrice so great a host at our desire
Should gather, eager to maintain our cause."

Then chode with him Anchises' valiant son:
"Polydamas, wherefore do they call thee wise,
Who biddest suffer endless tribulations
Cooped within walls? Never, how long soe'er
The Achaeans tarry here, will they lose heart;
But when they see us skulking from the field,
More fiercely will press on. So ours shall be
The sufferance, perishing in our native home,
If for long season they beleaguer us.
No food, if we be pent within our walls,
Shall Thebe send us, nor Maeonia wine,
But wretchedly by famine shall we die,
Though the great wall stand firm. Nay, though our lot
Should be to escape that evil death and doom,
And not by famine miserably to die;
Yet rather let us fight in armour clad
For children and grey fathers! Haply Zeus
Will help us yet; of his high blood are we.
Nay, even though we be abhorred of him,
Better straightway to perish gloriously
Fighting unto the last for fatherland,
Than die a death of lingering agony!"

Shouted they all who heard that gallant rede.
Swiftly with helms and shields and spears they stood
In close array. The eyes of mighty Zeus

From heaven beheld the Trojans armed for fight
Against the Danaans: then did he awake
Courage in these and those, that there might be
Strain of unflinching fight 'twixt host and host.
That day was Paris doomed, for Helen's sake
Fighting, by Philoctetes' hands to die.

To one place Strife incarnate drew them all,
The fearful Battle-queen, beheld of none,
But cloaked in clouds blood-raining: on she stalked
Swelling the mighty roar of battle, now
Rushed through Troy's squadrons, through Achaea's now;
Panic and Fear still waited on her steps
To make their father's sister glorious.
From small to huge that Fury's stature grew;
Her arms of adamant were blood-besprent,
The deadly lance she brandished reached the sky.
Earth quaked beneath her feet: dread blasts of fire
Flamed from her mouth: her voice pealed thunder-like
Kindling strong men. Swift closed the fronts of fight
Drawn by a dread Power to the mighty work.
Loud as the shriek of winds that madly blow
In early spring, when the tall woodland trees
Put forth their leaves--loud as the roar of fire
Blazing through sun-scorched brakes--loud as the voice
Of many waters, when the wide sea raves
Beneath the howling blast, with thunderous crash
Of waves, when shake the fearful shipman's knees;
So thundered earth beneath their charging feet.
Strife swooped on them: foe hurled himself on foe.

First did Aeneas of the Danaans slay
Harpalion, Arizelus' scion, born

In far Boeotia of Amphinome,
Who came to Troy to help the Argive men
With godlike Prothoenor. 'Neath his waist
Aeneas stabbed, and reft sweet life from him.
Dead upon him he cast Thersander's son,
For the barbed javelin pierced through Hyllus' throat
Whom Arethusa by Lethaeus bare
In Crete: sore grieved Idomeneus for his fall.

By this Peleides' son had swiftly slain
Twelve Trojan warriors with his father's spear.
First Cebrus fell, Harmon, Pasitheus then,
Hysminus, Schedius, and Imbrasius,
Phleges, Mnesaeus, Ennomus, Amphinous,
Phasis, Galenus last, who had his home

By Gargarus' steep--a mighty warrior he
Among Troy's mighties: with a countless host
To Troy he came: for Priam Dardanus' son
Promised him many gifts and passing fair.
Ah fool! his own doom never he foresaw,
Whose weird was suddenly to fall in fight
Ere he bore home King Priam's glorious gifts.

Doom the Destroyer against the Argives sped
Valiant Aeneas' friend, Eurymenes.
Wild courage spurred him on, that he might slay
Many--and then fill death's cup for himself.
Man after man he slew like some fierce beast,
And foes shrank from the terrible rage that burned
On his life's verge, nor reeked of imminent doom.
Yea, peerless deeds in that fight had he done,
Had not his hands grown weary, his spear-head

Bent utterly: his sword availed him not,
Snapped at the hilt by Fate. Then Meges' dart
Smote 'neath his ribs; blood spurted from his mouth,
And in death's agony Doom stood at his side.

Even as he fell, Epeius' henchmen twain,
Deileon and Amphion, rushed to strip
His armour; but Aeneas brave and strong
Chilled their hot hearts in death beside the dead.
As one in latter summer 'mid his vines
Kills wasps that dart about his ripening grapes,
And so, ere they may taste the fruit, they die;
So smote he them, ere they could seize the arms.

Menon and Amphinous Tydeides slew,
Both goodly men. Paris slew Hippasus' son
Demoleon, who in Laconia's land
Beside the outfall of Eurotas dwelt,
The stream deep-flowing, and to Troy he came
With Menelaus. Under his right breast
The shaft of Paris smote him unto death,
Driving his soul forth like a scattering breath.

Teucer slew Zechis, Medon's war-famed son,
Who dwelt in Phrygia, land of myriad flocks,
Below that haunted cave of fair-haired Nymphs
Where, as Endymion slept beside his kine,
Divine Selene watched him from on high,
And slid from heaven to earth; for passionate love
Drew down the immortal stainless Queen of Night.
And a memorial of her couch abides
Still 'neath the oaks; for mid the copses round
Was poured out milk of kine; and still do men

Marvelling behold its whiteness. Thou wouldst say
Far off that this was milk indeed, which is
A well-spring of white water: if thou draw
A little nigher, lo, the stream is fringed
As though with ice, for white stone rims it round.

Rushed on Alcaeus Meges, Phyleus' son,
And drave his spear beneath his fluttering heart.
Loosed were the cords of sweet life suddenly,
And his sad parents longed in vain to greet
That son returning from the woeful war
To Margasus and Phyllis lovely-girt,
Dwellers by lucent streams of Harpasus,
Who pours the full blood of his clamorous flow
Into Maeander madly rushing aye.

With Glaucus' warrior-comrade Scylaceus
Odeus' son closed in the fight, and stabbed
Over the shield-rim, and the cruel spear
Passed through his shoulder, and drenched his shield with blood.
Howbeit he slew him not, whose day of doom
Awaited him afar beside the wall
Of his own city; for when Illium's towers
Were brought low by that swift avenging host
Fleeing the war to Lycia then he came
Alone; and when he drew nigh to the town,
The thronging women met and questioned him
Touching their sons and husbands; and he told
How all were dead. They compassed him about,
And stoned the man with great stones, that he died.
So had he no joy of his winning home,
But the stones muffled up his dying groans,
And of the same his ghastly tomb was reared

Beside Bellerophon's grave and holy place
In Tlos, nigh that far-famed Chimaera's Crag.
Yet, though he thus fulfilled his day of doom,
As a God afterward men worshipped him
By Phoebus' hest, and never his honour fades.

Now Poeas' son the while slew Deioneus
And Acamas, Antenor's warrior son:
Yea, a great host of strong men laid he low.
On, like the War-god, through his foes he rushed,
Or as a river roaring in full flood
Breaks down long dykes, when, maddening round its rocks,
Down from the mountains swelled by rain it pours
An ever-flowing mightily-rushing stream
Whose foaming crests over its forelands sweep;
So none who saw him even from afar
Dared meet renowned Poeas' valiant son,
Whose breast with battle-fury was fulfilled,
Whose limbs were clad in mighty Hercules' arms
Of cunning workmanship; for on the belt
Gleamed bears most grim and savage, jackals fell,
And panthers, in whose eyes there seems to lurk
A deadly smile. There were fierce-hearted wolves,
And boars with flashing tusks, and mighty lions
All seeming strangely alive; and, there portrayed
Through all its breadth, were battles murder-rife.
With all these marvels covered was the belt;
And with yet more the quiver was adorned.
There Hermes was, storm-footed Son of Zeus,
Slaying huge Argus nigh to Inachus' streams,
Argus, whose sentinel eyes in turn took sleep.
And there was Phaethon from the Sun-car hurled
Into Eridanus. Earth verily seemed

Ablaze, and black smoke hovered on the air.
There Perseus slew Medusa gorgon-eyed
By the stars' baths and utmost bounds of earth
And fountains of deep-flowing Ocean, where
Night in the far west meets the setting sun.
There was the Titan Iapetus' great son
Hung from the beetling crag of Caucasus
In bonds of adamant, and the eagle tare
His liver unconsumed--he seemed to groan!
All these Hephaestus' cunning hands had wrought
For Hercules; and these to Poeas' son,
Most near of friends and dear, he gave to bear.

So glorying in those arms he smote the foe.
But Paris at the last to meet him sprang
Fearlessly, bearing in his hands his bow
And deadly arrows--but his latest day
Now met himself. A flying shaft he sped
Forth from the string, which sang as leapt the dart,
Which flew not vainly: yet the very mark
It missed, for Philoctetes swerved aside
A hair-breadth, and it smote above the breast
Cleodorus war-renowned, and cleft a path
Clear through his shoulder; for he had not now
The buckler broad which wont to fence from death
Its bearer, but was falling back from fight,
Being shieldless; for Polydamas' massy lance
Had cleft the shoulder-belt whereby his targe
Hung, and he gave back therefore, fighting still
With stubborn spear. But now the arrow of death
Fell on him, as from ambush leaping forth.
For so Fate willed, I trow, to bring dread doom
On noble-hearted Lernus' scion, born

Of Amphiale, in Rhodes the fertile land.

But soon as Poeas' battle-eager son
Marked him by Paris' deadly arrow slain,
Swiftly he strained his bow, shouting aloud:
"Dog! I will give thee death, will speed thee down
To the Unseen Land, who darest to brave me!
And so shall they have rest, who travail now
For thy vile sake. Destruction shall have end
When thou art dead, the author of our bane."

Then to his breast he drew the plaited cord.
The great bow arched, the merciless shaft was aimed
Straight, and the terrible point a little peered
Above the bow, in that constraining grip.
Loud sang the string, as the death-hissing shaft
Leapt, and missed not: yet was not Paris' heart
Stilled, but his spirit yet was strong in him;
For that first arrow was not winged with death:
It did but graze the fair flesh by his wrist.
Then once again the avenger drew the bow,
And the barbed shaft of Poeas' son had plunged,
Ere he could swerve, 'twixt flank and groin. No more
He abode the fight, but swiftly hasted back
As hastes a dog which on a lion rushed
At first, then fleeth terror-stricken back.
So he, his very heart with agony thrilled,
Fled from the war. Still clashed the grappling hosts,
Man slaying man: aye bloodier waxed the fray
As rained the blows: corpse upon corpse was flung
Confusedly, like thunder-drops, or flakes
Of snow, or hailstones, by the wintry blast
At Zeus' behest strewn over the long hills

And forest-boughs; so by a pitiless doom
Slain, friends with foes in heaps on heaps were strown.

Sorely groaned Paris; with the torturing wound
Fainted his spirit. Leeches sought to allay
His frenzy of pain. But now drew back to Troy
The Trojans, and the Danaans to their ships
Swiftly returned, for dark night put an end
To strife, and stole from men's limbs weariness,
Pouring upon their eyes pain-healing sleep.

But through the livelong night no sleep laid hold
On Paris: for his help no leech availed,
Though ne'er so willing, with his salves. His weird
Was only by Oenone's hands to escape
Death's doom, if so she willed. Now he obeyed
The prophecy, and he went--exceeding loth,
But grim necessity forced him thence, to face
The wife forsaken. Evil-boding fowl
Shrieked o'er his head, or darted past to left,
Still as he went. Now, as he looked at them,
His heart sank; now hope whispered, "Haply vain
Their bodings are!" but on their wings were borne
Visions of doom that blended with his pain.
Into Oenone's presence thus he came.
Amazed her thronging handmaids looked on him
As at the Nymph's feet that pale suppliant fell
Faint with the anguish of his wound, whose pangs
Stabbed him through brain and heart, yea, quivered through
His very bones, for that fierce venom crawled
Through all his inwards with corrupting fangs;
And his life fainted in him agony-thrilled.
As one with sickness and tormenting thirst

Consumed, lies parched, with heart quick-shuddering,
With liver seething as in flame, the soul,
Scarce conscious, fluttering at his burning lips,
Longing for life, for water longing sore;
So was his breast one fire of torturing pain.
Then in exceeding feebleness he spake:
"O reverenced wife, turn not from me in hate
For that I left thee widowed long ago!
Not of my will I did it: the strong Fates
Dragged me to Helen--oh that I had died
Ere I embraced her--in thine arms had died!
All, by the Gods I pray, the Lords of Heaven,
By all the memories of our wedded love,
Be merciful! Banish my bitter pain:
Lay on my deadly wound those healing salves
Which only can, by Fate's decree, remove
This torment, if thou wilt. Thine heart must speak
My sentence, to be saved from death or no.
Pity me--oh, make haste to pity me!
This venom's might is swiftly bringing death!
Heal me, while life yet lingers in my limbs!
Remember not those pangs of jealousy,
Nor leave me by a cruel doom to die
Low fallen at thy feet! This should offend
The Prayers, the Daughters of the Thunderer Zeus,
Whose anger followeth unrelenting pride
With vengeance, and the Erinnys executes
Their wrath. My queen, I sinned, in folly sinned;
Yet from death save me--oh, make haste to save!"

So prayed he; but her darkly-brooding heart
Was steeled, and her words mocked his agony:
"Thou comest unto me!--thou, who didst leave

Erewhile a wailing wife in a desolate home!--
Didst leave her for thy Tyndarid darling! Go,
Lie laughing in her arms for bliss! She is better
Than thy true wife--is, rumour saith, immortal!
Make haste to kneel to her but not to me!
Weep not to me, nor whimper pitiful prayers!
Oh that mine heart beat with a tigress' strength,
That I might tear thy flesh and lap thy blood
For all the pain thy folly brought on me!
Vile wretch! where now is Love's Queen glory-crowned?
Hath Zeus forgotten his daughter's paramour?
Have them for thy deliverers! Get thee hence
Far from my dwelling, curse of Gods and men!
Yea, for through thee, thou miscreant, sorrow came
On deathless Gods, for sons and sons' sons slain.
Hence from my threshold!--to thine Helen go!
Agonize day and night beside her bed:
There whimper, pierced to the heart with cruel pangs,
Until she heal thee of thy grievous pain."

So from her doors she drave that groaning man--
Ah fool! not knowing her own doom, whose weird
Was straightway after him to tread the path
Of death! So Fate had spun her destiny-thread.

Then, as he stumbled down through Ida's brakes,
Where Doom on his death-path was leading him
Painfully halting, racked with heart-sick pain,
Hera beheld him, with rejoicing soul
Throned in the Olympian palace-court of Zeus.
And seated at her side were handmaids four
Whom radiant-faced Selene bare to the Sun
To be unwearying ministers in Heaven,

In form and office diverse each from each;
For of these Seasons one was summer's queen,
And one of winter and his stormy star,
Of spring the third, of autumn-tide the fourth.
So in four portions parted is man's year
Ruled by these Queens in turn--but of all this
Be Zeus himself the Overseer in heaven.
And of those issues now these spake with her
Which baleful Fate in her all-ruining heart
Was shaping to the birth the new espousals
Of Helen, fatal to Deiphobus--
The wrath of Helenus, who hoped in vain
For that fair bride, and how, when he had fled,
Wroth with the Trojans, to the mountain-height,
Achaea's sons would seize him and would hale
Unto their ships--how, by his counselling
Strong Tydeus' son should with Odysseus scale
The great wall, and should slay Alcathous
The temple-warder, and should bear away
Pallas the Gracious, with her free consent,
Whose image was the sure defence of Troy;--
Yea, for not even a God, how wroth soe'er,
Had power to lay the City of Priam waste
While that immortal shape stood warder there.
No man had carven that celestial form,
But Cronos' Son himself had cast it down
From heaven to Priam's gold-abounding burg.

Of these things with her handmaids did the Queen
Of Heaven hold converse, and of many such,
But Paris, while they talked, gave up the ghost
On Ida: never Helen saw him more.
Loud wailed the Nymphs around him; for they still

Remembered how their nursling wont to lisp
His childish prattle, compassed with their smiles.
And with them mourned the neatherds light of foot,
Sorrowful-hearted; moaned the mountain-glens.

Then unto travail-burdened Priam's queen
A herdman told the dread doom of her son.
Wildly her trembling heart leapt when she heard;
With failing limbs she sank to earth and wailed:
"Dead! thou dead, O dear child! Grief heaped on grief
Hast thou bequeathed me, grief eternal! Best
Of all my sons, save Hector alone, wast thou!
While beats my heart, my grief shall weep for thee.
The hand of Heaven is in our sufferings:
Some Fate devised our ruin--oh that I
Had lived not to endure it, but had died
In days of wealthy peace! But now I see
Woes upon woes, and ever look to see
Worse things--my children slain, my city sacked
And burned with fire by stony-hearted foes,
Daughters, sons' wives, all Trojan women, haled
Into captivity with our little ones!"

So wailed she; but the King heard naught thereof,
But weeping ever sat by Hector's grave,
For most of all his sons he honoured him,
His mightiest, the defender of his land.
Nothing of Paris knew that pierced heart;
But long and loud lamented Helen; yet
Those wails were but for Trojan ears; her soul
With other thoughts was busy, as she cried:
"Husband, to me, to Troy, and to thyself
A bitter blow is this thy woeful death!

In misery hast thou left me, and I look
To see calamities more deadly yet.
Oh that the Spirits of the Storm had snatched
Me from the earth when first I fared with thee
Drawn by a baleful Fate! It might not be;
The Gods have meted ruin to thee and me.
With shuddering horror all men look on me,
All hate me! Place of refuge is there none
For me; for if to the Danaan host I fly,
With torments will they greet me. If I stay,
Troy's sons and daughters here will compass me
And rend me. Earth shall cover not my corpse,
But dogs and fowl of ravin shall devour.
Oh had Fate slain me ere I saw these woes!"

So cried she: but for him far less she mourned
Than for herself, remembering her own sin.
Yea, and Troy's daughters but in semblance wailed
For him: of other woes their hearts were full.
Some thought on parents, some on husbands slain,
These on their sons, on honoured kinsmen those.

One only heart was pierced with grief unfeigned,
Oenone. Not with them of Troy she wailed,
But far away within that desolate home
Moaning she lay on her lost husband's bed.
As when the copses on high mountains stand
White-veiled with frozen snow, which o'er the glens
The west-wind blasts have strown, but now the sun
And east-wind melt it fast, and the long heights
With water-courses stream, and down the glades
Slide, as they thaw, the heavy sheets, to swell
The rushing waters of an ice-cold spring,

So melted she in tears of anguished pain,
And for her own, her husband, agonised,
And cried to her heart with miserable moans:
"Woe for my wickedness! O hateful life!
I loved mine hapless husband--dreamed with him
To pace to eld's bright threshold hand in hand,
And heart in heart! The gods ordained not so.
Oh had the black Fates snatched me from the earth
Ere I from Paris turned away in hate!
My living love hath left me!--yet will I
Dare to die with him, for I loathe the light."

So cried she, weeping, weeping piteously,
Remembering him whom death had swallowed up,
Wasting, as melteth wax before the flame
Yet secretly, being fearful lest her sire
Should mark it, or her handmaids till the night
Rose from broad Ocean, flooding all the earth
With darkness bringing men release from toil.
Then, while her father and her maidens slept,
She slid the bolts back of the outer doors,
And rushed forth like a storm-blast. Fast she ran,
As when a heifer 'mid the mountains speeds,
Her heart with passion stung, to meet her mate,
And madly races on with flying feet,
And fears not, in her frenzy of desire,
The herdman, as her wild rush bears her on,
So she but find her mate amid the woods;
So down the long tracks flew Oenone's feet;
Seeking the awful pyre, to leap thereon.
No weariness she knew: as upon wings
Her feet flew faster ever, onward spurred
By fell Fate, and the Cyprian Queen. She feared

No shaggy beast that met her in the dark
Who erst had feared them sorely--rugged rock
And precipice of tangled mountain-slope,
She trod them all unstumbling; torrent-beds
She leapt. The white Moon-goddess from on high
Looked on her, and remembered her own love,
Princely Endymion, and she pitied her
In that wild race, and, shining overhead
In her full brightness, made the long tracks plain.

Through mountain-gorges so she won to where
Wailed other Nymphs round Alexander's corpse.
Roared up about him a great wall of fire;
For from the mountains far and near had come
Shepherds, and heaped the death-bale broad and high
For love's and sorrow's latest service done
To one of old their comrade and their king.
Sore weeping stood they round. She raised no wail,
The broken-hearted, when she saw him there,
But, in her mantle muffling up her face,
Leapt on the pyre: loud wailed that multitude.
There burned she, clasping Paris. All the Nymphs
Marvelled, beholding her beside her lord
Flung down, and heart to heart spake whispering:
"Verily evil-hearted Paris was,
Who left a leal true wife, and took for bride
A wanton, to himself and Troy a curse.
Ah fool, who recked not of the broken heart
Of a most virtuous wife, who more than life
Loved him who turned from her and loved her not!"

So in their hearts the Nymphs spake: but they twain
Burned on the pyre, never to hail again

The dayspring. Wondering herdmen stood around,
As once the thronging Argives marvelling saw
Evadne clasping mid the fire her lord
Capaneus, slain by Zeus' dread thunderbolt.
But when the blast of the devouring fire
Had made twain one, Oenone and Paris, now
One little heap of ashes, then with wine
Quenched they the embers, and they laid their bones
In a wide golden vase, and round them piled
The earth-mound; and they set two pillars there
That each from other ever turn away;
For the old jealousy in the marble lives.

BOOK XI

How the sons of Troy for the last time fought from her walls and her towers.

Troy's daughters mourned within her walls; might none
Go forth to Paris' tomb, for far away
From high-built Troy it lay. But the young men
Without the city toiled unceasingly
In fight wherein from slaughter rest was none,
Though dead was Paris; for the Achaeans pressed
Hard on the Trojans even unto Troy.
Yet these charged forth--they could not choose but so,
For Strife and deadly Enyo in their midst
Stalked, like the fell Erinyes to behold,
Breathing destruction from their lips like flame.
Beside them raged the ruthless-hearted Fates
Fiercely: here Panic-fear and Ares there
Stirred up the hosts: hard after followed
Dread With slaughter's gore besprent, that in one host
Might men see, and be strong, in the other fear;
And all around were javelins, spears, and darts
Murder-athirst from this side, that side, showered.
Aye, as they hurled together, armour clashed,
As foe with foe grappled in murderous fight.

There Neoptolemus slew Laodamas,
Whom Lycia nurtured by fair Xanthus' stream,
The stream revealed to men by Leto, bride
Of Thunderer Zeus, when Lycia's stony plain
Was by her hands uptorn mid agonies
Of travail-throes wherein she brought to light
Mid bitter pangs those babes of birth divine.
Nirus upon him laid he dead; the spear
Crashed through his jaw, and clear through mouth and tongue
Passed: on the lance's irresistible point
Shrieking was he impaled: flooded with gore
His mouth was as he cried. The cruel shaft,
Sped on by that strong hand, dashed him to earth
In throes of death. Evenor next he smote
Above the flank, and onward drave the spear
Into his liver: swiftly anguished death
Came upon him. Iphition next he slew:
He quelled Hippomedon, Hippasus' bold son,
Whom Ocyone the Nymph had borne beside
Sangarius' river-flow. Ne'er welcomed she
Her son's returning face, but ruthless Fate
With anguish thrilled her of her child bereaved.

Bremon Aeneas slew, and Andromachus,
Of Cnossus this, of hallowed Lyctus that:
On one spot both from their swift chariots fell;
This gasped for breath, his throat by the long spear
Transfixed; that other, by a massy stone,
Sped from a strong hand, on the temple struck,
Breathed out his life, and black doom shrouded him.
The startled steeds, bereft of charioteers,
Fleeing, mid all those corpses were confused,

The Fall of Troy

And princely Aeneas' henchmen seized on them
With hearts exulting in the goodly spoil.

There Philoctetes with his deadly shaft
Smote Peirasus in act to flee the war:
The tendons twain behind the knee it snapped,
And palsied all his speed. A Danaan marked,
And leapt on that maimed man with sweep of sword
Shearing his neck through. On the breast of earth
The headless body fell: the head far flung
Went rolling with lips parted as to shriek;
And swiftly fleeted thence the homeless soul.

Polydamas struck down Eurymachus
And Cleon with his spear. From Syme came
With Nireus' following these: cunning were both
In craft of fisher-folk to east the hook
Baited with guile, to drop into the sea
The net, from the boat's prow with deftest hands
Swiftly and straight to plunge the three-forked spear.
But not from bane their sea-craft saved them now.

Eurypylus battle-staunch laid Hellus low,
Whom Cleito bare beside Gygaea's mere,
Cleito the fair-cheeked. Face-down in the dust
Outstretched he lay: shorn by the cruel sword
From his strong shoulder fell the arm that held
His long spear. Still its muscles twitched, as though
Fain to uplift the lance for fight in vain;
For the man's will no longer stirred therein,
But aimlessly it quivered, even as leaps
The severed tail of a snake malignant-eyed,
Which cannot chase the man who dealt the wound;

So the right hand of that strong-hearted man
With impotent grip still clutched the spear for fight.

Aenus and Polydorus Odysseus slew,
Ceteians both; this perished by his spear,
That by his sword death-dealing. Sthenelus
Smote godlike Abas with a javelin-cast:
On through his throat and shuddering nape it rushed:
Stopped were his heart-beats, all his limbs collapsed.

Tydeides slew Laodocus; Melius fell
By Agamemnon's hand; Deiphobus
Smote Alcimus and Dryas: Hippasus,
How war-renowned soe'er, Agenor slew
Far from Peneius' river. Crushed by fate,
Love's nursing-debt to parents ne'er he paid.

Lamus and stalwart Lyncus Thoas smote,
And Meriones slew Lycon; Menelaus
Laid low Archelochus. Upon his home
Looked down Corycia's ridge, and that great rock
Of the wise Fire-god, marvellous in men's eyes;
For thereon, nightlong, daylong, unto him
Fire blazes, tireless and unquenchable.
Laden with fruit around it palm-trees grow,
While mid the stones fire plays about their roots.
Gods' work is this, a wonder to all time.

By Teucer princely Hippomedon's son was slain,
Menoetes: as the archer drew on him,
Rushed he to smite him; but already hand
And eye, and bow-craft keen were aiming straight
On the arching horn the shaft. Swiftly released

It leapt on the hapless man, while sang the string.
Stricken full front he heaved one choking gasp,
Because the fates on the arrow riding flew
Right to his heart, the throne of thought and strength
For men, whence short the path is unto death.

Far from his brawny hand Euryalus hurled
A massy stone, and shook the ranks of Troy.
As when in anger against long-screaming cranes
A watcher of the field leaps from the ground,
In swift hand whirling round his head the sling,
And speeds the stone against them, scattering
Before its hum their ranks far down the wind
Outspread, and they in huddled panic dart
With wild cries this way and that, who theretofore
Swept on in ordered lines; so shrank the foe
To right and left from that dread bolt of doom
Hurled of Euryalus. Not in vain it flew
Fate-winged; it shattered Meles' helm and head
Down to the eyes: so met him ghastly death.

Still man slew man, while earth groaned all around,
As when a mighty wind scourges the land,
And this way, that way, under its shrieking blasts
Through the wide woodland bow from the roots and fall
Great trees, while all the earth is thundering round;
So fell they in the dust, so clanged their arms,
So crashed the earth around. Still hot were they
For fell fight, still dealt bane unto their foes.

Nigh to Aeneas then Apollo came,
And to Eurymachus, brave Antenor's son;
For these against the mighty Achaeans fought

Shoulder to shoulder, as two strong oxen, matched
In age, yoked to a wain; nor ever ceased
From battling. Suddenly spake the God to these
In Polymestor's shape, the seer his mother
By Xanthus bare to the Far-darter's priest:
"Eurymachus, Aeneas, seed of Gods,
'Twere shame if ye should flinch from Argives! Nay,
Not Ares' self should joy to encounter you,
An ye would face him in the fray; for Fate
Hath spun long destiny-threads for thee and thee."

He spake, and vanished, mingling with the winds.
But their hearts felt the God's power: suddenly
Flooded with boundless courage were their frames,
Maddened their spirits: on the foe they leapt
Like furious wasps that in a storm of rage
Swoop upon bees, beholding them draw nigh
In latter-summer to the mellowing grapes,
Or from their hives forth-streaming thitherward;
So fiercely leapt these sons of Troy to meet
War-hardened Greeks. The black Fates joyed to see
Their conflict, Ares laughed, Enyo yelled
Horribly. Loud their glancing armour clanged:
They stabbed, they hewed down hosts of foes untold
With irresistible hands. The reeling ranks
Fell, as the swath falls in the harvest heat,
When the swift-handed reapers, ranged adown
The field's long furrows, ply the sickle fast;
So fell before their hands ranks numberless:
With corpses earth was heaped, with torrent blood
Was streaming: Strife incarnate o'er the slain
Gloated. They paused not from the awful toil,
But aye pressed on, like lions chasing sheep.

The Fall of Troy

Then turned the Greeks to craven flight; all feet
Unmaimed as yet fled from the murderous war.
Aye followed on Anchises' warrior son,
Smiting foes' backs with his avenging spear:
On pressed Eurymachus, while glowed the heart
Of Healer Apollo watching from on high.

As when a man descries a herd of swine
Draw nigh his ripening corn, before the sheaves
Fall neath the reapers' hands, and harketh on
Against them his strong dogs; as down they rush,
The spoilers see and quake; no more think they
Of feasting, but they turn in panic flight
Huddling: fast follow at their heels the hounds
Biting remorselessly, while long and loud
Squealing they flee, and joys the harvest's lord;
So rejoiced Phoebus, seeing from the war
Fleeing the mighty Argive host. No more
Cared they for deeds of men, but cried to the Gods
For swift feet, in whose feet alone was hope
To escape Eurymachus' and Aeneas' spears
Which lightened ever all along their rear.

But one Greek, over-trusting in his strength,
Or by Fate's malice to destruction drawn,
Curbed in mid flight from war's turmoil his steed,
And strove to wheel him round into the fight
To face the foe. But fierce Agenor thrust
Ere he was ware; his two-edged partizan
Shore though his shoulder; yea, the very bone
Of that gashed arm was cloven by the steel;
The tendons parted, the veins spirted blood:
Down by his horse's neck he slid, and straight

Fell mid the dead. But still the strong arm hung
With rigid fingers locked about the reins
Like a live man's. Weird marvel was that sight,
The bloody hand down hanging from the rein,
Scaring the foes yet more, by Ares' will.
Thou hadst said, "It craveth still for horsemanship!"
So bare the steed that sign of his slain lord.

Aeneas hurled his spear; it found the waist
Of Anthalus' son, it pierced the navel through,
Dragging the inwards with it. Stretched in dust,
Clutching with agonized hands at steel and bowels,
Horribly shrieked he, tore with his teeth the earth
Groaning, till life and pain forsook the man.
Scared were the Argives, like a startled team
Of oxen 'neath the yoke-band straining hard,
What time the sharp-fanged gadfly stings their flanks
Athirst for blood, and they in frenzy of pain
Start from the furrow, and sore disquieted
The hind is for marred work, and for their sake,
Lest haply the recoiling ploughshare light
On their leg-sinews, and hamstring his team;
So were the Danaans scared, so feared for them
Achilles' son, and shouted thunder-voiced:
"Cravens, why flee, like starlings nothing-worth
Scared by a hawk that swoopeth down on them?
Come, play the men! Better it is by far
To die in war than choose unmanly flight!"

Then to his cry they hearkened, and straightway
Were of good heart. Mighty of mood he leapt
Upon the Trojans, swinging in his hand
The lightening spear: swept after him his host

Of Myrmidons with hearts swelled with the strength
Resistless of a tempest; so the Greeks
Won breathing-space. With fury like his sire's
One after other slew he of the foe.
Recoiling back they fell, as waves on-rolled
By Boreas foaming from the deep to the strand,
Are caught by another blast that whirlwind-like
Leaps, in a short lull of the north-wind, forth,
Smites them full-face, and hurls them back from the shore;
So them that erewhile on the Danaans pressed
Godlike Achilles' son now backward hurled
A short space only brave Aeneas' spirit
Let him not flee, but made him bide the fight
Fearlessly; and Enyo level held
The battle's scales. Yet not against Aeneas
Achilles' son upraised his father's spear,
But elsewhither turned his fury: in reverence
For Aphrodite, Thetis splendour-veiled
Turned from that man her mighty son's son's rage
And giant strength on other hosts of foes.
There slew he many a Trojan, while the ranks
Of Greeks were ravaged by Aeneas' hand.
Over the battle-slain the vultures joyed,
Hungry to rend the hearts and flesh of men.
But all the Nymphs were wailing, daughters born
Of Xanthus and fair-flowing Simois.

So toiled they in the fight: the wind's breath rolled
Huge dust-clouds up; the illimitable air
Was one thick haze, as with a sudden mist:
Earth disappeared, faces were blotted out;
Yet still they fought on; each man, whomso he met,
Ruthlessly slew him, though his very friend

It might be--in that turmoil none could tell
Who met him, friend or foe: blind wilderment
Enmeshed the hosts. And now had all been blent
Confusedly, had perished miserably,
All falling by their fellows' murderous swords,
Had not Cronion from Olympus helped
Their sore strait, and he swept aside the dust
Of conflict, and he calmed those deadly winds.
Yet still the hosts fought on; but lighter far
Their battle-travail was, who now discerned
Whom in the fray to smite, and whom to spare.
The Danaans now forced back the Trojan host,
The Trojans now the Danaan ranks, as swayed
The dread fight to and fro. From either side
Darts leapt and fell like snowflakes. Far away
Shepherds from Ida trembling watched the strife,
And to the Heaven-abiders lifted hands
Of supplication, praying that all their foes
Might perish, and that from the woeful war
Troy might win breathing-space, and see at last
The day of freedom: the Gods hearkened not.
Far other issues Fate devised, nor recked
Of Zeus the Almighty, nor of none beside
Of the Immortals. Her unpitying soul
Cares naught what doom she spinneth with her thread
Inevitable, be it for men new-born
Or cities: all things wax and wane through her.
So by her hest the battle-travail swelled
'Twixt Trojan chariot-lords and Greeks that closed
In grapple of fight--they dealt each other death
Ruthlessly: no man quailed, but stout of heart
Fought on; for courage thrusts men into war.

The Fall of Troy

But now when many had perished in the dust,
Then did the Argive might prevail at last
By stern decree of Pallas; for she came
Into the heart of battle, hot to help
The Greeks to lay waste Priam's glorious town.
Then Aphrodite, who lamented sore
For Paris slain, snatched suddenly away
Renowned Aeneas from the deadly strife,
And poured thick mist about him. Fate forbade
That hero any longer to contend
With Argive foes without the high-built wall.
Yea, and his mother sorely feared the wrath
Of Pallas passing-wise, whose heart was keen
To help the Danaans now--yea, feared lest she
Might slay him even beyond his doom, who spared
Not Ares' self, a mightier far than he.

No more the Trojans now abode the edge
Of fight, but all disheartened backward drew.
For like fierce ravening beasts the Argive men
Leapt on them, mad with murderous rage of war.
Choked with their slain the river-channels were,
Heaped was the field; in red dust thousands fell,
Horses and men; and chariots overturned
Were strewn there: blood was streaming all around
Like rain, for deadly Doom raged through the fray.

Men stabbed with swords, and men impaled on spears
Lay all confusedly, like scattered beams,
When on the strand of the low-thundering sea
Men from great girders of a tall ship's hull
Strike out the bolts and clamps, and scatter wide
Long planks and timbers, till the whole broad beach

Is paved with beams o'erplashed by darkling surge;
So lay in dust and blood those slaughtered men,
Rapture and pain of fight forgotten now.

A remnant from the pitiless strife escaped
Entered their stronghold, scarce eluding doom.
Children and wives from their limbs blood-besprent
Received their arms bedabbled with foul gore;
And baths for all were heated. Leeches ran
Through all the town in hot haste to the homes
Of wounded men to minister to their hurts.
Here wives and daughters moaned round men come back
From war, there cried on many who came not
Here, men stung to the soul by bitter pangs
Groaned upon beds of pain; there, toil-spent men
Turned them to supper. Whinnied the swift steeds
And neighed o'er mangers heaped. By tent and ship
Far off the Greeks did even as they of Troy.

When o'er the streams of Ocean Dawn drove up
Her splendour-flashing steeds, and earth's tribes waked,
Then the strong Argives' battle-eager sons
Marched against Priam's city lofty-towered,
Save some that mid the tents by wounded men
Tarried, lest haply raiders on the ships
Might fall, to help the Trojans, while these fought
The foe from towers, while rose the flame of war.

Before the Scaean gate fought Capaneus' son
And godlike Diomedes. High above
Deiphobus battle-staunch and strong Polites
With many comrades, stoutly held them back
With arrows and huge stones. Clanged evermore

The smitten helms and shields that fenced strong men
From bitter doom and unrelenting fate,

Before the Gate Idaean Achilles' son
Set in array the fight: around him toiled
His host of battle-cunning Myrmidons.
Helenus and Agenor gallant-souled,
Down-hailing darts, against them held the wall,
Aye cheering on their men. No spurring these
Needed to fight hard for their country's walls.

Odysseus and Eurypylus made assault
Unresting on the gates that fated the plain
And looked to the swift ships. From wall and tower
With huge stones brave Aeneas made defence.

In battle-stress by Simons Teucer toiled.
Each endured hardness at his several post.

Then round war-wise Odysseus men renowned,
By that great captain's battle cunning ruled,
Locked shields together, raised them o'er their heads
Ranged side by side, that many were made one.
Thou hadst said it was a great hall's solid roof,
Which no tempestuous wind-blast misty wet
Can pierce, nor rain from heaven in torrents poured.
So fenced about with shields firm stood the ranks
Of Argives, one in heart for fight, and one
In that array close-welded. From above
The Trojans hailed great stones; as from a rock
Rolled these to earth. Full many a spear and dart
And galling javelin in the pierced shields stood;
Some in the earth stood; many glanced away

With bent points falling baffled from the shields
Battered on all sides. But that clangorous din
None feared; none flinched; as pattering drops of rain
They heard it. Up to the rampart's foot they marched:
None hung back; shoulder to shoulder on they came
Like a long lurid cloud that o'er the sky
Cronion trails in wild midwinter-tide.
On that battalion moved, with thunderous tread
Of tramping feet: a little above the earth
Rose up the dust; the breeze swept it aside
Drifting away behind the men. There went
A sound confused of voices with them, like
The hum of bees that murmur round the hives,
And multitudinous panting, and the gasp
Of men hard-breathing. Exceeding glad the sons
Of Atreus, glorying in them, saw that wall
Unwavering of doom-denouncing war.
In one dense mass against the city-gate
They hurled themselves, with twibills strove to breach
The long walls, from their hinges to upheave
The gates, and dash to earth. The pulse of hope
Beat strong in those proud hearts. But naught availed
Targes nor levers, when Aeneas' might
Swung in his hands a stone like a thunderbolt,
Hurled it with uttermost strength, and dashed to death
All whom it caught beneath the shields, as when
A mountain's precipice-edge breaks off and falls
On pasturing goats, and all that graze thereby
Tremble; so were those Danaans dazed with dread.
Stone after stone he hurled on the reeling ranks,
As when amid the hills Olympian Zeus
With thunderbolts and blazing lightnings rends
From their foundations crags that rim a peak,

And this way, that way, sends them hurtling down;
Then the flocks tremble, scattering in wild flight;
So quailed the Achaeans, when Aeneas dashed
To sudden fragments all that battle-wall
Moulded of adamant shields, because a God
Gave more than human strength. No man of them
Could lift his eyes unto him in that fight,
Because the arms that lapped his sinewy limbs
Flashed like the heaven-born lightnings. At his side
Stood, all his form divine in darkness cloaked,
Ares the terrible, and winged the flight
Of what bare down to the Argives doom or dread.
He fought as when Olympian Zeus himself
From heaven in wrath smote down the insolent bands
Of giants grim, and shook the boundless earth,
And sea, and ocean, and the heavens, when reeled
The knees of Atlas neath the rush of Zeus.
So crumbled down beneath Aeneas' bolts
The Argive squadrons. All along the wall
Wroth with the foeman rushed he: from his hands
Whatso he lighted on in onslaught-haste
Hurled he; for many a battle-staying bolt
Lay on the walls of those staunch Dardan men.
With such Aeneas stormed in giant might,
With such drave back the thronging foes. All round
The Trojans played the men. Sore travail and pain
Had all folk round the city: many fell,
Argives and Trojans. Rang the battle-cries:
Aeneas cheered the war-fain Trojans on
To fight for home, for wives, and their own souls
With a good heart: war-staunch Achilles' son
Shouted: "Flinch not, ye Argives, from the walls,
Till Troy be taken, and sink down in flames!"

And round these twain an awful measureless roar
Rang, daylong as they fought: no breathing-space
Came from the war to them whose spirits burned,
These, to smite Ilium, those, to guard her safe.

But from Aeneas valiant-souled afar
Fought Aias, speeding midst the men of Troy
Winged death; for now his arrow straight through air
Flew, now his deadly dart, and smote them down
One after one: yet others cowered away
Before his peerless prowess, and abode
The fight no more, but fenceless left the wall

Then one, of all the Locrians mightiest,
Fierce-souled Alcimedon, trusting in his prince
And his own might and valour of his youth,
All battle-eager on a ladder set
Swift feet, to pave for friends a death-strewn path
Into the town. Above his head he raised

The screening shield; up that dread path he went
Hardening his heart from trembling, in his hand
Now shook the threatening spear, now upward climbed
Fast high in air he trod the perilous way.
Now on the Trojans had disaster come,
But, even as above the parapet
His head rose, and for the first time and the last
From her high rampart he looked down on Troy,
Aeneas, who had marked, albeit afar,
That bold assault, rushed on him, dashed on his head
So huge a stone that the hero's mighty strength
Shattered the ladder. Down from on high he rushed
As arrow from the string: death followed him

As whirling round he fell; with air was blent
His lost life, ere he crashed to the stony ground.
Strong spear, broad shield, in mid fall flew from his hands,
And from his head the helm: his corslet came
Alone with him to earth. The Locrian men
Groaned, seeing their champion quelled by evil doom;
For all his hair and all the stones around
Were brain-bespattered: all his bones were crushed,
And his once active limbs besprent with gore.

Then godlike Poeas' war-triumphant son
Marked where Aeneas stormed along the wall
In lion-like strength, and straightway shot a shaft
Aimed at that glorious hero, neither missed
The man: yet not through his unyielding targe
To the fair flesh it won, being turned aside
By Cytherea and the shield, but grazed
The buckler lightly: yet not all in vain
Fell earthward, but between the targe and helm
Smote Medon: from the tower he fell, as falls
A wild goat from a crag, the hunter's shaft
Deep in its heart: so nerveless-flung he fell,
And fled away from him the precious life.
Wroth for his friend, a stone Aeneas hurled,
And Philoctetes' stalwart comrade slew,
Toxaechmes; for he shattered his head and crushed
Helmet and skull-bones; and his noble heart
Was stilled. Loud shouted princely Poeas' son:
"Aeneas, thou, forsooth, dost deem thyself
A mighty champion, fighting from a tower
Whence craven women war with foes! Now if
Thou be a man, come forth without the wall
In battle-harness, and so learn to know

In spear-craft and in bow-craft Poeas' son!"

So cried he; but Anchises' valiant seed,
How fain soe'er, naught answered, for the stress
Of desperate conflict round that wall and burg
Ceaselessly raging: pause from fight was none:
Yea, for long time no respite had there been
For the war-weary from that endless toil.

BOOK XII

How the Wooden Horse was fashioned, and brought into Troy by her people.

When round the walls of Troy the Danaan host
Had borne much travail, and yet the end was not,
By Calchas then assembled were the chiefs;
For his heart was instructed by the hests
Of Phoebus, by the flights of birds, the stars,
And all the signs that speak to men the will
Of Heaven; so he to that assembly cried:
"No longer toil in leaguer of yon walls;
Some other counsel let your hearts devise,
Some stratagem to help the host and us.
For here but yesterday I saw a sign:
A falcon chased a dove, and she, hard pressed,
Entered a cleft of the rock; and chafing he
Tarried long time hard by that rift, but she
Abode in covert. Nursing still his wrath,
He hid him in a bush. Forth darted she,
In folly deeming him afar: he swooped,
And to the hapless dove dealt wretched death.
Therefore by force essay we not to smite Troy,
but let cunning stratagem avail."

He spake; but no man's wit might find a way
To escape their grievous travail, as they sought
To find a remedy, till Laertes' son
Discerned it of his wisdom, and he spake:
"Friend, in high honour held of the Heavenly Ones,
If doomed it be indeed that Priam's burg
By guile must fall before the war-worn Greeks,
A great Horse let us fashion, in the which
Our mightiest shall take ambush. Let the host
Burn all their tents, and sail from hence away
To Tenedos; so the Trojans, from their towers
Gazing, shall stream forth fearless to the plain.
Let some brave man, unknown of any in Troy,
With a stout heart abide without the Horse,
Crouching beneath its shadow, who shall say:
"`Achaea's lords of might, exceeding fain
Safe to win home, made this their offering
For safe return, an image to appease
The wrath of Pallas for her image stolen
From Troy.' And to this story shall he stand,
How long soe'er they question him, until,
Though never so relentless, they believe,
And drag it, their own doom, within the town.
Then shall war's signal unto us be given--
To them at sea, by sudden flash of torch,
To the ambush, by the cry, `Come forth the Horse!'
When unsuspecting sleep the sons of Troy."

He spake, and all men praised him: most of all
Extolled him Calchas, that such marvellous guile
He put into the Achaeans' hearts, to be
For them assurance of triumph, but for Troy
Ruin; and to those battle-lords he cried:

The Fall of Troy

"Let your hearts seek none other stratagem,
Friends; to war-strong Odysseus' rede give ear.
His wise thought shall not miss accomplishment.
Yea, our desire even now the Gods fulfil.
Hark! for new tokens come from the Unseen!
Lo, there on high crash through the firmament
Zeus' thunder and lightning! See, where birds to right
Dart past, and scream with long-resounding cry!
Go to, no more in endless leaguer of Troy
Linger we. Hard necessity fills the foe
With desperate courage that makes cowards brave;
For then are men most dangerous, when they stake
Their lives in utter recklessness of death,
As battle now the aweless sons of Troy
All round their burg, mad with the lust of fight."

But cried Achilles' battle-eager son:
"Calchas, brave men meet face to face their foes!
Who skulk behind their walls, and fight from towers,
Are nidderings, hearts palsied with base fear.
Hence with all thought of wile and stratagem!
The great war-travail of the spear beseems
True heroes. Best in battle are the brave."

But answer made to him Laertes' seed:
"Bold-hearted child of aweless Aeacus' son,
This as beseems a hero princely and brave,
Dauntlessly trusting in thy strength, thou say'st.
Yet thine invincible sire's unquailing might
Availed not to smite Priam's wealthy burg,
Nor we, for all our travail. Nay, with speed,
As counselleth Calchas, go we to the ships,
And fashion we the Horse by Epeius' hands,

Who in the woodwright's craft is chiefest far
Of Argives, for Athena taught his lore."

Then all their mightiest men gave ear to him
Save twain, fierce-hearted Neoptolemus
And Philoctetes mighty-souled; for these
Still were insatiate for the bitter fray,
Still longed for turmoil of the fight. They bade
Their own folk bear against that giant wall
What things soe'er for war's assaults avail,
In hope to lay that stately fortress low,
Seeing Heaven's decrees had brought them both to war.
Yea, they had haply accomplished all their will,
But from the sky Zeus showed his wrath; he shook
The earth beneath their feet, and all the air
Shuddered, as down before those heroes twain
He hurled his thunderbolt: wide echoes crashed
Through all Dardania. Unto fear straightway
Turned were their bold hearts: they forgat their might,
And Calchas' counsels grudgingly obeyed.
So with the Argives came they to the ships
In reverence for the seer who spake from Zeus
Or Phoebus, and they obeyed him utterly.

What time round splendour-kindled heavens the stars
From east to west far-flashing wheel, and when
Man doth forget his toil, in that still hour
Athena left the high mansions of the Blest,
Clothed her in shape of a maiden tender-fleshed,
And came to ships and host. Over the head
Of brave Epeius stood she in his dream,
And bade him build a Horse of tree: herself
Would labour in his labour, and herself

Stand by his side, to the work enkindling him.
Hearing the Goddess' word, with a glad laugh
Leapt he from careless sleep: right well he knew
The Immortal One celestial. Now his heart
Could hold no thought beside; his mind was fixed
Upon the wondrous work, and through his soul
Marched marshalled each device of craftsmanship.

When rose the dawn, and thrust back kindly night
To Erebus, and through the firmament streamed
Glad glory, then Epeius told his dream
To eager Argives--all he saw and heard;
And hearkening joyed they with exceeding joy.
Straightway to tall-tressed Ida's leafy glades
The sons of Atreus sent swift messengers.
These laid the axe unto the forest-pines,
And hewed the great trees: to their smiting rang
The echoing glens. On those far-stretching hills
All bare of undergrowth the high peaks rose:
Open their glades were, not, as in time past,
Haunted of beasts: there dry the tree-trunks rose
Wooing the winds. Even these the Achaeans hewed
With axes, and in haste they bare them down
From those shagged mountain heights to Hellespont's shores.
Strained with a strenuous spirit at the work
Young men and mules; and all the people toiled
Each at his task obeying Epeius's hest.
For with the keen steel some were hewing beams,
Some measuring planks, and some with axes lopped
Branches away from trunks as yet unsawn:
Each wrought his several work. Epeius first
Fashioned the feet of that great Horse of Wood:
The belly next he shaped, and over this

Moulded the back and the great loins behind,
The throat in front, and ridged the towering neck
With waving mane: the crested head he wrought,
The streaming tail, the ears, the lucent eyes--
All that of lifelike horses have. So grew
Like a live thing that more than human work,
For a God gave to a man that wondrous craft.
And in three days, by Pallas's decree,
Finished was all. Rejoiced thereat the host
Of Argos, marvelling how the wood expressed
Mettle, and speed of foot--yea, seemed to neigh.
Godlike Epeius then uplifted hands
To Pallas, and for that huge Horse he prayed:
"Hear, great-souled Goddess: bless thine Horse and me!"
He spake: Athena rich in counsel heard,
And made his work a marvel to all men
Which saw, or heard its fame in days to be.

But while the Danaans o'er Epeius' work
Joyed, and their routed foes within the walls
Tarried, and shrank from death and pitiless doom,
Then, when imperious Zeus far from the Gods
Had gone to Ocean's streams and Tethys' caves,
Strife rose between the Immortals: heart with heart
Was set at variance. Riding on the blasts
Of winds, from heaven to earth they swooped: the air
Crashed round them. Lighting down by Xanthus' stream
Arrayed they stood against each other, these
For the Achaeans, for the Trojans those;
And all their souls were thrilled with lust of war:
There gathered too the Lords of the wide Sea.
These in their wrath were eager to destroy
The Horse of Guile and all the ships, and those

The Fall of Troy

Fair Ilium. But all-contriving Fate
Held them therefrom, and turned their hearts to strife
Against each other. Ares to the fray
Rose first, and on Athena rushed. Thereat
Fell each on other: clashed around their limbs
The golden arms celestial as they charged.
Round them the wide sea thundered, the dark earth
Quaked 'neath immortal feet. Rang from them all
Far-pealing battle-shouts; that awful cry
Rolled up to the broad-arching heaven, and down
Even to Hades' fathomless abyss:
Trembled the Titans there in depths of gloom.
Ida's long ridges sighed, sobbed clamorous streams
Of ever-flowing rivers, groaned ravines
Far-furrowed, Argive ships, and Priam's towers.
Yet men feared not, for naught they knew of all
That strife, by Heaven's decree. Then her high peaks
The Gods' hands wrenched from Ida's crest, and hurled
Against each other: but like crumbling sands
Shivered they fell round those invincible limbs,
Shattered to small dust. But the mind of Zeus,
At the utmost verge of earth, was ware of all:
Straight left he Ocean's stream, and to wide heaven
Ascended, charioted upon the winds,
The East, the North, the West-wind, and the South:
For Iris rainbow-plumed led 'neath the yoke
Of his eternal car that stormy team,
The car which Time the immortal framed for him
Of adamant with never-wearying hands.
So came he to Olympus' giant ridge.
His wrath shook all the firmament, as crashed
From east to west his thunders; lightnings gleamed,
As thick and fast his thunderbolts poured to earth,

And flamed the limitless welkin. Terror fell
Upon the hearts of those Immortals: quaked
The limbs of all--ay, deathless though they were!
Then Themis, trembling for them, swift as thought
Leapt down through clouds, and came with speed to them--
For in the strife she only had no part
And stood between the fighters, and she cried:
"Forbear the conflict! O, when Zeus is wroth,
It ill beseems that everlasting Gods
Should fight for men's sake, creatures of a day:
Else shall ye be all suddenly destroyed;
For Zeus will tear up all the hills, and hurl
Upon you: sons nor daughters will he spare,
But bury 'neath one ruin of shattered earth
All. No escape shall ye find thence to light,
In horror of darkness prisoned evermore."

Dreading Zeus' menace gave they heed to her,
From strife refrained, and cast away their wrath,
And were made one in peace and amity.
Some heavenward soared, some plunged into the sea,
On earth stayed some. Amid the Achaean host
Spake in his subtlety Laertes' son:
"O valorous-hearted lords of the Argive host,
Now prove in time of need what men ye be,
How passing-strong, how flawless-brave! The hour
Is this for desperate emprise: now, with hearts
Heroic, enter ye yon carven horse,
So to attain the goal of this stern war.
For better it is by stratagem and craft
Now to destroy this city, for whose sake
Hither we came, and still are suffering
Many afflictions far from our own land.

Come then, and let your hearts be stout and strong
For he who in stress of fight hath turned to bay
And snatched a desperate courage from despair,
Oft, though the weaker, slays a mightier foe.
For courage, which is all men's glory, makes
The heart great. Come then, set the ambush, ye
Which be our mightiest, and the rest shall go
To Tenedos' hallowed burg, and there abide
Until our foes have haled within their walls
Us with the Horse, as deeming that they bring
A gift unto Tritonis. Some brave man,
One whom the Trojans know not, yet we lack,
To harden his heart as steel, and to abide
Near by the Horse. Let that man bear in mind
Heedfully whatsoe'er I said erewhile.
And let none other thought be in his heart,
Lest to the foe our counsel be revealed."

Then, when all others feared, a man far-famed
Made answer, Sinon, marked of destiny
To bring the great work to accomplishment.
Therefore with worship all men looked on him,
The loyal of heart, as in the midst he spake:
"Odysseus, and all ye Achaean chiefs,
This work for which ye crave will I perform--
Yea, though they torture me, though into fire
Living they thrust me; for mine heart is fixed
Not to escape, but die by hands of foes,
Except I crown with glory your desire."

Stoutly he spake: right glad the Argives were;
And one said: "How the Gods have given to-day
High courage to this man! He hath not been

Heretofore valiant. Heaven is kindling him
To be the Trojans' ruin, but to us
Salvation. Now full soon, I trow, we reach
The goal of grievous war, so long unseen."

So a voice murmured mid the Achaean host.
Then, to stir up the heroes, Nestor cried:
"Now is the time, dear sons, for courage and strength:
Now do the Gods bring nigh the end of toil:
Now give they victory to our longing hands.
Come, bravely enter ye this cavernous Horse.
For high renown attendeth courage high.
Oh that my limbs were mighty as of old,
When Aeson's son for heroes called, to man
Swift Argo, when of the heroes foremost I
Would gladly have entered her, but Pelias
The king withheld me in my own despite.
Ah me, but now the burden of years--O nay,
As I were young, into the Horse will I
Fearlessly! Glory and strength shall courage give."

Answered him golden-haired Achilles' son:
"Nestor, in wisdom art thou chief of men;
But cruel age hath caught thee in his grip:
No more thy strength may match thy gallant will;
Therefore thou needs must unto Tenedos' strand.
We will take ambush, we the youths, of strife
Insatiate still, as thou, old sire, dost bid."

Then strode the son of Neleus to his side,
And kissed his hands, and kissed the head of him
Who offered thus himself the first of all
To enter that huge horse, being peril-fain,

And bade the elder of days abide without.
Then to the battle-eager spake the old:
"Thy father's son art thou! Achilles' might
And chivalrous speech be here! O, sure am I
That by thine hands the Argives shall destroy
The stately city of Priam. At the last,
After long travail, glory shall be ours,
Ours, after toil and tribulation of war;
The Gods have laid tribulation at men's feet
But happiness far off, and toil between:
Therefore for men full easy is the path
To ruin, and the path to fame is hard,
Where feet must press right on through painful toil."

He spake: replied Achilles' glorious son:
"Old sire, as thine heart trusteth, be it vouchsafed
In answer to our prayers; for best were this:
But if the Gods will otherwise, be it so.
Ay, gladlier would I fall with glory in fight
Than flee from Troy, bowed 'neath a load of shame."

Then in his sire's celestial arms he arrayed
His shoulders; and with speed in harness sheathed
Stood the most mighty heroes, in whose healers
Was dauntless spirit. Tell, ye Queens of Song,
Now man by man the names of all that passed
Into the cavernous Horse; for ye inspired
My soul with all my song, long ere my cheek
Grew dark with manhood's beard, what time I fed
My goodly sheep on Smyrna's pasture-lea,
From Hermus thrice so far as one may hear
A man's shout, by the fane of Artemis,
In the Deliverer's Grove, upon a hill

Neither exceeding low nor passing high.

Into that cavernous Horse Achilles' son
First entered, strong Menelaus followed then,
Odysseus, Sthenelus, godlike Diomede,
Philoctetes and Menestheus, Anticlus,
Thoas and Polypoetes golden-haired,
Aias, Eurypylus, godlike Thrasymede,
Idomeneus, Meriones, far-famed twain,
Podaleirius of spears, Eurymachus,
Teucer the godlike, fierce Ialmenus,
Thalpius, Antimachus, Leonteus staunch,
Eumelus, and Euryalus fair as a God,
Amphimachus, Demophoon, Agapenor,
Akamas, Meges stalwart Phyleus' son--
Yea, more, even all their chiefest, entered in,
So many as that carven Horse could hold.
Godlike Epeius last of all passed in,
The fashioner of the Horse; in his breast lay
The secret of the opening of its doors
And of their closing: therefore last of all
He entered, and he drew the ladders up
Whereby they clomb: then made he all secure,
And set himself beside the bolt. So all
In silence sat 'twixt victory and death.

But the rest fired the tents, wherein erewhile
They slept, and sailed the wide sea in their ships.
Two mighty-hearted captains ordered these,
Nestor and Agamemnon lord of spears.
Fain had they also entered that great Horse,
But all the host withheld them, bidding stay
With them a-shipboard, ordering their array:

For men far better work the works of war
When their kings oversee them; therefore these
Abode without, albeit mighty men.
So came they swiftly unto Tenedos' shore,
And dropped the anchor-stones, then leapt in haste
Forth of the ships, and silent waited there
Keen-watching till the signal-torch should flash.

But nigh the foe were they in the Horse, and now
Looked they for death, and now to smite the town;
And on their hopes and fears uprose the dawn.

Then marked the Trojans upon Hellespont's strand
The smoke upleaping yet through air: no more
Saw they the ships which brought to them from Greece
Destruction dire. With joy to the shore they ran,
But armed them first, for fear still haunted them
Then marked they that fair-carven Horse, and stood
Marvelling round, for a mighty work was there.
A hapless-seeming man thereby they spied,
Sinon; and this one, that one questioned him
Touching the Danaans, as in a great ring
They compassed him, and with unangry words
First questioned, then with terrible threatenings.
Then tortured they that man of guileful soul
Long time unceasing. Firm as a rock abode
The unquivering limbs, the unconquerable will.
His ears, his nose, at last they shore away
In every wise tormenting him, until
He should declare the truth, whither were gone
The Danaans in their ships, what thing the Horse
Concealed within it. He had armed his mind
With resolution, and of outrage foul

Recked not; his soul endured their cruel stripes,
Yea, and the bitter torment of the fire;
For strong endurance into him Hera breathed;
And still he told them the same guileful tale:
"The Argives in their ships flee oversea
Weary of tribulation of endless war.
This horse by Calchas' counsel fashioned they
For wise Athena, to propitiate
Her stern wrath for that guardian image stol'n
From Troy. And by Odysseus' prompting I
Was marked for slaughter, to be sacrificed
To the sea-powers, beside the moaning waves,
To win them safe return. But their intent
I marked; and ere they spilt the drops of wine,
And sprinkled hallowed meal upon mine head,
Swiftly I fled, and, by the help of Heaven,
I flung me down, clasping the Horse's feet;
And they, sore loth, perforce must leave me there
Dreading great Zeus's daughter mighty-souled."

In subtlety so he spake, his soul untamed
By pain; for a brave man's part is to endure
To the uttermost. And of the Trojans some
Believed him, others for a wily knave
Held him, of whose mind was Laocoon.
Wisely he spake: "A deadly fraud is this,"
He said, "devised by the Achaean chiefs!"
And cried to all straightway to burn the Horse,
And know if aught within its timbers lurked.

Yea, and they had obeyed him, and had 'scaped
Destruction; but Athena, fiercely wroth
With him, the Trojans, and their city, shook

The Fall of Troy

Earth's deep foundations 'neath Laocoon's feet.
Straight terror fell on him, and trembling bowed
The knees of the presumptuous: round his head
Horror of darkness poured; a sharp pang thrilled
His eyelids; swam his eyes beneath his brows;
His eyeballs, stabbed with bitter anguish, throbbed
Even from the roots, and rolled in frenzy of pain.
Clear through his brain the bitter torment pierced
Even to the filmy inner veil thereof;
Now bloodshot were his eyes, now ghastly green;
Anon with rheum they ran, as pours a stream
Down from a rugged crag, with thawing snow
Made turbid. As a man distraught he seemed:
All things he saw showed double, and he groaned
Fearfully; yet he ceased not to exhort
The men of Troy, and recked not of his pain.
Then did the Goddess strike him utterly blind.
Stared his fixed eyeballs white from pits of blood;
And all folk groaned for pity of their friend,
And dread of the Prey-giver, lest he had sinned
In folly against her, and his mind was thus
Warped to destruction yea, lest on themselves
Like judgment should be visited, to avenge
The outrage done to hapless Sinon's flesh,
Whereby they hoped to wring the truth from him.
So led they him in friendly wise to Troy,
Pitying him at the last. Then gathered all,
And o'er that huge Horse hastily cast a rope,
And made it fast above; for under its feet
Smooth wooden rollers had Epeius laid,
That, dragged by Trojan hands, it might glide on
Into their fortress. One and all they haled
With multitudinous tug and strain, as when

Down to the sea young men sore-labouring drag
A ship; hard-crushed the stubborn rollers groan,
As, sliding with weird shrieks, the keel descends
Into the sea-surge; so that host with toil
Dragged up unto their city their own doom,
Epeius' work. With great festoons of flowers
They hung it, and their own heads did they wreathe,
While answering each other pealed the flutes.
Grimly Enyo laughed, seeing the end
Of that dire war; Hera rejoiced on high;
Glad was Athena. When the Trojans came
Unto their city, brake they down the walls,
Their city's coronal, that the Horse of Death
Might be led in. Troy's daughters greeted it
With shouts of salutation; marvelling all
Gazed at the mighty work where lurked their doom.

But still Laocoon ceased not to exhort
His countrymen to burn the Horse with fire:
They would not hear, for dread of the Gods' wrath.
But then a yet more hideous punishment
Athena visited on his hapless sons.
A cave there was, beneath a rugged cliff
Exceeding high, unscalable, wherein
Dwelt fearful monsters of the deadly brood
Of Typhon, in the rock-clefts of the isle
Calydna that looks Troyward from the sea.
Thence stirred she up the strength of serpents twain,
And summoned them to Troy. By her uproused
They shook the island as with earthquake: roared
The sea; the waves disparted as they came.
Onward they swept with fearful-flickering tongues:
Shuddered the very monsters of the deep:

Xanthus' and Simois' daughters moaned aloud,
The River-nymphs: the Cyprian Queen looked down
In anguish from Olympus. Swiftly they came
Whither the Goddess sped them: with grim jaws
Whetting their deadly fangs, on his hapless sons
Sprang they. All Trojans panic-stricken fled,
Seeing those fearsome dragons in their town.
No man, though ne'er so dauntless theretofore,
Dared tarry; ghastly dread laid hold on all
Shrinking in horror from the monsters. Screamed
The women; yea, the mother forgat her child,
Fear-frenzied as she fled: all Troy became
One shriek of fleers, one huddle of jostling limbs:
The streets were choked with cowering fugitives.
Alone was left Laocoon with his sons,
For death's doom and the Goddess chained their feet.
Then, even as from destruction shrank the lads,
Those deadly fangs had seized and ravined up
The twain, outstretching to their sightless sire
Agonized hands: no power to help had he.
Trojans far off looked on from every side
Weeping, all dazed. And, having now fulfilled
Upon the Trojans Pallas' awful hest,
Those monsters vanished 'neath the earth; and still
Stands their memorial, where into the fane
They entered of Apollo in Pergamus
The hallowed. Therebefore the sons of Troy
Gathered, and reared a cenotaph for those
Who miserably had perished. Over it
Their father from his blind eyes rained the tears:
Over the empty tomb their mother shrieked,
Boding the while yet worse things, wailing o'er
The ruin wrought by folly of her lord,

Dreading the anger of the Blessed Ones.
As when around her void nest in a brake
In sorest anguish moans the nightingale
Whose fledglings, ere they learned her plaintive song,
A hideous serpent's fangs have done to death,
And left the mother anguish, endless woe,
And bootless crying round her desolate home;
So groaned she for her children's wretched death,
So moaned she o'er the void tomb; and her pangs
Were sharpened by her lord's plight stricken blind.

While she for children and for husband moaned--
These slain, he of the sun's light portionless--
The Trojans to the Immortals sacrificed,
Pouring the wine. Their hearts beat high with hope
To escape the weary stress of woeful war.
Howbeit the victims burned not, and the flames
Died out, as though 'neath heavy-hissing rain;
And writhed the smoke-wreaths blood-red, and the thighs
Quivering from crumbling altars fell to earth.
Drink-offerings turned to blood, Gods' statues wept,
And temple-walls dripped gore: along them rolled
Echoes of groaning out of depths unseen;
And all the long walls shuddered: from the towers
Came quick sharp sounds like cries of men in pain;
And, weirdly shrieking, of themselves slid back
The gate-bolts. Screaming "Desolation!" wailed
The birds of night. Above that God-built burg
A mist palled every star; and yet no cloud
Was in the flashing heavens. By Phoebus' fane
Withered the bays that erst were lush and green.
Wolves and foul-feeding jackals came and howled
Within the gates. Ay, other signs untold

The Fall of Troy

Appeared, portending woe to Dardanus' sons
And Troy: yet no fear touched the Trojans' hearts
Who saw all through the town those portents dire:
Fate crazed them all, that midst their revelling
Slain by their foes they might fill up their doom.

One heart was steadfast, and one soul clear-eyed,
Cassandra. Never her words were unfulfilled;
Yet was their utter truth, by Fate's decree,
Ever as idle wind in the hearers' ears,
That no bar to Troy's ruin might be set.
She saw those evil portents all through Troy
Conspiring to one end; loud rang her cry,
As roars a lioness that mid the brakes
A hunter has stabbed or shot, whereat her heart
Maddens, and down the long hills rolls her roar,
And her might waxes tenfold; so with heart
Aflame with prophecy came she forth her bower.
Over her snowy shoulders tossed her hair
Streaming far down, and wildly blazed her eyes.
Her neck writhed, like a sapling in the wind
Shaken, as moaned and shrieked that noble maid:
"O wretches! into the Land of Darkness now
We are passing; for all round us full of fire
And blood and dismal moan the city is.
Everywhere portents of calamity
Gods show: destruction yawns before your feet.
Fools! ye know not your doom: still ye rejoice
With one consent in madness, who to Troy
Have brought the Argive Horse where ruin lurks!
Oh, ye believe not me, though ne'er so loud
I cry! The Erinyes and the ruthless Fates,
For Helen's spousals madly wroth, through Troy

Dart on wild wings. And ye, ye are banqueting there
In your last feast, on meats befouled with gore,
When now your feet are on the Path of Ghosts!"

Then cried a scoffing voice an ominous word:
"Why doth a raving tongue of evil speech,
Daughter of Priam, make thy lips to cry
Words empty as wind? No maiden modesty
With purity veils thee: thou art compassed round
With ruinous madness; therefore all men scorn
Thee, babbler! Hence, thine evil bodings speak
To the Argives and thyself! For thee doth wait
Anguish and shame yet bitterer than befell
Presumptuous Laocoon. Shame it were
In folly to destroy the Immortals' gift."

So scoffed a Trojan: others in like sort
Cried shame on her, and said she spake but lies,
Saying that ruin and Fate's heavy stroke
Were hard at hand. They knew not their own doom,
And mocked, and thrust her back from that huge Horse
For fain she was to smite its beams apart,
Or burn with ravening fire. She snatched a brand
Of blazing pine-wood from the hearth and ran
In fury: in the other hand she bare
A two-edged halberd: on that Horse of Doom
She rushed, to cause the Trojans to behold
With their own eyes the ambush hidden there.
But straightway from her hands they plucked and flung
Afar the fire and steel, and careless turned
To the feast; for darkened o'er them their last night.
Within the horse the Argives joyed to hear
The uproar of Troy's feasters setting at naught

Cassandra, but they marvelled that she knew
So well the Achaeans' purpose and device.

As mid the hills a furious pantheress,
Which from the steading hounds and shepherd-folk
Drive with fierce rush, with savage heart turns back
Even in departing, galled albeit by darts:
So from the great Horse fled she, anguish-racked
For Troy, for all the ruin she foreknew.

BOOK XIII

How Troy in the night was taken and sacked with fire and slaughter.

So feasted they through Troy, and in their midst
Loud pealed the flutes and pipes: on every hand
Were song and dance, laughter and cries confused
Of banqueters beside the meats and wine.
They, lifting in their hands the beakers brimmed,
Recklessly drank, till heavy of brain they grew,
Till rolled their fluctuant eyes. Now and again
Some mouth would babble the drunkard's broken words.
The household gear, the very roof and walls
Seemed as they rocked: all things they looked on seemed
Whirled in wild dance. About their eyes a veil
Of mist dropped, for the drunkard's sight is dimmed,
And the wit dulled, when rise the fumes to the brain:
And thus a heavy-headed feaster cried:
"For naught the Danaans mustered that great host
Hither! Fools, they have wrought not their intent,
But with hopes unaccomplished from our town
Like silly boys or women have they fled."

So cried a Trojan wit-befogged with wine,
Fool, nor discerned destruction at the doors.

The Fall of Troy

When sleep had locked his fetters everywhere
Through Troy on folk fulfilled of wine and meat,
Then Sinon lifted high a blazing torch
To show the Argive men the splendour of fire.
But fearfully the while his heart beat, lest
The men of Troy might see it, and the plot
Be suddenly revealed. But on their beds
Sleeping their last sleep lay they, heavy with wine.
The host saw, and from Tenedos set sail.

Then nigh the Horse drew Sinon: softly he called,
Full softly, that no man of Troy might hear,
But only Achaea's chiefs, far from whose eyes
Sleep hovered, so athirst were they for fight.
They heard, and to Odysseus all inclined
Their ears: he bade them urgently go forth
Softly and fearlessly; and they obeyed
That battle-summons, pressing in hot haste
To leap to earth: but in his subtlety
He stayed them from all thrusting eagerly forth.
But first himself with swift unfaltering hands,
Helped of Epeius, here and there unbarred
The ribs of the Horse of beams: above the planks
A little he raised his head, and gazed around
On all sides, if he haply might descry
One Trojan waking yet. As when a wolf,
With hunger stung to the heart, comes from the hills,
And ravenous for flesh draws nigh the flock
Penned in the wide fold, slinking past the men
And dogs that watch, all keen to ward the sheep,
Then o'er the fold-wall leaps with soundless feet;
So stole Odysseus down from the Horse: with him
Followed the war-fain lords of Hellas' League,

Orderly stepping down the ladders, which
Epeius framed for paths of mighty men,
For entering and for passing forth the Horse,
Who down them now on this side, that side, streamed
As fearless wasps startled by stroke of axe
In angry mood pour all together forth
From the tree-bole, at sound of woodman's blow;
So battle-kindled forth the Horse they poured
Into the midst of that strong city of Troy
With hearts that leapt expectant. [With swift hands
Snatched they the brands from dying hearths, and fired
Temple and palace. Onward then to the gates
Sped they,] and swiftly slew the slumbering guards,
[Then held the gate-towers till their friends should come.]
Fast rowed the host the while; on swept the ships
Over the great flood: Thetis made their paths
Straight, and behind them sent a driving wind
Speeding them, and the hearts Achaean glowed.
Swiftly to Hellespont's shore they came, and there
Beached they the keels again, and deftly dealt
With whatso tackling appertains to ships.
Then leapt they aland, and hasted on to Troy
Silent as sheep that hurry to the fold
From woodland pasture on an autumn eve;
So without sound of voices marched they on
Unto the Trojans' fortress, eager all
To help those mighty chiefs with foes begirt.
Now these--as famished wolves fierce-glaring round
Fall on a fold mid the long forest-hills,
While sleeps the toil-worn watchman, and they rend
The sheep on every hand within the wall
In darkness, and all round [are heaped the slain;
So these within the city smote and slew,

As swarmed the awakened foe around them; yet,
Fast as they slew, aye faster closed on them
Those thousands, mad to thrust them from the gates.]
Slipping in blood and stumbling o'er the dead
[Their line reeled,] and destruction loomed o'er them,
Though Danaan thousands near and nearer drew.

But when the whole host reached the walls of Troy,
Into the city of Priam, breathing rage
Of fight, with reckless battle-lust they poured;
And all that fortress found they full of war
And slaughter, palaces, temples, horribly
Blazing on all sides; glowed their hearts with joy.
In deadly mood then charged they on the foe.
Ares and fell Enyo maddened there:
Blood ran in torrents, drenched was all the earth,
As Trojans and their alien helpers died.
Here were men lying quelled by bitter death
All up and down the city in their blood;
Others on them were falling, gasping forth
Their life's strength; others, clutching in their hands
Their bowels that looked through hideous gashes forth,
Wandered in wretched plight around their homes:
Others, whose feet, while yet asleep they lay,
Had been hewn off, with groans unutterable
Crawled mid the corpses. Some, who had rushed to fight,
Lay now in dust, with hands and heads hewn off.
Some were there, through whose backs, even as they fled,
The spear had passed, clear through to the breast, and some
Whose waists the lance had pierced, impaling them
Where sharpest stings the anguish-laden steel.
And all about the city dolorous howls
Of dogs uprose, and miserable moans

Of strong men stricken to death; and every home
With awful cries was echoing. Rang the shrieks
Of women, like to screams of cranes, which see
An eagle stooping on them from the sky,
Which have no courage to resist, but scream
Long terror-shrieks in dread of Zeus's bird;
So here, so there the Trojan women wailed,
Some starting from their sleep, some to the ground
Leaping: they thought not in that agony
Of robe and zone; in naught but tunics clad
Distraught they wandered: others found nor veil
Nor cloak to cast about them, but, as came
Onward their foes, they stood with beating hearts
Trembling, as lettered by despair, essaying,
All-hapless, with their hands alone to hide
Their nakedness. And some in frenzy of woe:
Their tresses tore, and beat their breasts, and screamed.
Others against that stormy torrent of foes
Recklessly rushed, insensible of fear,
Through mad desire to aid the perishing,
Husbands or children; for despair had given
High courage. Shrieks had startled from their sleep
Soft little babes whose hearts had never known
Trouble--and there one with another lay
Gasping their lives out! Some there were whose dreams
Changed to a sudden vision of doom. All round
The fell Fates gloated horribly o'er the slain.
And even as swine be slaughtered in the court
Of a rich king who makes his folk a feast,
So without number were they slain. The wine
Left in the mixing-bowls was blent with blood
Gruesomely. No man bare a sword unstained
With murder of defenceless folk of Troy,

Though he were but a weakling in fair fight.
And as by wolves or jackals sheep are torn,
What time the furnace-breath of midnoon-heat
Darts down, and all the flock beneath the shade
Are crowded, and the shepherd is not there,
But to the homestead bears afar their milk;
And the fierce brutes leap on them, tear their throats,
Gorge to the full their ravenous maws, and then
Lap the dark blood, and linger still to slay
All in mere lust of slaughter, and provide
An evil banquet for that shepherd-lord;
So through the city of Priam Danaans slew
One after other in that last fight of all.
No Trojan there was woundless, all men's limbs
With blood in torrents spilt were darkly dashed.

Nor seetheless were the Danaans in the fray:
With beakers some were smitten, with tables some,
Thrust in the eyes of some were burning brands
Snatched from the hearth; some died transfixed with spits
Yet left within the hot flesh of the swine
Whereon the red breath of the Fire-god beat;
Others struck down by bills and axes keen
Gasped in their blood: from some men's hands were shorn
The fingers, who, in wild hope to escape
The imminent death, had clutched the blades of swords.
And here in that dark tumult one had hurled
A stone, and crushed the crown of a friend's head.
Like wild beasts trapped and stabbed within a fold
On a lone steading, frenziedly they fought,
Mad with despair-enkindled rage, beneath
That night of horror. Hot with battle-lust
Here, there, the fighters rushed and hurried through

The palace of Priam. Many an Argive fell
Spear-slain; for whatso Trojan in his halls
Might seize a sword, might lift a spear in hand,
Slew foes--ay, heavy though he were with wine.

Upflashed a glare unearthly through the town,
For many an Argive bare in hand a torch
To know in that dim battle friends from foes.

Then Tydeus' son amid the war-storm met
Spearman Coroebus, lordly Mygdon's son,
And 'neath the left ribs pierced him with the lance
Where run the life-ways of man's meat and drink;
So met him black death borne upon the spear:
Down in dark blood he fell mid hosts of slain.
Ah fool! the bride he won not, Priam's child
Cassandra, yea, his loveliest, for whose sake
To Priam's burg but yesterday he came,
And vaunted he would thrust the Argives back
From Ilium. Never did the Gods fulfil
His hope: the Fates hurled doom upon his head.
With him the slayer laid Eurydamas low,
Antenor's gallant son-in-law, who most
For prudence was pre-eminent in Troy.
Then met he Ilioneus the elder of days,
And flashed his terrible sword forth. All the limbs
Of that grey sire were palsied with his fear:
He put forth trembling hands, with one he caught
The swift avenging sword, with one he clasped
The hero's knees. Despite his fury of war,
A moment paused his wrath, or haply a God
Held back the sword a space, that that old man
Might speak to his fierce foe one word of prayer.

Piteously cried he, terror-overwhelmed:
"I kneel before thee, whosoe'er thou be
Of mighty Argives. Oh compassionate
My suppliant hands! Abate thy wrath! To slay
The young and valiant is a glorious thing;
But if thou smite an old man, small renown
Waits on thy prowess. Therefore turn from me
Thine hands against young men, if thou dost hope
Ever to come to grey hairs such as mine."

So spake he; but replied strong Tydeus' son:
"Old man, I look to attain to honoured age;
But while my Strength yet waxeth, will not I
Spare any foe, but hurl to Hades all.
The brave man makes an end of every foe."

Then through his throat that terrible warrior drave
The deadly blade, and thrust it straight to where
The paths of man's life lead by swiftest way
Blood-paved to doom: death palsied his poor strength
By Diomedes' hands. Thence rushed he on
Slaying the Trojans, storming in his might
All through their fortress: pierced by his long spear
Eurycoon fell, Perimnestor's son renowned.
Amphimedon Aias slew: Agamemnon smote
Damastor's son: Idomeneus struck down
Mimas: by Meges Deiopites died.
Achilles' son with his resistless lance
Smote godlike Pammon; then his javelin pierced
Polites in mid-rush: Antiphonus
Dead upon these he laid, all Priam's sons.
Agenor faced him in the fight, and fell:
Hero on hero slew he; everywhere

Stalked at his side Death's black doom manifest:
Clad in his sire's might, whomso he met he slew.
Last, on Troy's king in murderous mood he came.
By Zeus the Hearth-lord's altar. Seeing him,
Old Priam knew him and quaked not; for he longed
Himself to lay his life down midst his sons;
And craving death to Achilles' seed he spake:
"Fierce-hearted son of Achilles strong in war,
Slay me, and pity not my misery.
I have no will to see the sun's light more,
Who have suffered woes so many and so dread.
With my sons would I die, and so forget
Anguish and horror of war. Oh that thy sire
Had slain me, ere mine eyes beheld aflame
Illium, had slain me when I brought to him
Ransom for Hector, whom thy father slew.
He spared me--so the Fates had spun my thread
Of destiny. But thou, glut with my blood
Thy fierce heart, and let me forget my pain."
Answered Achilles' battle-eager son:
"Fain am I, yea, in haste to grant thy prayer.
A foe like thee will I not leave alive;
For naught is dearer unto men than life."

With one stroke swept he off that hoary head
Lightly as when a reaper lops an ear
In a parched cornfield at the harvest-tide.
With lips yet murmuring low it rolled afar
From where with quivering limbs the body lay
Amidst dark-purple blood and slaughtered men.
So lay he, chiefest once of all the world
In lineage, wealth, in many and goodly sons.
Ah me, not long abides the honour of man,

But shame from unseen ambush leaps on him
So clutched him Doom, so he forgat his woes.

Yea, also did those Danaan car-lords hurl
From a high tower the babe Astyanax,
Dashing him out of life. They tore the child
Out of his mother's arms, in wrathful hate
Of Hector, who in life had dealt to them
Such havoc; therefore hated they his seed,
And down from that high rampart flung his child--
A wordless babe that nothing knew of war!
As when amid the mountains hungry wolves
Chase from the mother's side a suckling calf,
And with malignant cunning drive it o'er
An echoing cliffs edge, while runs to and fro
Its dam with long moans mourning her dear child,
And a new evil followeth hard on her,
For suddenly lions seize her for a prey;
So, as she agonized for her son, the foe
To bondage haled with other captive thralls
That shrieking daughter of King Eetion.
Then, as on those three fearful deaths she thought
Of husband, child, and father, Andromaehe
Longed sore to die. Yea, for the royally-born
Better it is to die in war, than do
The service of the thrall to baser folk.
All piteously the broken-hearted cried:
"Oh hurl my body also from the wall,
Or down the cliff, or cast me midst the fire,
Ye Argives! Woes are mine unutterable!
For Peleus' son smote down my noble father
In Thebe, and in Troy mine husband slew,
Who unto me was all mine heart's desire,

Who left me in mine halls one little child,
My darling and my pride--of all mine hopes
In him fell merciless Fate hath cheated me!
Oh therefore thrust this broken-hearted one
Now out of life! Hale me not overseas
Mingled with spear-thralls; for my soul henceforth
Hath no more pleasure in life, since God hath slain
My nearest and my dearest! For me waits
Trouble and anguish and lone homelessness!"

So cried she, longing for the grave; for vile
Is life to them whose glory is swallowed up
Of shame: a horror is the scorn of men.
But, spite her prayers, to thraldom dragged they her.

In all the homes of Troy lay dying men,
And rose from all a lamentable cry,
Save only Antenor's halls; for unto him
The Argives rendered hospitality's debt,
For that in time past had his roof received
And sheltered godlike Menelaus, when
He with Odysseus came to claim his own.
Therefore the mighty sons of Achaea showed
Grace to him, as to a friend, and spared his life
And substance, fearing Themis who seeth all.

Then also princely Anchises' noble son--
Hard had he fought through Priam's burg that night
With spear and valour, and many had he slain--
When now he saw the city set aflame
By hands of foes, saw her folk perishing
In multitudes, her treasures spoiled, her wives
And children dragged to thraldom from their homes,

No more he hoped to see the stately walls
Of his birth-city, but bethought him now
How from that mighty ruin to escape.
And as the helmsman of a ship, who toils
On the deep sea, and matches all his craft
Against the winds and waves from every side
Rushing against him in the stormy time,
Forspent at last, both hand and heart, when now
The ship is foundering in the surge, forsakes
The helm, to launch forth in a little boat,
And heeds no longer ship and lading; so
Anchises' gallant son forsook the town
And left her to her foes, a sea of fire.
His son and father alone he snatched from death;
The old man broken down with years he set
On his broad shoulders with his own strong hands,
And led the young child by his small soft hand,
Whose little footsteps lightly touched the ground;
And, as he quaked to see that work of deaths
His father led him through the roar of fight,
And clinging hung on him the tender child,
Tears down his soft cheeks streaming. But the man
O'er many a body sprang with hurrying feet,
And in the darkness in his own despite
Trampled on many. Cypris guided them,
Earnest to save from that wild ruin her son,
His father, and his child. As on he pressed,
The flames gave back before him everywhere:
The blast of the Fire-god's breath to right and left
Was cloven asunder. Spears and javelins hurled
Against him by the Achaeans harmless fell.
Also, to stay them, Calchas cried aloud:
"Forbear against Aeneas' noble head

To hurl the bitter dart, the deadly spear!
Fated he is by the high Gods' decree
To pass from Xanthus, and by Tiber's flood
To found a city holy and glorious
Through all time, and to rule o'er tribes of men
Far-sundered. Of his seed shall lords of earth
Rule from the rising to the setting sun.
Yea, with the Immortals ever shall he dwell,
Who is son of Aphrodite lovely-tressed.
From him too is it meet we hold our hands
Because he hath preferred his father and son
To gold, to all things that might profit a man
Who fleeth exiled to an alien land.
This one night hath revealed to us a man
Faithful to death to his father and his child."

Then hearkened they, and as a God did all
Look on him. Forth the city hasted he
Whither his feet should bear him, while the foe
Made havoc still of goodly-builded Troy.

Then also Menelaus in Helen's bower
Found, heavy with wine, ill-starred Deiphobus,
And slew him with the sword: but she had fled
And hidden her in the palace. O'er the blood
Of that slain man exulted he, and cried:
"Dog! I, even I have dealt thee unwelcome death
This day! No dawn divine shall meet thee again
Alive in Troy--ay, though thou vaunt thyself
Spouse of the child of Zeus the thunder-voiced!
Black death hath trapped thee slain in my wife's bower!
Would I had met Alexander too in fight
Ere this, and plucked his heart out! So my grief

Had been a lighter load. But he hath paid
Already justice' debt, hath passed beneath
Death's cold dark shadow. Ha, small joy to thee
My wife was doomed to bring! Ay, wicked men
Never elude pure Themis: night and day
Her eyes are on them, and the wide world through
Above the tribes of men she floats in air,
Holpen of Zeus, for punishment of sin."

On passed he, dealing merciless death to foes,
For maddened was his soul with jealousy.
Against the Trojans was his bold heart full
Of thoughts of vengeance, which were now fulfilled
By the dread Goddess Justice, for that theirs
Was that first outrage touching Helen, theirs
That profanation of the oaths, and theirs
That trampling on the blood of sacrifice
When their presumptuous souls forgat the Gods.
Therefore the Vengeance-friends brought woes on them
Thereafter, and some died in fighting field,
Some now in Troy by board and bridal bower.

Menelaus mid the inner chambers found
At last his wife, there cowering from the wrath
Of her bold-hearted lord. He glared on her,
Hungering to slay her in his jealous rage.
But winsome Aphrodite curbed him, struck
Out of his hand the sword, his onrush reined,
Jealousy's dark cloud swept she away, and stirred
Love's deep sweet well-springs in his heart and eyes.
Swept o'er him strange amazement: powerless all
Was he to lift the sword against her neck,
Seeing her splendour of beauty. Like a stock

Of dead wood in a mountain forest, which
No swiftly-rushing blasts of north-winds shake,
Nor fury of south-winds ever, so he stood,
So dazed abode long time. All his great strength
Was broken, as he looked upon his wife.
And suddenly had he forgotten all
Yea, all her sins against her spousal-troth;
For Aphrodite made all fade away,
She who subdueth all immortal hearts
And mortal. Yet even so he lifted up
From earth his sword, and made as he would rush
Upon his wife but other was his intent,
Even as he sprang: he did but feign, to cheat
Achaean eyes. Then did his brother stay
His fury, and spake with pacifying words,
Fearing lest all they had toiled for should be lost:
"Forbear wrath, Menelaus, now: 'twere shame
To slay thy wedded wife, for whose sake we
Have suffered much affliction, while we sought
Vengeance on Priam. Not, as thou dost deem,
Was Helen's the sin, but his who set at naught
The Guest-lord, and thine hospitable board;
So with death-pangs hath God requited him."

Then hearkened Menelaus to his rede.
But the Gods, palled in dark clouds, mourned for Troy,
A ruined glory save fair-tressed Tritonis
And Hera: their hearts triumphed, when they saw
The burg of god-descended Priam destroyed.
Yet not the wise heart Trito-born herself
Was wholly tearless; for within her fane
Outraged Cassandra was of Oileus son
Lust-maddened. But grim vengeance upon him

The Fall of Troy

Ere long the Goddess wreaked, repaying insult
With mortal sufferance. Yea, she would not look
Upon the infamy, but clad herself
With shame and wrath as with a cloak: she turned
Her stern eyes to the temple-roof, and groaned
The holy image, and the hallowed floor
Quaked mightily. Yet did he not forbear
His mad sin, for his soul was lust-distraught.

Here, there, on all sides crumbled flaming homes
In ruin down: scorched dust with smoke was blent:
Trembled the streets to the awful thunderous crash.
Here burned Aeneas' palace, yonder flamed
Antimachus' halls: one furnace was the height
Of fair-built Pergamus; flames were roaring round
Apollo's temple, round Athena's fane,
And round the Hearth-lord's altar: flames licked up
Fair chambers of the sons' sons of a king;
And all the city sank down into hell.

Of Trojans some by Argos' sons were slain,
Some by their own roofs crashing down in fire,
Giving at once in death and tomb to them:
Some in their own throats plunged the steel, when foes
And fire were in the porch together seen:
Some slew their wives and children, and flung themselves
Dead on them, when despair had done its work
Of horror. One, who deemed the foe afar,
Caught up a vase, and, fain to quench the flame,
Hasted for water. Leapt unmarked on him
An Argive, and his spirit, heavy with wine,
Was thrust forth from the body by the spear.
Clashed the void vase above him, as he fell

Backward within the house. As through his hall
Another fled, the burning roof-beam crashed
Down on his head, and swift death came with it.
And many women, as in frenzied flight
They rushed forth, suddenly remembered babes
Left in their beds beneath those burning roofs:
With wild feet sped they back--the house fell in
Upon them, and they perished, mother and child.
Horses and dogs in panic through the town
Fled from the flames, trampling beneath their feet
The dead, and dashing into living men
To their sore hurt. Shrieks rang through all the town.
In through his blazing porchway rushed a man
To rescue wife and child. Through smoke and flame
Blindly he groped, and perished while he cried
Their names, and pitiless doom slew those within.

The fire-glow upward mounted to the sky,
The red glare o'er the firmament spread its wings,
And all the tribes of folk that dwelt around
Beheld it, far as Ida's mountain-crests,
And sea-girt Tenedos, and Thracian Samos.
And men that voyaged on the deep sea cried:
"The Argives have achieved their mighty task
After long toil for star-eyed Helen's sake.
All Troy, the once queen-city, burns in fire:
For all their prayers, no God defends them now;
For strong Fate oversees all works of men,
And the renownless and obscure to fame
She raises, and brings low the exalted ones.
Oft out of good is evil brought, and good
From evil, mid the travail and change of life."

The Fall of Troy

So spake they, who from far beheld the glare
Of Troy's great burning. Compassed were her folk
With wailing misery: through her streets the foe
Exulted, as when madding blasts turmoil
The boundless sea, what time the Altar ascends
To heaven's star-pavement, turned to the misty south
Overagainst Arcturus tempest-breathed,
And with its rising leap the wild winds forth,
And ships full many are whelmed 'neath ravening seas;
Wild as those stormy winds Achaea's sons
Ravaged steep Ilium while she burned in flame.
As when a mountain clothed with shaggy woods
Burns swiftly in a fire-blast winged with winds,
And from her tall peaks goeth up a roar,
And all the forest-children this way and that
Rush through the wood, tormented by the flame;
So were the Trojans perishing: there was none
To save, of all the Gods. Round these were staked
The nets of Fate, which no man can escape.

Then were Demophoon and Acamas
By mighty Theseus' mother Aethra met.
Yearning to see them was she guided on
To meet them by some Blessed One, the while
'Wildered from war and fire she fled. They saw
In that red glare a woman royal-tall,
Imperial-moulded, and they weened that this
Was Priam's queen, and with swift eagerness
Laid hands on her, to lead her captive thence
To the Danaans; but piteously she moaned:
"Ah, do not, noble sons of warrior Greeks,
To your ships hale me, as I were a foe!
I am not of Trojan birth: of Danaans came

My princely blood renowned. In Troezen's halls
Pittheus begat me, Aegeus wedded me,
And of my womb sprang Theseus glory-crowned.
For great Zeus' sake, for your dear parents' sake,
I pray you, if the seed of Theseus came
Hither with Atreus' sons, O bring ye me
Unto their yearning eyes. I trow they be
Young men like you. My soul shall be refreshed
If living I behold those chieftains twain."

Hearkening to her they called their sire to mind,
His deeds for Helen's sake, and how the sons
Of Zeus the Thunderer in the old time smote
Aphidnae, when, because these were but babes,
Their nurses hid them far from peril of fight;
And Aethra they remembered--all she endured
Through wars, as mother-in-law at first, and thrall
Thereafter of Helen. Dumb for joy were they,
Till spake Demophoon to that wistful one:
"Even now the Gods fulfil thine heart's desire:
We whom thou seest are the sons of him,
Thy noble son: thee shall our loving hands
Bear to the ships: with joy to Hellas' soil
Thee will we bring, where once thou wast a queen."

Then his great father's mother clasped him round
With clinging arms: she kissed his shoulders broad,
His head, his breast, his bearded lips she kissed,
And Acamas kissed withal, the while she shed
Glad tears on these who could not choose but weep.
As when one tarries long mid alien men,
And folk report him dead, but suddenly
He cometh home: his children see his face,

And break into glad weeping; yea, and he,
His arms around them, and their little heads
Upon his shoulders, sobs: echoes the home
With happy mourning's music-beating wings;
So wept they with sweet sighs and sorrowless moans.

Then, too, affliction-burdened Priam's child,
Laodice, say they, stretched her hands to heaven,
Praying the mighty Gods that earth might gape
To swallow her, ere she defiled her hand
With thralls' work; and a God gave ear, and rent
Deep earth beneath her: so by Heaven's decree
Did earth's abysmal chasm receive the maid
In Troy's last hour. Electra's self withal,
The Star-queen lovely-robed, shrouded her form
In mist and cloud, and left the Pleiad-band,
Her sisters, as the olden legend tells.
Still riseth up in sight of toil-worn men
Their bright troop in the skies; but she alone
Hides viewless ever, since the hallowed town
Of her son Dardanus in ruin fell,
When Zeus most high from heaven could help her not,
Because to Fate the might of Zeus must bow;
And by the Immortals' purpose all these things
Had come to pass, or by Fate's ordinance.

Still on Troy's folk the Argives wreaked their wrath,
And battle's issues Strife Incarnate held.

BOOK XIV.

How the conquerors sailed from Troy unto judgment of tempest and shipwreck.

    Then rose from Ocean Dawn the golden-throned
Up to the heavens; night into Chaos sank.
And now the Argives spoiled fair-fenced Troy,
And took her boundless treasures for a prey.
Like river-torrents seemed they, that sweep down,
By rain, floods swelled, in thunder from the hills,
And seaward hurl tall trees and whatsoe'er
Grows on the mountains, mingled with the wreck
Of shattered cliff and crag; so the long lines
Of Danaans who had wasted Troy with fire
Seemed, streaming with her plunder to the ships.
Troy's daughters therewithal in scattered bands
They haled down seaward--virgins yet unwed,
And new-made brides, and matrons silver-haired,
And mothers from whose bosoms foes had torn
Babes for the last time closing lips on breasts.

    Amidst of these Menelaus led his wife
Forth of the burning city, having wrought
A mighty triumph--joy and shame were his.

The Fall of Troy

Cassandra heavenly-fair was haled the prize
Of Agamemnon: to Achilles' son
Andromache had fallen: Hecuba
Odysseus dragged unto his ship. The tears
Poured from her eyes as water from a spring;
Trembled her limbs, fear-frenzied was her heart;
Rent were her hoary tresses and besprent
With ashes of the hearth, cast by her hands
When she saw Priam slain and Troy aflame.
And aye she deeply groaned for thraldom's day
That trapped her vainly loth. Each hero led
A wailing Trojan woman to his ship.
Here, there, uprose from these the wild lament,
The woeful-mingling cries of mother and babe.
As when with white-tusked swine the herdmen drive
Their younglings from the hill-pens to the plain
As winter closeth in, and evermore
Each answereth each with mingled plaintive cries;
So moaned Troy's daughters by their foes enslaved,
Handmaid and queen made one in thraldom's lot.

But Helen raised no lamentation: shame
Sat on her dark-blue eyes, and cast its flush
Over her lovely cheeks. Her heart beat hard
With sore misgiving, lest, as to the ships
She passed, the Achaeans might mishandle her.
Therefore with fluttering soul she trembled sore;
And, her head darkly mantled in her veil,
Close-following trod she in her husband's steps,
With cheek shame-crimsoned, like the Queen of Love,
What time the Heaven-abiders saw her clasped
In Ares' arms, shaming in sight of all
The marriage-bed, trapped in the myriad-meshed

Toils of Hephaestus: tangled there she lay
In agony of shame, while thronged around
The Blessed, and there stood Hephaestus' self:
For fearful it is for wives to be beheld
By husbands' eyes doing the deed of shame.
Lovely as she in form and roseate blush
Passed Helen mid the Trojan captives on
To the Argive ships. But the folk all around
Marvelled to see the glory of loveliness
Of that all-flawless woman. No man dared
Or secretly or openly to cast
Reproach on her. As on a Goddess all
Gazed on her with adoring wistful eyes.
As when to wanderers on a stormy sea,
After long time and passion of prayer, the sight
Of fatherland is given; from deadly deeps
Escaped, they stretch hands to her joyful-souled;
So joyed the Danaans all, no man of them
Remembered any more war's travail and pain.
Such thoughts Cytherea stirred in them, for grace
To Helen starry-eyed, and Zeus her sire.

Then, when he saw that burg beloved destroyed,
Xanthus, scarce drawing breath from bloody war,
Mourned with his Nymphs for ruin fallen on Troy,
Mourned for the city of Priam blotted out.
As when hail lashes a field of ripened wheat,
And beats it small, and smites off all the ears
With merciless scourge, and levelled with the ground
Are stalks, and on the earth is all the grain
Woefully wasted, and the harvest's lord
Is stricken with deadly grief; so Xanthus' soul
Was utterly whelmed in grief for Ilium made

A desolation; grief undying was his,
Immortal though he was. Mourned Simois
And long-ridged Ida: all who on Ida dwelt
Wailed from afar the ruin of Priam's town.

But with loud laughter of glee the Argives sought
Their galleys, chanting the triumphant might
Of victory, chanting now the Blessed Gods,
Now their own valour, and Epeius' work
Ever renowned. Their song soared up to heaven,
Like multitudinous cries of daws, when breaks
A day of sunny calm and windless air
After a ruining storm: from their glad hearts
So rose the joyful clamour, till the Gods
Heard and rejoiced in heaven, all who had helped
With willing hands the war-fain Argive men.
But chafed those others which had aided Troy,
Beholding Priam's city wrapped in flame,
Yet powerless for her help to override
Fate; for not Cronos' Son can stay the hand
Of Destiny, whose might transcendeth all
The Immortals, and Zeus sanctioneth all her deeds.

The Argives on the flaming altar-wood
Laid many thighs of oxen, and made haste
To spill sweet wine on their burnt offerings,
Thanking the Gods for that great work achieved.
And loudly at the feast they sang the praise
Of all the mailed men whom the Horse of Tree
Had ambushed. Far-famed Sinon they extolled
For that dire torment he endured of foes;
Yea, song and honour-guerdons without end
All rendered him: and that resolved soul

Glad-hearted joyed for the Argives victory,
And for his own misfeaturing sorrowed not.
For to the wise and prudent man renown
Is better far than gold, than goodlihead,
Than all good things men have or hope to win.

So, feasting by the ships all void of fear,
Cried one to another ever and anon:
"We have touched the goal of this long war, have won
Glory, have smitten our foes and their great town!
Now grant, O Zeus, to our prayers safe home-return!"
But not to all the Sire vouchsafed return.

Then rose a cunning harper in their midst.
And sang the song of triumph and of peace
Re-won, and with glad hearts untouched by care
They heard; for no more fear of war had they,
But of sweet toil of law-abiding days
And blissful, fleeting hours henceforth they dreamed.
All the War's Story in their eager ears
He sang--how leagued peoples gathering met
At hallowed Aulis--how the invincible strength
Of Peleus' son smote fenced cities twelve
In sea-raids, how he marched o'er leagues on leagues
Of land, and spoiled eleven--all he wrought
In fight with Telephus and Eetion--
How he slew giant Cycnus--all the toil
Of war that through Achilles' wrath befell
The Achaeans--how he dragged dead Hector round
His own Troy's wall, and how he slew in fight
Penthesileia and Tithonus' son:--
How Aias laid low Glaucus, lord of spears,
Then sang he how the child of Aeacus' son

The Fall of Troy

Struck down Eurypylus, and how the shafts
Of Philoctetes dealt to Paris death.
Then the song named all heroes who passed in
To ambush in the Horse of Guile, and hymned
The fall of god-descended Priam's burg;
The feast he sang last, and peace after war;
Then many another, as they listed, sang.

But when above those feasters midnight's stars
Hung, ceased the Danaans from the feast and wine,
And turned to sleep's forgetfulness of care,
For that with yesterday's war-travail all
Were wearied; wherefore they, who fain all night
Had revelled, needs must cease: how loth soe'er,
Sleep drew them thence; here, there, soft slumbered they.

But in his tent Menelaus lovingly
With bright-haired Helen spake; for on their eyes
Sleep had not fallen yet. The Cyprian Queen
Brooded above their souls, that olden love
Might be renewed, and heart-ache chased away.

Helen first brake the silence, and she said:
"O Menelaus, be not wroth with me!
Not of my will I left thy roof, thy bed,
But Alexander and the sons of Troy
Came upon me, and snatched away, when thou
Wast far thence. Oftentimes did I essay
By the death-noose to perish wretchedly,
Or by the bitter sword; but still they stayed
Mine hand, and still spake comfortable words
To salve my grief for thee and my sweet child.
For her sake, for the sake of olden love,

And for thine own sake, I beseech thee now,
Forget thy stern displeasure against thy wife."

Answered her Menelaus wise of wit:
"No more remember past griefs: seal them up
Hid in thine heart. Let all be locked within
The dim dark mansion of forgetfulness.
What profits it to call ill deeds to mind?"

Glad was she then: fear flitted from her heart,
And came sweet hope that her lord's wrath was dead.
She cast her arms around him, and their eyes
With tears were brimming as they made sweet moan;
And side by side they laid them, and their hearts
Thrilled with remembrance of old spousal joy.
And as a vine and ivy entwine their stems
Each around other, that no might of wind
Avails to sever them, so clung these twain
Twined in the passionate embrace of love.

When came on these too sorrow-drowning sleep,
Even then above his son's head rose and stood
Godlike Achilles' mighty shade, in form
As when he lived, the Trojans' bane, the joy
Of Greeks, and kissed his neck and flashing eyes
Lovingly, and spake comfortable words:
"All hail, my son! Vex not thine heart with grief
For thy dead sire; for with the Blessed Gods
Now at the feast I sit. Refrain thy soul
From sorrow, and plant my strength within thy mind.
Be foremost of the Argives ever; yield
To none in valour, but in council bow
Before thine elders: so shall all acclaim

Thy courtesy. Honour princely men and wise;
For the true man is still the true man's friend,
Even as the vile man cleaveth to the knave.
If good thy thought be, good shall be thy deeds:
But no man shall attain to Honour's height,
Except his heart be right within: her stem
Is hard to climb, and high in heaven spread
Her branches: only they whom strength and toil
Attend, strain up to pluck her blissful fruit,
Climbing the Tree of Honour glow-crowned.
Thou therefore follow fame, and let thy soul
Be not in sorrow afflicted overmuch,
Nor in prosperity over-glad. To friends,
To comrades, child and wife, be kindly of heart,
Remembering still that near to all men stand
The gates of doom, the mansions of the dead:
For humankind are like the flower of grass,
The blossom of spring; these fade the while those bloom:
Therefore be ever kindly with thy kind.
Now to the Argives say--to Atreus' son
Agamemnon chiefly--if my battle-toil
Round Priam's walls, and those sea-raids I led
Or ever I set foot on Trojan land,
Be in their hearts remembered, to my tomb
Be Priam's daughter Polyxeina led--
Whom as my portion of the spoil I claim--
And sacrificed thereon: else shall my wrath
Against them more than for Briseis burn.
The waves of the great deep will I turmoil
To bar their way, upstirring storm on storm,
That through their own mad folly pining away
Here they may linger long, until to me
They pour drink-offerings, yearning sore for home.

But, when they have slain the maiden, I grudge not
That whoso will may bury her far from me."

Then as a wind-breath swift he fleeted thence,
And came to the Elysian Plain, whereto
A path to heaven reacheth, for the feet
Ascending and descending of the Blest.
Then the son started up from sleep, and called
His sire to mind, and glowed the heart in him.

When to wide heaven the Child of Mist uprose,
Scattering night, unveiling earth and air,
Then from their rest upsprang Achaea's sons
Yearning for home. With laughter 'gan they hale
Down to the sea the keels: but lo, their haste
Was reined in by Achilles' mighty son:

He assembled them, and told his sire's behest:
"Hearken, dear sons of Argives battle-staunch,
To this my glorious father's hest, to me
Spoken in darkness slumbering on my bed:
He saith, he dwells with the Immortal Gods:
He biddeth you and Atreus' son the king
To bring, as his war-guerdon passing-fair,
To his dim dark tomb Polyxeina queenly-robed,
To slay her there, but far thence bury her.
But if ye slight him, and essay to sail
The sea, he threateneth to stir up the waves
To bar your path upon the deep, and here
Storm-bound long time to hold you, ships and men."

Then hearkened they, and as to a God they prayed;
For even now a storm-blast on the sea

Upheaved the waves, broad-backed and thronging fast
More than before beneath the madding wind.
Tossed the great deep, smit by Poseidon's hands
For a grace to strong Achilles. All the winds
Swooped on the waters. Prayed the Dardans all
To Achilles, and a man to his fellow cried:
"Great Zeus's seed Achilles verily was;
Therefore is he a God, who in days past
Dwelt among us; for lapse of dateless time
Makes not the sons of Heaven to fade away."

Then to Achilles' tomb the host returned,
And led the maid, as calf by herdmen dragged
For sacrifice, from woodland pastures torn
From its mother's side, and lowing long and loud
It moans with anguished heart; so Priam's child
Wailed in the hands of foes. Down streamed her tears
As when beneath the heavy sacks of sand
Olives clear-skinned, ne'er blotched by drops of storm,
Pour out their oil, when the long levers creak
As strong men strain the cords; so poured the tears
Of travail-burdened Priam's daughter, haled
To stern Achilles' tomb, tears blent with moans.
Drenched were her bosom-folds, glistened the drops
On flesh clear-white as costly ivory.

Then, to crown all her griefs, yet sharper pain
Fell on the heart of hapless Hecuba.
Then did her soul recall that awful dream,
The vision of sleep of that night overpast:
Herseemed that on Achilles' tomb she stood
Moaning, her hair down-streaming to the ground,
And from her breasts blood dripped to earth the while,

And drenched the tomb. Fear-haunted touching this,
Foreboding all calamity, she wailed
Piteously; far rang her wild lament.
As a dog moaning at her master's door,
Utters long howls, her teats with milk distent,
Whose whelps, ere their eyes opened to the light,
Her lords afar have flung, a prey to kites;
And now with short sharp cries she plains, and now
Long howling: the weird outcry thrills the air;
So wailed and shrieked for her child Hecuba:
"Ah me! what sorrows first or last shall I
Lament heart-anguished, who am full of woes?
Those unimagined ills my sons, my king
Have suffered? or my city, or daughters shamed?
Or my despair, my day of slavery?
Oh, the grim fates have caught me in a net
Of manifold ills! O child, they have spun for thee
Dread weird of unimagined misery!
They have thrust thee away, when near was Hymen's hymn,
From thine espousals, marked thee for destruction
Dark, unendurable, unspeakable!
For lo, a dead man's heart, Achilles' heart,
Is by our blood made warm with life to-day!
O child, dear child, that I might die with thee,
That earth might swallow me, ere I see thy doom!"
So cried she, weeping never-ceasing tears,
For grief on bitter grief encompassed her.
But when these reached divine Achilles' tomb,
Then did his son unsheathe the whetted sword,
His left hand grasped the maid, and his right hand
Was laid upon the tomb, and thus he cried:
"Hear, father, thy son's prayer, hear all the prayers
Of Argives, and be no more wroth with us!

The Fall of Troy

Lo, unto thee now all thine heart's desire
Will we fulfil. Be gracious to us thou,
And to our praying grant sweet home-return."

Into the maid's throat then he plunged the blade
Of death: the dear life straightway sobbed she forth,
With the last piteous moan of parting breath.
Face-downward to the earth she fell: all round
Her flesh was crimsoned from her neck, as snow
Stained on a mountain-side with scarlet blood
Rushing, from javelin-smitten boar or bear.
The maiden's corpse then gave they, to be borne
Unto the city, to Antenor's home,
For that, when Troy yet stood, he nurtured her
In his fair halls, a bride for his own son
Eurymachus. The old man buried her,
King Priam's princess-child, nigh his own house,
By Ganymedes' shrine, and overagainst
The temple of Pallas the Unwearied One.
Then were the waves stilled, and the blast was hushed
To sleep, and all the sea-flood lulled to calm.

Swift with glad laughter hied they to the ships,
Hymning Achilles and the Blessed Ones.
A feast they made, first severing thighs of kine
For the Immortals. Gladsome sacrifice
Steamed on all sides: in cups of silver and gold
They drank sweet wine: their hearts leaped up with hope
Of winning to their fatherland again.
But when with meats and wine all these were filled,
Then in their eager ears spake Neleus' son:
"Hear, friends, who have 'scaped the long turmoil of war,
That I may say to you one welcome word:

Now is the hour of heart's delight, the hour
Of home-return. Away! Achilles soul
Hath ceased from ruinous wrath; Earth-shaker stills
The stormy wave, and gentle breezes blow;
No more the waves toss high. Haste, hale the ships
Down to the sea. Now, ho for home-return!"

Eager they heard, and ready made the ships.
Then was a marvellous portent seen of men;
For all-unhappy Priam's queen was changed
From woman's form into a pitiful hound;
And all men gathered round in wondering awe.
Then all her body a God transformed to stone--
A mighty marvel for men yet unborn!
At Calchas' bidding this the Achaeans bore
In a swift ship to Hellespont's far side.
Then down to the sea in haste they ran the keels:
Their wealth they laid aboard, even all the spoil
Taken, or ever unto Troy they came,
From conquered neighbour peoples; therewithal
Whatso they took from Ilium, wherein most
They joyed, for untold was the sum thereof.
And followed with them many a captive maid
With anguished heart: so went they aboard the ships.
But Calchas would not with that eager host
Launch forth; yea, he had fain withheld therefrom
All the Achaeans, for his prophet-soul
Foreboded dread destruction looming o'er
The Argives by the Rocks Capherean.
But naught they heeded him; malignant
Fate Deluded men's souls: only Amphilochus
The wise in prophet-lore, the gallant son
Of princely Amphiaraus, stayed with him.

Fated were these twain, far from their own land,
To reach Pamphylian and Cilician burgs;
And this the Gods thereafter brought to pass.

But now the Achaeans cast the hawsers loose
From shore: in haste they heaved the anchor-stones.
Roared Hellespont beneath swift-flashing oars;
Crashed the prows through the sea. About the bows
Much armour of slain foes was lying heaped:
Along the bulwarks victory-trophies hung
Countless. With garlands wreathed they all the ships,
Their heads, the spears, the shields wherewith they had fought
Against their foes. The chiefs stood on the prows,
And poured into the dark sea once and again
Wine to the Gods, to grant them safe return.
But with the winds their prayers mixed; far away
Vainly they floated blent with cloud and air.

With anguished hearts the captive maids looked back
On Ilium, and with sobs and moans they wailed,
Striving to hide their grief from Argive eyes.
Clasping their knees some sat; in misery some
Veiled with their hands their faces; others nursed
Young children in their arms: those innocents
Not yet bewailed their day of bondage, nor
Their country's ruin; all their thoughts were set
On comfort of the breast, for the babe's heart
Hath none affinity with sorrow. All
Sat with unbraided hair and pitiful breasts
Scored with their fingers. On their cheeks there lay
Stains of dried tears, and streamed thereover now
Fresh tears full fast, as still they gazed aback
On the lost hapless home, wherefrom yet rose

The flames, and o'er it writhed the rolling smoke.
Now on Cassandra marvelling they gazed,
Calling to mind her prophecy of doom;
But at their tears she laughed in bitter scorn,
In anguish for the ruin of her land.

Such Trojans as had scaped from pitiless war
Gathered to render now the burial-dues
Unto their city's slain. Antenor led
To that sad work: one pyre for all they raised.

But laughed with triumphing hearts the Argive men,
As now with oars they swept o'er dark sea-ways,
Now hastily hoised the sails high o'er the ships,
And fleeted fast astern Dardania-land,
And Hero Achilles' tomb. But now their hearts,
How blithe soe'er, remembered comrades slain,
And sorely grieved, and wistfully they looked
Back to the alien's land; it seemed to them
Aye sliding farther from their ships. Full soon
By Tenedos' beaches slipt they: now they ran
By Chrysa, Sminthian Phoebus' holy place,
And hallowed Cilla. Far away were glimpsed
The windy heights of Lesbos. Rounded now
Was Lecton's foreland, where is the last peak
Of Ida. In the sails loud hummed the wind,
Crashed round the prows the dark surge: the long waves
Showed shadowy hollows, far the white wake gleamed.

Now had the Argives all to the hallowed soil
Of Hellas won, by perils of the deep
Unscathed, but for Athena Daughter of Zeus
The Thunderer, and her indignation's wrath.

When nigh Euboea's windy heights they drew,
She rose, in anger unappeasable
Against the Locrian king, devising doom
Crushing and pitiless, and drew nigh to Zeus
Lord of the Gods, and spake to him apart
In wrath that in her breast would not be pent:
"Zeus, Father, unendurable of Gods
Is men's presumption! They reck not of thee,
Of none of the Blessed reck they, forasmuch
As vengeance followeth after sin no more;
And ofttimes more afflicted are good men
Than evil, and their misery hath no end.
Therefore no man regardeth justice: shame
Lives not with men! And I, I will not dwell
Hereafter in Olympus, not be named
Thy daughter, if I may not be avenged
On the Achaeans' reckless sin! Behold,
Within my very temple Oileus' son
Hath wrought iniquity, hath pitied not
Cassandra stretching unregarded hands
Once and again to me; nor did he dread
My might, nor reverenced in his wicked heart
The Immortal, but a deed intolerable
He did. Therefore let not thy spirit divine
Begrudge mine heart's desire, that so all men
May quake before the manifest wrath of Gods."

Answered the Sire with heart-assuaging words:
"Child, not for the Argives' sake withstand I thee;
But all mine armoury which the Cyclops' might
To win my favour wrought with tireless hands,
To thy desire I give. O strong heart, hurl
A ruining storm thyself on the Argive fleet."

Then down before the aweless Maid he cast
Swift lightning, thunder, and deadly thunderbolt;
And her heart leapt, and gladdened was her soul.
She donned the stormy Aegis flashing far,
Adamantine, massy, a marvel to the Gods,
Whereon was wrought Medusa's ghastly head,
Fearful: strong serpents breathing forth the blast
Of ravening fire were on the face thereof.
Crashed on the Queen's breast all the Aegis-links,
As after lightning crashes the firmament.
Then grasped she her father's weapons, which no God
Save Zeus can lift, and wide Olympus shook.
Then swept she clouds and mist together on high;
Night over earth was poured, haze o'er the sea.
Zeus watched, and was right glad as broad heaven's floor
Rocked 'neath the Goddess's feet, and crashed the sky,
As though invincible Zeus rushed forth to war.
Then sped she Iris unto Acolus,
From heaven far-flying over misty seas,
To bid him send forth all his buffering winds
O'er iron-bound Caphereus' cliffs to sweep
Ceaselessly, and with ruin of madding blasts
To upheave the sea. And Iris heard, and swift
She darted, through cloud-billows plunging down--
Thou hadst said: "Lo, in the sky dark water and fire!"
And to Aeolia came she, isle of caves,
Of echoing dungeons of mad-raging winds
With rugged ribs of mountain overarched,
Whereby the mansion stands of Aeolus
Hippotas' son. Him found she therewithin
With wife and twelve sons; and she told to him
Athena's purpose toward the homeward-bound
Achaeans. He denied her not, but passed

Forth of his halls, and in resistless hands
Upswung his trident, smiting the mountain-side
Within whose chasm-cell the wild winds dwelt
Tempestuously shrieking. Ever pealed
Weird roarings of their voices round its vaults.
Cleft by his might was the hill-side; forth they poured.
He bade them on their wings bear blackest storm
To upheave the sea, and shroud Caphereus' heights.
Swiftly upsprang they, ere their king's command
Was fully spoken. Mightily moaned the sea
As they rushed o'er it; waves like mountain-cliffs
From all sides were uprolled. The Achaeans' hearts
Were terror-palsied, as the uptowering surge
Now swung the ships up high through palling mist,
Now hurled them rolled as down a precipice
To dark abysses. Up through yawning deeps
Some power resistless belched the boiling sand
From the sea's floor. Tossed in despair, fear-dazed,
Men could not grasp the oar, nor reef the sail
About the yard-arm, howsoever fain,
Ere the winds rent it, could not with the sheets
Trim the torn canvas, buffeted so were they
By ruining blasts. The helmsman had no power
To guide the rudder with his practised hands,
For those ill winds hurled all confusedly.
No hope of life was left them: blackest night,
Fury of tempest, wrath of deathless Gods,
Raged round them. Still Poseidon heaved and swung
The merciless sea, to work the heart's desire
Of his brother's glorious child; and she on high
Stormed with her lightnings, ruthless in her rage.
Thundered from heaven Zeus, in purpose fixed
To glorify his daughter. All the isles

And mainlands round were lashed by leaping seas
Nigh to Euboea, where the Power divine
Scourged most with unrelenting stroke on stroke
The Argives. Groan and shriek of perishing men
Rang through the ships; started great beams and snapped
With ominous sound, for ever ship on ship
With shivering timbers crashed. With hopeless toil
Men strained with oars to thrust back hulls that reeled
Down on their own, but with the shattered planks
Were hurled into the abyss, to perish there
By pitiless doom; for beams of foundering ships
From this, from that side battered out their lives,
And crushed were all their bodies wretchedly.
Some in the ships fell down, and like dead men
Lay there; some, in the grip of destiny,
Clinging to oars smooth-shaven, tried to swim;
Some upon planks were tossing. Roared the surge
From fathomless depths: it seemed as though sea, sky,
And land were blended all confusedly.

Still from Olympus thundering Atrytone
Wielded her Father's power unshamed, and still
The welkin shrieked around. Her ruin of wrath
Now upon Aias hurled she: on his ship
Dashed she a thunderbolt, and shivered it
Wide in a moment into fragments small,
While earth and air yelled o'er the wreck, and whirled
And plunged and fell the whole sea down thereon.
They in the ship were all together flung
Forth: all about them swept the giant waves,
Round them leapt lightnings flaming through the dark.
Choked with the strangling surf of hissing brine,
Gasping out life, they drifted o'er the sea.

But even in death those captive maids rejoiced,
As some ill-starred ones, clasping to their breasts
Their babes, sank in the sea; some flung their arms
Round Danaans' horror-stricken heads, and dragged
These down with them, so rendering to their foes
Requital for foul outrage down to them.
And from on high the haughty Trito-born
Looked down on all this, and her heart was glad.

But Aias floated now on a galley's plank,
Now through the brine with strong hands oared his path,
Like some old Titan in his tireless might.
Cleft was the salt sea-surge by the sinewy hands
Of that undaunted man: the Gods beheld
And marvelled at his courage and his strength.
But now the billows swung him up on high
Through misty air, as though to a mountain's peak,
Now whelmed him down, as they would bury him
In ravening whirlpits: yet his stubborn hands
Toiled on unwearied. Aye to right and left
Flashed lightnings down, and quenched them in the sea;
For not yet was the Child of Thunderer Zeus
Purposed to smite him dead, despite her wrath,
Ere he had drained the cup of travail and pain
Down to the dregs; so in the deep long time
Affliction wore him down, tormented sore
On every side. Grim Fates stood round the man
Unnumbered; yet despair still kindled strength.
He cried: "Though all the Olympians banded come
In wrath, and rouse against me all the sea,
I will escape them!" But no whit did he
Elude the Gods' wrath; for the Shaker of Earth
In fierceness of his indignation marked

Where his hands clung to the Gyraean Rock,
And in stern anger with an earthquake shook
Both sea and land. Around on all sides crashed
Caphereus' cliffs: beneath the Sea-king's wrath
The surf-tormented beaches shrieked and roared.
The broad crag rifted reeled into the sea,
The rock whereto his desperate hands had clung;
Yet did he writhe up round its jutting spurs,
While flayed his hands were, and from 'neath his nails
The blood ran. Wrestling with him roared the waves,
And the foam whitened all his hair and beard.

Yet had he 'scaped perchance his evil doom,
Had not Poseidon, wroth with his hardihood,
Cleaving the earth, hurled down the chasm the rock,
As in the old time Pallas heaved on high
Sicily, and on huge Enceladus
Dashed down the isle, which burns with the burning yet
Of that immortal giant, as he breathes
Fire underground; so did the mountain-crag,
Hurled from on high, bury the Locrian king,
Pinning the strong man down, a wretch crushed flat.
And so on him death's black destruction came
Whom land and sea alike were leagued to slay.

Still over the great deep were swept the rest
Of those Achaeans, crouching terror-dazed
Down in the ships, save those that mid the waves
Had fallen. Misery encompassed all;
For some with heavily-plunging prows drave on,
With keels upturned some drifted. Here were masts
Snapped from the hull by rushing gusts, and there
Were tempest-rifted wrecks of scattered beams;

The Fall of Troy

And some had sunk, whelmed in the mighty deep,
Swamped by the torrent downpour from the clouds:
For these endured not madness of wind-tossed sea
Leagued with heaven's waterspout; for streamed the sky
Ceaselessly like a river, while the deep
Raved round them. And one cried: "Such floods on men
Fell only when Deucalion's deluge came,
When earth was drowned, and all was fathomless sea!"

So cried a Danaan, seeing soul-appalled
That wild storm. Thousands perished; corpses thronged
The great sea-highways: all the beaches were
Too strait for them: the surf belched multitudes
Forth on the land. The heavy-booming sea
With weltering beams of ships was wholly paved,
And here and there the grey waves gleamed between.

So found they each his several evil fate,
Some whelmed beneath broad-rushing billows, some
Wretchedly perishing with their shattered ships
By Nauplius' devising on the rocks.
Wroth for that son whom they had done to death,
He; when the storm rose and the Argives died,
Rejoiced amid his sorrow, seeing a God
Gave to his hands revenge, which now he wreaked
Upon the host he hated, as o'er the deep
They tossed sore-harassed. To his sea-god sire
He prayed that all might perish, ships and men
Whelmed in the deep. Poseidon heard his prayer,
And on the dark surge swept them nigh his land.
He, like a harbour-warder, lifted high
A blazing torch, and so by guile he trapped
The Achaean men, who deemed that they had won

A sheltering haven: but sharp reefs and crags
Gave awful welcome unto ships and men,
Who, dashed to pieces on the cruel rocks
In the black night, crowned ills with direr ills.
Some few escaped, by a God or Power unseen
Plucked from death's hand. Athena now rejoiced
Her heart within, and now was racked with fears
For prudent-souled Odysseus; for his weird
Was through Poseidon's wrath to suffer woes
Full many.

      But Earth-shaker's jealousy now
Burned against those long walls and towers uppiled
By the strong Argives for a fence against
The Trojans' battle-onset. Swiftly then
He swelled to overbrimming all the sea
That rolls from Euxine down to Hellespont,
And hurled it on the shore of Troy: and Zeus,
For a grace unto the glorious Shaker of Earth,
Poured rain from heaven: withal Far-darter bare
In that great work his part; from Ida's heights
Into one channel led he all her streams,
And flooded the Achaeans' work. The sea
Dashed o'er it, and the roaring torrents still
Rushed on it, swollen by the rains of Zeus;
And the dark surge of the wide-moaning sea
Still hurled them back from mingling with the deep,
Till all the Danaan walls were blotted out
Beneath their desolating flood. Then earth
Was by Poseidon chasm-cleft: up rushed
Deluge of water, slime and sand, while quaked
Sigeum with the mighty shock, and roared
The beach and the foundations of the land

The Fall of Troy

Dardanian. So vanished, whelmed from sight,
That mighty rampart. Earth asunder yawned,
And all sank down, and only sand was seen,
When back the sea rolled, o'er the beach outspread
Far down the heavy-booming shore. All this
The Immortals' anger wrought. But in their ships
The Argives storm-dispersed went sailing on.
So came they home, as heaven guided each,
Even all that 'scaped the fell sea-tempest blasts.

www.bookjungle.com email: sales@bookjungle.com fax: 630-214-0564 mail: Book Jungle PO Box 2226 Champaign, IL 61825

The Codes Of Hammurabi And Moses
W. W. Davies

QTY

The discovery of the Hammurabi Code is one of the greatest achievements of archaeology, and is of paramount interest, not only to the student of the Bible, but also to all those interested in ancient history...

Religion   **ISBN:** *1-59462-338-4*   Pages:132
MSRP *$12.95*

The Theory of Moral Sentiments
Adam Smith

QTY

This work from 1749. contains original theories of conscience amd moral judgment and it is the foundation for systemof morals.

Philosophy   **ISBN:** *1-59462-777-0*   Pages:536
MSRP *$19.95*

Jessica's First Prayer
Hesba Stretton

QTY

In a screened and secluded corner of one of the many railway-bridges which span the streets of London there could be seen a few years ago, from five o'clock every morning until half past eight, a tidily set-out coffee-stall, consisting of a trestle and board, upon which stood two large tin cans, with a small fire of charcoal burning under each so as to keep the coffee boiling during the early hours of the morning when the work-people were thronging into the city on their way to their daily toil...

Childrens   **ISBN:** *1-59462-373-2*   Pages:84
MSRP *$9.95*

My Life and Work
Henry Ford

QTY

Henry Ford revolutionized the world with his implementation of mass production for the Model T automobile. Gain valuable business insight into his life and work with his own auto-biography... "We have only started on our development of our country we have not as yet, with all our talk of wonderful progress, done more than scratch the surface. The progress has been wonderful enough but..."

Biographies/   **ISBN:** *1-59462-198-5*   **Pages:300**
MSRP *$21.95*

www.bookjungle.com email: sales@bookjungle.com fax: 630-214-0564 mail: Book Jungle PO Box 2226 Champaign, IL 61825

The Art of Cross-Examination
Francis Wellman

QTY

I presume it is the experience of every author, after his first book is published upon an important subject, to be almost overwhelmed with a wealth of ideas and illustrations which could readily have been included in his book, and which to his own mind, at least, seem to make a second edition inevitable. Such certainly was the case with me; and when the first edition had reached its sixth impression in five months, I rejoiced to learn that it seemed to my publishers that the book had met with a sufficiently favorable reception to justify a second and considerably enlarged edition. ..

Reference   ISBN: *1-59462-647-2*   **Pages:412**   *MSRP $19.95*

On the Duty of Civil Disobedience
Henry David Thoreau

QTY

Thoreau wrote his famous essay, On the Duty of Civil Disobedience, as a protest against an unjust but popular war and the immoral but popular institution of slave-owning. He did more than write—he declined to pay his taxes, and was hauled off to gaol in consequence. Who can say how much this refusal of his hastened the end of the war and of slavery ?

Law   ISBN: *1-59462-747-9*   **Pages:48**   *MSRP $7.45*

Dream Psychology Psychoanalysis for Beginners
Sigmund Freud

QTY

Sigmund Freud, born Sigismund Schlomo Freud (May 6, 1856 - September 23, 1939), was a Jewish-Austrian neurologist and psychiatrist who co-founded the psychoanalytic school of psychology. Freud is best known for his theories of the unconscious mind, especially involving the mechanism of repression; his redefinition of sexual desire as mobile and directed towards a wide variety of objects; and his therapeutic techniques, especially his understanding of transference in the therapeutic relationship and the presumed value of dreams as sources of insight into unconscious desires.

Psychology   ISBN: *1-59462-905-6*   **Pages:196**   *MSRP $15.45*

The Miracle of Right Thought
Orison Swett Marden

QTY

Believe with all of your heart that you will do what you were made to do. When the mind has once formed the habit of holding cheerful, happy, prosperous pictures, it will not be easy to form the opposite habit. It does not matter how improbable or how far away this realization may see, or how dark the prospects may be, if we visualize them as best we can, as vividly as possible, hold tenaciously to them and vigorously struggle to attain them, they will gradually become actualized, realized in the life. But a desire, a longing without endeavor, a yearning abandoned or held indifferently will vanish without realization.

Self Help   ISBN: *1-59462-644-8*   **Pages:360**   *MSRP $25.45*

www.bookjungle.com email: sales@bookjungle.com fax: 630-214-0564 mail: Book Jungle PO Box 2226 Champaign, IL 61825

QTY

| ☐ | **The Rosicrucian Cosmo-Conception Mystic Christianity** by *Max Heindel* | ISBN: *1-59462-188-8* | **$38.95** |

The Rosicrucian Cosmo-conception is not dogmatic, neither does it appeal to any other authority than the reason of the student. It is: not controversial, but is: sent forth in the, hope that it may help to clear... *New Age/Religion Pages 646*

| ☐ | **Abandonment To Divine Providence** by *Jean-Pierre de Caussade* | ISBN: *1-59462-228-0* | **$25.95** |

"The Rev. Jean Pierre de Caussade was one of the most remarkable spiritual writers of the Society of Jesus in France in the 18th Century. His death took place at Toulouse in 1751. His works have gone through many editions and have been republished... *Inspirational/Religion Pages 400*

| ☐ | **Mental Chemistry** by *Charles Haanel* | ISBN: *1-59462-192-6* | **$23.95** |

Mental Chemistry allows the change of material conditions by combining and appropriately utilizing the power of the mind. Much like applied chemistry creates something new and unique out of careful combinations of chemicals the mastery of mental chemistry... *New Age Pages 354*

| ☐ | **The Letters of Robert Browning and Elizabeth Barret Barrett 1845-1846 vol II** | ISBN: *1-59462-193-4* | **$35.95** |

by *Robert Browning* and *Elizabeth Barrett* *Biographies Pages 596*

| ☐ | **Gleanings In Genesis (volume I)** by *Arthur W. Pink* | ISBN: *1-59462-130-6* | **$27.45** |

Appropriately has Genesis been termed "the seed plot of the Bible" for in it we have, in germ form, almost all of the great doctrines which are afterwards fully developed in the books of Scripture which follow... *Religion/Inspirational Pages 420*

| ☐ | **The Master Key** by *L. W. de Laurence* | ISBN: *1-59462-001-6* | **$30.95** |

In no branch of human knowledge has there been a more lively increase of the spirit of research during the past few years than in the study of Psychology, Concentration and Mental Discipline. The requests for authentic lessons in Thought Control, Mental Discipline and... *New Age/Business Pages 422*

| ☐ | **The Lesser Key Of Solomon Goetia** by *L. W. de Laurence* | ISBN: *1-59462-092-X* | **$9.95** |

This translation of the first book of the "Lernegton" which is now for the first time made accessible to students of Talismanic Magic was done, after careful collation and edition, from numerous Ancient Manuscripts in Hebrew, Latin, and French... *New Age/Occult Pages 92*

| ☐ | **Rubaiyat Of Omar Khayyam** by *Edward Fitzgerald* | ISBN:*1-59462-332-5* | **$13.95** |

Edward Fitzgerald, whom the world has already learned, in spite of his own efforts to remain within the shadow of anonymity, to look upon as one of the rarest poets of the century, was born at Bredfield, in Suffolk, on the 31st of March, 1809. He was the third son of John Purcell... *Music Pages 172*

| ☐ | **Ancient Law** by *Henry Maine* | ISBN: *1-59462-128-4* | **$29.95** |

The chief object of the following pages is to indicate some of the earliest ideas of mankind, as they are reflected in Ancient Law, and to point out the relation of those ideas to modern thought. *Religiom/History Pages 452*

| ☐ | **Far-Away Stories** by *William J. Locke* | ISBN: *1-59462-129-2* | **$19.45** |

"Good wine needs no bush, but a collection of mixed vintages does. And this book is just such a collection. Some of the stories I do not want to remain buried for ever in the museum files of dead magazine-numbers an author's not unpardonable vanity..." *Fiction Pages 272*

| ☐ | **Life of David Crockett** by *David Crockett* | ISBN: *1-59462-250-7* | **$27.45** |

"Colonel David Crockett was one of the most remarkable men of the times in which he lived. Born in humble life, but gifted with a strong will, an indomitable courage, and unremitting perseverance... *Biographies/New Age Pages 424*

| ☐ | **Lip-Reading** by *Edward Nitchie* | ISBN: *1-59462-206-X* | **$25.95** |

Edward B. Nitchie, founder of the New York School for the Hard of Hearing, now the Nitchie School of Lip-Reading, Inc, wrote "LIP-READING Principles and Practice". The development and perfecting of this meritorious work on lip-reading was an undertaking... *How-to Pages 400*

| ☐ | **A Handbook of Suggestive Therapeutics, Applied Hypnotism, Psychic Science** | ISBN: *1-59462-214-0* | **$24.95** |

by *Henry Munro* *Health/New Age/Health/Self-help Pages 376*

| ☐ | **A Doll's House: and Two Other Plays** by *Henrik Ibsen* | ISBN: *1-59462-112-8* | **$19.95** |

Henrik Ibsen created this classic when in revolutionary 1848 Rome. Introducing some striking concepts in playwriting for the realist genre, this play has been studied the world over. *Fiction/Classics/Plays 308*

| ☐ | **The Light of Asia** by *sir Edwin Arnold* | ISBN: *1-59462-204-3* | **$13.95** |

In this poetic masterpiece, Edwin Arnold describes the life and teachings of Buddha. The man who was to become known as Buddha to the world was born as Prince Gautama of India but he rejected the worldly riches and abandoned the reigns of power when... *Religion/History/Biographies Pages 170*

| ☐ | **The Complete Works of Guy de Maupassant** by *Guy de Maupassant* | ISBN: *1-59462-157-8* | **$16.95** |

"For days and days, nights and nights, I had dreamed of that first kiss which was to consecrate our engagement, and I knew not on what spot I should put my lips..." *Fiction/Classics Pages 240*

| ☐ | **The Art of Cross-Examination** by *Francis L. Wellman* | ISBN: *1-59462-309-0* | **$26.95** |

Written by a renowned trial lawyer, Wellman imparts his experience and uses case studies to explain how to use psychology to extract desired information through questioning. *How-to/Science/Reference Pages 408*

| ☐ | **Answered or Unanswered?** by *Louisa Vaughan* | ISBN: *1-59462-248-5* | **$10.95** |

Miracles of Faith in China *Religion Pages 112*

| ☐ | **The Edinburgh Lectures on Mental Science (1909)** by *Thomas* | ISBN: *1-59462-008-3* | **$11.95** |

This book contains the substance of a course of lectures recently given by the writer in the Queen Street Hail, Edinburgh. Its purpose is to indicate the Natural Principles governing the relation between Mental Action and Material Conditions... *New Age/Psychology Pages 148*

| ☐ | **Ayesha** by *H. Rider Haggard* | ISBN: *1-59462-301-5* | **$24.95** |

Verily and indeed it is the unexpected that happens! Probably if there was one person upon the earth from whom the Editor of this, and of a certain previous history, did not expect to hear again... *Classics Pages 380*

| ☐ | **Ayala's Angel** by *Anthony Trollope* | ISBN: *1-59462-352-X* | **$29.95** |

The two girls were both pretty, but Lucy who was twenty-one who supposed to be simple and comparatively unattractive, whereas Ayala was credited, as her Bombwhat romantic name might show, with poetic charm and a taste for romance. Ayala when her father died was nineteen... *Fiction Pages 484*

| ☐ | **The American Commonwealth** by *James Bryce* | ISBN: *1-59462-286-8* | **$34.45** |

An interpretation of American democratic political theory. It examines political mechanics and society from the perspective of Scotsman James Bryce *Politics Pages 572*

| ☐ | **Stories of the Pilgrims** by *Margaret P. Pumphrey* | ISBN: *1-59462-116-0* | **$17.95** |

This book explores pilgrims religious oppression in England as well as their escape to Holland and eventual crossing to America on the Mayflower, and their early days in New England... *History Pages 268*

www.bookjungle.com *email: sales@bookjungle.com fax: 630-214-0564 mail: Book Jungle PO Box 2226 Champaign, IL 61825*

QTY

The Fasting Cure *by Sinclair Upton*   ISBN: *1-59462-222-1*   **$13.95**
In the Cosmopolitan Magazine for May, 1910, and in the Contemporary Review (London) for April, 1910, I published an article dealing with my experiences in fasting. I have written a great many magazine articles, but never one which attracted so much attention...   New Age/Self Help/Health Pages 164

Hebrew Astrology *by Sepharial*   ISBN: *1-59462-308-2*   **$13.45**
In these days of advanced thinking it is a matter of common observation that we have left many of the old landmarks behind and that we are now pressing forward to greater heights and to a wider horizon than that which represented the mind-content of our progenitors...   Astrology Pages 144

Thought Vibration or The Law of Attraction in the Thought World   ISBN: *1-59462-127-6*   **$12.95**
by William Walker Atkinson   Psychology/Religion Pages 144

Optimism *by Helen Keller*   ISBN: *1-59462-108-X*   **$15.95**
Helen Keller was blind, deaf, and mute since 19 months old, yet famously learned how to overcome these handicaps, communicate with the world, and spread her lectures promoting optimism. An inspiring read for everyone...   Biographies/Inspirational Pages 84

Sara Crewe *by Frances Burnett*   ISBN: *1-59462-360-0*   **$9.45**
In the first place, Miss Minchin lived in London. Her home was a large, dull, tall one, in a large, dull square, where all the houses were alike, and all the sparrows were alike, and where all the door-knockers made the same heavy sound...   Childrens/Classic Pages 88

The Autobiography of Benjamin Franklin *by Benjamin Franklin*   ISBN: *1-59462-135-7*   **$24.95**
The Autobiography of Benjamin Franklin has probably been more extensively read than any other American historical work, and no other book of its kind has had such ups and downs of fortune. Franklin lived for many years in England, where he was agent...   Biographies/History Pages 332

Name	
Email	
Telephone	
Address	
City, State ZIP	

☐ Credit Card   ☐ Check / Money Order

Credit Card Number	
Expiration Date	
Signature	

Please Mail to: Book Jungle
                      PO Box 2226
                      Champaign, IL 61825
or Fax to: 630-214-0564

ORDERING INFORMATION

web: *www.bookjungle.com*
email: *sales@bookjungle.com*
fax: *630-214-0564*
mail: *Book Jungle PO Box 2226 Champaign, IL 61825*
or PayPal *to sales@bookjungle.com*

Please contact us for bulk discounts

DIRECT-ORDER TERMS

20% Discount if You Order Two or More Books
Free Domestic Shipping!
Accepted: Master Card, Visa, Discover, American Express

www.ingramcontent.com/pod-product-compliance
Lightning Source LLC
Chambersburg PA
CBHW082107230426
43671CB00015B/2626